'Full of warmth, humour, optimism and sometimes painful honesty, *Both Not Half* is a brilliant, fresh and moving memoir that explores race and colour, fusion and mingling' **William Dalrymple, author of *The Anarchy***

'A journey that will resonate with anyone on their own quest for cohesion' **Laila Woozeer, author of *Not Quite White***

'I can't wait for my daughter to read this book' **Nikesh Patel**

'A beautiful and profound story' **Nihal Arthanayake**

'*Both Not Half* is a moving, challenging and fascinating page-turner … that contains important lessons for progressive politics in a divided age' **Grace Blakeley, author of *Vulture Capitalism***

'Anyone who's ever struggled to make sense of who they are and where they belong should read this book' **Nadia Whittome MP**

'A hopeful manifesto for our times' **Kavita Puri, author of *Partition Voices***

'An unexpected and enthralling journey … I loved it' **Samira Ahmed**

'In a world where we all long for a sense of belonging, Jassa shows us the richness of complexity and compassion' **Anita Anand, author of *Sophia: Princess, Suffragette, Revolutionary***

'A paean to self-definition and belonging in a confusing world' **Sanjeev Bhaskar**

'An important voice of our generation and for generations to come' **Parminder Nagra, star of *Bend it Like Beckham***

'The sort of book that should become required reading in all of our schools' **Hashi Mohamed, author of *People Like Us***

'Brilliantly researched and dripping with personal colour' **Ranvir Singh**

'A vital book for our times' **Aanchal Malhotra, author of *Remnants of Partition***

'A timely plea for a politics that embraces hybridity'
Peter Mitchell, author of *Imperial Nostalgia*

'Beautifully moving … A must-read for all'
Jaspreet Kaur, author of *Brown Girl Like Me*

'Stunning and transparent' **Sharan Dhaliwal, author of *Burning My Roti***

'Intensely relatable' **Vaneet Mehta, author of *Bisexual Men Exist***

'Touching, essential and moving' **Andy Nyman, author of *The Golden Rules of Acting***

'Ahluwalia asks us to re-wire our minds, to push back against cultural divisions which demand simplistic labels that alienate us from others'
Ritch C. Savin-Williams, author of *Bi*

'Timely and eloquent' **Tim Walker**

About the Author

Jassa Ahluwalia is a British actor, writer, filmmaker and trade unionist. Born in Coventry to a white English mum and a brown Punjabi dad in 1990, he attended school in Leicester and was raised in an extended family environment. He spoke English in the playground, Punjabi with his grandparents, and spent various summer holidays in India.

He came to prominence as Rocky in the hit BBC Three series *Some Girls*, followed by starring roles in *Unforgotten*, *Ripper Street*, and *Peaky Blinders*. Jassa created the hashtag #BothNotHalf to explore mixed identity in light of his own British-Indian heritage. His TEDx talk on 'How Language Shapes Identity' has clocked up over 180k views and his BBC One documentary *Am I English?* won an Asian Media Award in 2022.

JASSA AHLUWALIA

BOTH NOT HALF

A Radical New Approach to Mixed Heritage Identity

BLINK
bringing you closer

First published in the UK by Blink Publishing
An imprint of The Zaffre Publishing Group
A Bonnier Books UK company
4th Floor, Victoria House
Bloomsbury Square,
London, WC1B 4DA
England

Owned by Bonnier Books
Sveavägen 56, Stockholm, Sweden

Hardback – 9781788708319
Ebook – 9781788708302
Audio – 9781785120336

A CIP catalogue of this book is available from the British Library.

Designed by EnvyDesignLtd
Printed and bound by Clays Ltd, Elcograf S.p.A

1 3 5 7 9 10 8 6 4 2

Blink Publishing is an imprint of Bonnier Books UK
www.bonnierbooks.co.uk

For BG, partitioned but never divided

ਆਪਣਾ ਮੂਲੁ ਪਛਾਣੁ

aapnaa mool pachhaan

Recognise your origin

GURU GRANTH SAHIB

پڑھ پڑھ علم تے فاضل ہویو

وے کدے اپنے آپ نوں پڑھیا نائیں

paṛh paṛh 'ilm te faazil hoyo
ve kade apne aap noon paṛhya naaeen

You read and read and become a scholar,
and yet you have never read your self

BULLEH SHAH

CONTENTS

1

ALONE IN THE JUNGLE

The call rings up the curtain, always,
on a mystery of transfiguration.
JOSEPH CAMPBELL, *THE HERO WITH A THOUSAND FACES*

MY FIRST PERFORMANCE ever caught on camera was in India. It was late February 1994, I was three years old, and I had stage fright. I was at my great uncle and aunty's house in Moga, Punjab, surrounded by women I didn't know, all decked out in brightly coloured salwars, clapping along to music I wasn't familiar with. Where was the bhangra? I had come prepared for bhangra. I was sporting a bright red kurta, complete with an embroidered black waistcoat, and handkerchiefs tied to my little fingers. Apart from my blonde hair and white skin, I was the very image of a Punjabi folk dancer. As my dad operated the camcorder, my mum tried to coax me into letting loose, but I couldn't find my rhythm. After all, I'd never been to a sangeet (a pre-wedding party arranged by and for the women of the bride and groom's families) and Asha Bhosle's 'Chham Chham Nachdi Phiran' wasn't doing it for me.

But the next day, my dad's cousin's wedding day, the dhol player arrived and filled the gully with the sound I longed for. It didn't matter that I was now dressed in the pageboy's outfit that had been made for my maternal aunty's New Forest wedding the previous spring. My gold silk shorts, short-sleeved white shirt and bow tie, made from the same embroidery used in my aunty's bodice, did nothing to hold me back. The unmetalled Punjab street was my stage. I was totally unfazed by the crowd watching me. A few uncles joined in periodically, as did my mum who was holding my darker-skinned baby sister, Ramanique, but I was unstoppable. Bhangra was in my bones. If the dhol was playing, I was dancing. I only stopped when my mum, worried I was going to get heatstroke, tipped the drummer generously and persuaded him to take a break.

This was my first experience of India. Music, dance and joy. When the father of the bride, my grandad's younger brother, Uncle Jagir, saw us off at the train station, he held out his hand to shake mine. I duly obliged. But a few moments later, I was holding up my arms for a hug. He scooped me up and I wrapped myself around his neck. I felt safe here. This was home. Another home.

A child of the nineties

My white English mum and my brown Punjabi dad met in their mid-20s in the mid-1980s in Coventry, where I would later be born in Walsgrave Hospital on 12 September 1990. They got to know each other over the course of a year through mutual friends on the postgrad course my dad was doing in computer-aided design. Marriage was discussed early on, but it took my dad a bit of time to pluck up the courage to tell his parents about his white girlfriend. Anticipating resistance from my grandad, my mum, a professional artist, got to work in her studio on a large watercolour of Harmandir Sahib (the Golden Temple).

With this peace offering in hand, my mum went to meet my grandad to see if she would pass muster. 'It was very formal,' my mum recalls. 'I was taken into the sitting room and essentially got cross-examined as to what my intentions were. We talked about how we'd bring up children, how we'd deal with the whole faith thing, my attitude towards Sikhism, understanding the difficulties of a mixed marriage. It was a real reality check type of discussion. How was I going to deal with all of that?'

Thankfully, my mum had come prepared. She said that when it came to kids, she saw it as her obligation to raise us as 50% Punjabi, 50% English. But, given that we'd be growing up in the UK, she knew she'd have to work harder to make us aware of our Sikh and Indian identities. Going to India to see family, connecting to those roots and learning Punjabi would be integral to both her marriage and her parenting. My grandad approved of her sincere commitment and gave his blessing to the engagement. The painting of Harmandir Sahib hung in pride of place in my grandparents' living room for the rest of their lives.

My dad then visited my mum's father for his permission, but he needn't have bothered. Whereas my mum had faced an inquisition, my dad was met with laughter. My mum's relationship with her parents was strained following their divorce and my grandpa was certain that his opinion held very little sway. With this perfunctory blessing, a wedding date was set for 1989. Even though they had their families onside, society continued to remind them that they were an atypical match.

While waiting in a queue at an opticians, the receptionist looked straight through my dad to ask my mum what time her appointment was. My mum didn't have an appointment: my dad did. And he was clearly standing in front of her in the line. Since moving to the UK as a child in 1973, my dad had grown up carrying a cricket bat to the park, regardless of whether there was a match to play; he was well attuned to and unsurprised by the racism and violence he encountered. My mum, on the other hand, by her own admission, was entirely ignorant and initially suspected he had a bit of a chip on his shoulder.

It wasn't long, though, before the world started to look different to my mum. Her naivety gave way to reality when she attended an old school friend's wedding. They were in the reception line to congratulate the newlyweds; my mum had just given the groom a hug and my dad followed, holding out his hand for a handshake. The groom kept his hands by his side. My dad kept his hand out. The moment became an eternity and the queue started to back up. Finally, prompted by the bride, the groom relented. But just as he raised his arm, my dad dropped his and walked away. Legend.

Returning from another wedding in London, a Sikh

wedding this time, my mum and dad were walking back to where they had parked in Peckham when a car screamed past carrying a group of young men. They shouted something that my mum didn't quite catch, but my dad did. 'He grabbed my arm and just said "run",' my mum tells me, her voice catching in her throat as the memory floods her eyes. I feel it too. 'I felt so wonderful in my beautiful salwar kameez, turquoise with gold thread and hand-painted details.' The shout my dad had heard was 'paki-lover'.

On 28 May 1989, the conference room at Brandon Hall Hotel was converted into a gurdwara and my parents' Anand Karaj was performed. My grandpa, architect James A. Roberts, had led the refurbishment of the hotel, grounding the Sikh wedding ceremony in my mum's family heritage. It was a glorious sunny day, a bhangra troupe tore up the croquet lawn and my mum's family threw themselves into the occasion, including the Milni (a pre-wedding gathering) where corresponding relatives compete to pick each other up. I find it deeply moving to look at their wedding photos. They were still in their 20s; I'm in my 30s and unmarried. I see now what I never saw as a child: their youth, their nerves, their hopes. Resplendent in red and gold, white and brown, they were taking a step into the unknown.

And then I arrived. A living, breathing unknown. On 12 September 1990, I was born far whiter and blonder than anyone had expected; even the hospital staff made a joke about the milkman. But there I was: a mixed heritage child of the nineties, the decade of multiculturalism.

*

'The nineties was a period of great progress and cultural flourishing and, in many ways, was the golden decade for British South Asians,' journalist Kavita Puri told me when I interviewed her in 2021 to discuss her BBC Radio 4 documentary series *Three Pounds in My Pocket*.

In 1993, British South Asian club night Bombay Jungle became a regular and rammed fixture at the Wag Club in Soho. Two years later, the LGBTQ+ club night Club Kali was born. But I was at home (obviously), dancing away to Birmingham's Balwinder Safri, who formed the bhangra group the Safri Boyz in 1990. As the decade wore on, brown excellence was on the ascent. *Goodness Gracious Me* became a TV sensation in 1998, and I delighted in shouting out 'Cheque, please!' and following the adventures of Skipinder, The Punjabi Kangaroo. (Such was the impact of the show, I never realised then that 'goodness gracious me' was a reference to Peter Sellers' cod-Indian accent, and only discovered this when I hosted an event to celebrate its silver anniversary with Nina Wadia, Kulvinder Ghir and writer Sanjeev Kohli in 2023.) 'Brimful of Asha' blared in the car while I revelled in singing the lyric 'everybody needs a bosom for a pillow' without getting told off for being rude. And I was developing an interest in music making myself. Enthralled by the percussive sounds of the tabla at the gurdwara, I came home from a 1997 trip to India with my own pair and began lessons. The following year saw the release of Panjabi MC's *Legalised*, the album that featured the song 'Mundian To Bach Ke', which went on to become a smash hit. Talvin Singh won the Mercury Prize in 1999, giving me a mainstream tabla hero. And Nitin Sawhney released his iconic album *Beyond Skin*. As the decade was coming to a close, *East is East* hit cinema screens. I was too young to see it in theatres, but on VHS I would see a brown dad, a white mum and mixed kids. Lines like 'this jungly family of half-breeds' made me laugh; Grandad called me 'jungly' when I climbed the trees in the back garden.

I was seeing faces like my father's on TV, hearing tabla and dhol beats on the radio, and I was too young to understand that these were groundbreaking moments. Nothing about my existence seemed extraordinary. During my earliest years, the world was full of joy and possibility. I hadn't been around to see brown solidarity begin to fracture along religious lines in 1984, when Indira Gandhi ordered a military attack on the Golden Temple, leading to her assassination by her Sikh bodyguards and, subsequently, anti-Sikh pogroms in Delhi and across the country. Nor was I old enough to have known about the Islamist book burnings of Salman Rushdie's 1988 novel *The Satanic Verses*, prompting some Hindus and Sikhs to distance themselves from their skinfolk. I was only two years old when Stephen Lawrence was murdered in April 1993, and I was too young to register the 1995 Srebrenica massacre and how the British government's support for an arms embargo, preventing Bosnian Muslims from defending themselves, saw some British South Asians make Islam their salient identity. I grew up in ignorant bliss, in Leicester, a mixed heritage city that reflected all that I was.

The 1991 census reveals just over 94% of the UK

population identified as white, but in Leicester, ethnic minorities constituted 28%, and Asians made up almost a quarter of the city. It's impossible to say with any accuracy what the mixed population of the UK or Leicester was at that time – 'mixed' only came into usage on the 2001 census, when I was ten years old. Prior to the millennium, 'mixed' did not exist in census data despite mixed people existing under British authority for hundreds of years; 'mixed races' get a whole table to themselves in the first census of the whole of British India (1871–72) and numbered 108,402 in total.[1] Limited though the data is, over the course of my childhood, Leicester became increasingly diverse. By the time of my 21st birthday, it was pretty much fifty-fifty white and ethnic minorities. It was only then, in my 20s, that I discovered our local Diwali celebrations are among the largest outside of India. Growing up in Leicester, they were just a regular fixture, like the Christmas tree going up by the clocktower, the Sikh Vaisakhi parade or the Caribbean Carnival (which is one of the largest outside of London). The culture was fluid and accommodated me easily. And it has continued to evolve. The 2021 census shows Leicester to be 'the first plural city in the UK where no ethnic group has a majority'.[2]

But why am I talking about Leicester? I was born in Coventry, where my parents met and lived. How did Leicester become my hometown?

When I was three years old, I moved to Leicester to live with my Punjabi grandparents. That's how I remember it. For my parents, I was simply staying with Grandad and BG (my grandmother, *biji* in Punjabi, though I've always written it BG) during school term times so that I could start my education earlier than Coventry council would allow. There was also a practical reason for packing me off. My sister was now on the scene, my dad had been made redundant and was doing an MBA, and my mum's interior design business was in its infancy. Cash was tight and childcare was costly. Plus, multigenerational parenting is a South Asian cultural norm. And my grandad was a teacher at the local primary school. It all made sense. This became my new normal. Weekdays in Leicester, weekends in Coventry, Punjabi and BG's roti at home and English and canteen lunches at school.

Mr Walia, as my grandad was known, was never my teacher. He taught the older kids and retired before there was a chance of me becoming his pupil. But he kept a watchful eye over me and would hear about my achievements and disgraces via the staff room. I was a mini celebrity: 'Mr Walia's grandson'. My grandad was one of the few male teachers and the only brown man on the premises who wore a turban. The staff, the student body and most other parents I met all knew who I was. I had always thought of this as being rather fun – it perhaps explains why I feel comfortable being recognised as an actor – but while writing this book, something new occurred to me: I had never had to explain myself. My ability to speak Punjabi was taken for granted, my enthusiasm and knowledge when it came to events like Diwali required no backstory, and my surname wasn't an anomaly. *I* wasn't an anomaly. Growing up in the nineties, living in Leicester, with my Sikh grandad roaming the school corridors, I was simply able to be.

Towards the end of my primary school years, my parents moved into the house next door to Grandad and BG, and Leicester became my undisputed home. For me and my sister, our ritual was peanut butter toast, a couple of hours to play in the garden or with our Gujarati mates down the road, followed by the sabji or dhal of the day. My parents would then get back from work and we'd rush over to greet them, catch up on the day and perhaps watch a bit of TV together, and then bed. This routine began to shift into a more nuclear family setup complete with evening activities once my sister had joined me at secondary school, but BG was a fount of love, warmth and exceptional food that we were always coming back to.

BG is perhaps the main reason I speak Punjabi. My dad immersed me in the language from birth, my mum mixed Punjabi words into her speech and was adept at disciplining me – '*chup kar, baite ja, hatt ja*': 'be quiet, sit down, stop it' – and I briefly forgot English after a 1995 summer holiday to India with my grandad. He only realised what had happened on the flight home when the British Airways steward asked if I wanted a colouring book. I stared blankly back before asking my grandad, '*Ki kendhi hai?*': 'What's she saying?' Thankfully, the elasticity of youth allowed my English to come back quickly, but my Indian accent persisted a little longer. The story goes that I was at a supermarket with my mum, just the two of us, and I was sitting in the trolley when all of a sudden I shouted out in a strong Indian accent, 'Mummy, I want bananas!' My mum panicked and completed our shopping in record time.

I eventually lost my Indian accent, but I never stopped speaking Punjabi; it was the only language with which I could fully access BG's love. She could speak English if she needed to, but not as fluently or as comfortably as she did Punjabi. She had been well educated in India, working as a teacher before eventually emigrating to the UK to join Grandad, but she had always struggled with (and hated) English. *'Meinu ki patha si mein England chule jaana!'* 'How was I to know I'd end up in England!'

Perhaps knowing what it felt like to grapple with a second tongue, BG never made me feel silly for making mistakes. She allowed me to stumble my way through, mixing up tenses, genders and agreements. She'd repeat things back to me matter-of-factly where necessary, but most of the time, she let things slide. When I speak to people who struggled to pick up their ancestral language, there's always a common theme: a sense of humiliation. No doubt well intentioned, there's a particular kind of elder who feels it necessary to call out every mistake a child makes while simultaneously piling the pressure on them to speak. No one likes to feel stupid or shamed and inevitably those kids grow up, in the best-case scenario, able to understand the language but speak very little; or, worst case, reject the language entirely and later lament their loss and blame themselves as they begin to contemplate their place in the world. Learning Punjabi was not my achievement, it was my family's. If you're reading this and feeling guilty for not being able to speak whatever language you grew up with, recognise that it was never your responsibility and forgive yourself. It's never too late to learn.

I still make mistakes. I'm still learning. Grammar police frequently kick down my door. (Sometimes when they're asking me how they can get their grandkids to speak Punjabi.) But I've learnt to resist arrest. For most of us, language is about being understood and making connections, not an academic test.

It's also worth emphasising that our ancestral tongues are not preternaturally difficult. I often hear this as part of people's regret: that because they didn't learn as a kid, they're now doomed. The issue is not alphabets or grammar but resources. No one doubts that with enough dedication you can become fluent enough in Russian or Chinese to make profound human connection. So why not Punjabi? It is infuriating to me that I can use Duolingo to learn Klingon or High Valyrian, but not Punjabi (or a number of other real languages). I have no issue with people wanting to learn fictitious languages – go wild – but wouldn't it be wonderful if learning our ancestral tongues was just as accessible.

Undoubtedly, my whiteness also played a part in the wider encouragement I received with my Punjabi. Looking the way I did, especially as a young child with blonde hair, there was no expectation on me to be able to speak by the kinds of uncles and aunties who would crack the mother tongue whip with their own brown progeny. Nor did white people feel threatened by me. I was a novelty, and I was lauded for my efforts. This was white privilege in action: I was afforded grace where others were policed. And as a burgeoning performer, I knew how to put on a show. White people would gawp in amazement and brown folk would cheer me on. What a difference it would make if all kids received this kind of encouragement.

*

I was in my teens when I became aware that my early upbringing was not typical. Until then, I'd genuinely not reflected on my home life. It was only after I was a couple of years into secondary school that realisation dawned. And it was quite a sudden moment. I have a clear memory of explaining my multigenerational, split-city and dual-home childhood to a couple of friends at a sleepover. We were holding court in the kitchen; I was sitting on a stool and I was staring down at the terracotta tiles. The tiles stick in my mind for some reason. Perhaps I was avoiding eye contact. It felt strange to suddenly have a history and a domestic setup that others found unconventional. But I didn't feel othered. Again, I'm sure my whiteness insulated me. Instead of feeling pressure to assimilate, I became the guy with an interesting backstory. And while many of my brown peers played down their ethnic identities in order to achieve proximity to the white default, I leant into my Indian identity in order to court the attention and admiration I'd grown up with. I even went as far as attending a black-tie school prom wearing a white silk kurta pyjama with a black achkan (a knee-length jacket) and a black turban tied for me by my grandad. I styled it with my father's gold sarpech, which my mum had designed for their wedding, complete with a peacock feather. I was, quite literally, peacocking.

I was so comfortable in my identity that I happily went

around during my teens, proudly introducing myself as 'half-Indian-half-British' and was perplexed by John Agard's poem 'Half-Caste' when we studied it for GCSE English:

> wha yu mean
> when yu say half-caste
> yu mean tchaikovsky
> sit down at dah piano
> an mix a black key
> wid a white key
> is a half-caste symphony[3]

This was just one excerpt that I was expected to critique. It's remarkable that this was in no way a turning point for my sense of self. Reading the poem now, I find myself grinning at Agard's sardonic description of English weather as being perpetually 'half-caste'. But as a young teen, I had no sudden recognition of my own experience in his words. Nor do I remember my teacher encouraging me to reflect on my own identity. I was not Black, nor did I recognise 'half-caste' as a slur. If anything, I quite liked that there was a special term that described me. I didn't properly understand that 'caste', derived from the Latin *castus*, meant chaste or pure, with 'half-caste' literally meaning 'half-pure'. But while I was taught about the concept of racial chastity, I have no recollection of the word 'half' being discussed. Fractionality was simply an objective fact. Just as some of my white friends called themselves half Irish or quarter French, I was half Indian. And most importantly, I never felt like I was opening myself up to accusations of not being enough, even when a clear example presented itself.

It was during a rather dull maths class and I was somewhere near the back, performing a song under my breath for my brown classmates. It was inspired by my grandparents' mispronunciations and my parents' love of Louis Armstrong:

> I say guarantee and you say *gruntee*,
> I say warranty and you say *wruntee*.
> Guarantee, *gruntee*,
> Warranty, *wruntee*,
> Let's call the whole thing off ...[4]

We were in hysterics. My Gujarati friend offered up his own verses. But our teacher, a South Asian woman, was not impressed and asked me to stay behind after class. I was expecting a lecture on the follies of showmanship, but what I got came as a surprise: I was reprimanded for doing an Indian accent. This was a first. I was sure she knew my heritage, but perhaps she'd forgotten? I said something along the lines of, 'I sometimes forget people don't see me as Indian' thinking she might actually be looking out for me. But no, she told me my impersonations were offensive and I should put a stop to it.

Why had my Gujarati friend been spared this lecture? I felt weird. Humiliated. And angry. But I was a teenager. Everything made me feel weird, humiliated and angry. The moment passed quickly and I paid it no heed. Ms S. was known for being a bit prim and she'd only been covering our class that day. But that slightly sick feeling, of having my sense of self wrenched from me, however briefly, etched itself into my memory, unresolved and tagged 'for adulthood'.

Adulthood

Exams were passed and I completed the first year of an undergraduate degree in modern languages at University College London. Growing up traversing cultural boundaries, I felt a natural affinity to studying languages. I also had an inkling that I may have to drop out at some point to pursue my career as a performer, and I figured that languages would always be useful, regardless of whether or not I had a qualification. Alongside Spanish, I opted to study Russian. I had wanted to study Hindi, but none of the universities I was looking at offered it and none of my teachers or careers advisers at that time seemed to know that SOAS University of London existed. I settled for Russian on the basis that Russia had a burgeoning film industry, was a large landmass (lots of places to travel) and the alphabet looked pretty badass. Plus, Punjabi sounds transferred remarkably well into Russian. And it served me well.

My first taste of the film industry big leagues was doing the voice of a Russian partisan in Amit Gupta's 2011 film, *Resistance*, starring Andrea Riseborough and Michael Sheen. Meeting Amit was thrilling and inspiring. Here was a brown man from Leicester, directing veritable stars, in a real movie. When he came to do his second feature in 2012, *Jadoo*, inspired by his family's restaurant on Leicester's Golden Mile, I joined the crew in my hometown as a location assistant. While I rejoiced in meeting Kulvinder Ghir, wowing him with my Punjabi and hearing about his own mixed heritage kids, the industry was teaching me to be grateful for my whiteness and to accept that I wasn't brown enough. There was no role for someone like me in *Jadoo*. The options were Nikesh Patel or Tom Mison.

But I *was* grateful. Grateful to be working when my brown peers were struggling to get a foot on the ladder. Grateful, for example, for the chance to play a scheming Victorian cockney in season two of *Ripper Street*, when South Asian faces would only get a brief look-in in season four as part of an imperial storyline.

My big break came with playing the loveable bad boy Rocky in BBC Three's *Some Girls*. Despite my background, my character was coded as white. I would joke around in Punjabi over lunch with my co-star Mandeep Dhillon, but it never occurred to me to suggest a mixed heritage backstory for myself. It would have been easy enough; my parents are never seen and the show was pioneering when it came to representation on screen. Likewise, when I was cast as Nicola Walker's son in *Unforgotten*, I loved riffing in Punjabi with Sanjeev Bhaskar, but I didn't think to suggest my unseen father could look like him. My Indian ancestry was my personal life; I was professionally white.

But tremors from the deep were beginning to cause ripples on the surface of my being: brief glimpses that something was being suppressed. Three moments stick in my mind: an audition, a radio play and a self-tape.

The audition

I grew up watching Disney's 1967 animated classic *The Jungle Book* religiously as a child. I was so obsessed that one monsoon season trip to India I made a point of packing my red underpants so that I could re-enact my hero's adventures in the pouring rain. So when the opportunity arose in 2013 to audition to play Mowgli in a theatre production, I was ecstatic. But it was only when I was in the room, as the director gave me notes, erroneously correcting my pronunciation of *bandar-log* (monkey people), that I realised why Rudyard Kipling's famous man-cub had resonated with me so strongly and for so long. I remember the moment of realisation well, staring at my script on the floor, trying to process my shock and feeling exposed. How had it never occurred to me before? He was a young boy, caught between two worlds, searching for belonging. This was me. This was my story. The energy in the room was electric. And I never heard back. The role went to a white actor. I moved on.

The radio play

In 2014, with my face safely out of sight, I spent a couple of days in BBC Drama Studio 60A playing both Indian and British First World War soldiers in the Radio 4 drama *Tommies*. I was even kept on for an extra hour to coach some of my brown colleagues, who needed help with their Punjabi. Bringing my full self to my work was a new and thrilling experience. As was meeting the series' narrator Indira Varma at the read-through, an actor of mixed Indian and Swiss heritage. But I knew that this job was a rare quirk of radio. There was no way

I'd be playing a Punjabi-speaking soldier on film or TV, not least because such productions were rare to nonexistent. It would be foolish to get my hopes up. And while I saw myself reflected in Indira Varma's heritage, she served as another reminder that I was not brown enough. She had played Kiran in *Bride and Prejudice*, whereas I'd recently depicted the 19th-century Nantucket whaler Owen Coffin in BBC drama *The Whale*. Later in 2014, I was briefly in contention to play Varma's son in a major BBC TV drama set in Russia, but my hopes were dashed when new creatives were brought on board and the casting went in a more traditional (whiter) direction. I moved on.

The self-tape

Before doing *Tommies*, I'd been out to Hollywood to see what it was all about. There, I met with manager Susan Calogerakis, known for launching Bradley Cooper's career, and duly signed with her. Out of everyone I'd met in LA, I felt she really understood me. And a year later, when I was asked to audition for a film called *Burn Your Maps*, I discovered I was right.

The character, Ismail, was described as 'East Indian, lanky, awkward, with a bad haircut' but Susan had got me in the room. She knew I had what it took. And shooting my self-tape felt unlike anything I'd done before. Immense reserves came bursting out of me: accent, mannerisms, physicality. I became Ismail and I loved every moment of it.

The film tells the story of an eight-year-old white American boy who, after a family tragedy, announces to his parents that he is a Mongolian goat herder. An uplifting, off-beat journey of self-discovery ensues, exploring identity, belonging and the meaning of home. While writing this, I watched my audition tape back for the first time since I sent it off. It's fascinating to see the joy I was radiating. But during my introduction to the camera, my confusion is equally clear. 'I really often feel this … erm … like I'm floating in the void between two worlds … I'm finding it very hard as I'm growing up to be aware of … to live within one world whilst being really aware of the absence of the other.' The role eventually went to *Life of Pi* star Suraj Sharma.

Neither Mowgli, nor *Tommies*, nor Ismail triggered my own journey of self-discovery. My sense of vulnerability, confusion and the sheer weight of the challenge stopped me from walking that path. I was prepared to engage if the opportunity presented itself, within the safe framework of a role, but going after an answer of my own accord felt like a hopeless task. It was easier to trust that my white appearance would keep me in work, and hope for a break.

I had briefly wondered whether I was looking for my break in the wrong place. And the awareness I spoke of in my Ismail self-tape was born of that search. In 2014, inspired by my visit to LA, I decided to go on a similar adventure in Mumbai. Perhaps Bollywood held the answer.

*

In March 2014, I'd blagged a ticket to the Empire awards and had found myself on a table next to Tom Cruise. Sat one table along was *Jadoo* star Amara Karan, who introduced me to her friend, producer and consultant Julian Alcantara, who had links to Bollywood and kindly offered to share some contacts. Over the course of a week, I met with the likes of Shanoo Sharma at Yash Raj Films, Seher Latif, who cast *The Lunchbox*, starring Irrfan Khan, and Mukesh Chhabra, who would go on to cast the Netflix hits *Sacred Games* and *Delhi Crime*. Not one of them was impressed by my tale of shaking Tom Cruise's hand and several others I met had no idea who he was. Bollywood was its own massive ecosystem, dominated by Hindi, and there was no desperate need for a novelty gora who only spoke Punjabi. My irrelevance seemed to be underlined by the fact that the film *2 States* had hit cinemas just as I'd arrived in town: a mixed-marriage love story about a Punjabi boy from the north and a Tamil girl from the south. There was no need for foreign faces when it came to Bollywood culture-clash dramas. Slightly deflated, I checked out from my budget hotel near the airport and boarded a plane to Amritsar. My trip wouldn't be wasted.

It was during this long overdue trip to Punjab and time spent in my pind – the ancestral village where both my grandad and my dad had grown up, where I too had spent time during my childhood summer holidays – that the first major ripple disturbed the surface of my life. After a long day sat in the courtyard on manjas, eating, talking and admiring the calf that was still being weaned, the time came for me and my dad to head back with Uncle Jagir to his house in Moga. As we bounced along the dirt road towards Kot Ise Khan, I was thinking about my uncles and the conversations they'd been having about their twilight years and their wish to see my grandad at least once more before they died. And I began to think about my own connection to India, to these people who had been synonymous with Punjab since before I could remember. Frustration rose up: I spoke Punjabi but I didn't have the vocabulary to communicate complex thoughts and emotions; I hadn't been able to properly share the nuances of how I felt about my parents' divorce a few years earlier. And then an intense grief. I tried not to cry. We were only travelling down the road, not back to the UK, but huge tears forced their way out and my chest heaved. My dad asked what was wrong and if I'd been able to speak coherently I might have said, 'I'm afraid of growing up, growing distant from India, family dying and being left untethered. Without these uncles and aunties here in India, who held me as a child, who am I?'

The implications of this question were terrifying and I wasn't ready for it. I cried it out and sought solace in what I knew and what I could control. That summer, my sister and I borrowed a DSLR camera and a microphone and interviewed BG about her life: her earliest memories, Partition and moving to the UK. It was something we'd been meaning to do for a while, and I'd later do the same with Grandad. Whatever happened, I'd have those videos to watch, forever.

The call to adventure

The following spring, I attended a Punjabi wedding with my dad. The groom, Gurpreet, was an old family friend who I'd see during school holidays when his mum and dad would drive up from east London to visit grandad and BG. Gurpreet was slightly older than me and therefore cool. We played cricket in the garden with my sister and his younger brother, went off exploring on our bikes, and we spent many hours dissecting the intricacies of *The Matrix* sequels. He was like a cousin and I was certain that this wedding would feel like a family affair.

But as I arrived in the hotel lobby, it struck me that I didn't fit. I was attending with my dad, his Hindu Punjabi partner and her daughter. They appeared to be a perfect nuclear family of three brown faces. And then there was me. It dawned on me that I could probably call myself 'Steve, from work' for the whole evening and get away with it.

I'm rarely identified as my dad's son in public. I didn't notice it as a kid, nor did it bother me as a teen. Indeed, I once delighted in convincing a stranger on a train that I was adopted; my dad was sitting next to me and played along. But as I got older, an anxiety crept in. On a trip to New York for my sister's drama school graduation, we visited Coney Island together and rode Cyclone, the famous wooden roller coaster. My main memory of that outing was how quick my dad was to inform the woman on the kiosk that he was my dad (she hadn't asked) lest we were mistaken for an age gap couple out on a date. There was a similar occurrence in a hotel spa, when a group of people came into the sauna while my dad was kneading a knot in my shoulder. And I'm not alone in these experiences.

In response to my TEDx talk in 2020, Alisha Mohindra

tweeted a few examples of her own experiences as a white-presenting person of mixed heritage: 'It's been as outrageous as people questioning how I could possibly be the daughter of my father. People have assumed I was his 'young partner' (sorry, it's so gross) before considering that a man with dark skin could have a daughter with light skin.' Our collective ignorance has made families like mine and Alisha's seem so anomalous that we are assumed to be our parents' lovers before we are recognised as their children.

For me, these incidents were never serious, rarely discussed and treated with levity. But the blended family configuration in which we'd arrived at this wedding in 2015 was new. As other guests glanced our way, I felt powerless and uncomfortable.

My fears were soon made manifest when the photographer logging the arrivals beckoned us forward and, upon seeing me, remarked, 'One family at a time, please.' 'He's my son,' my dad chuckled politely. 'She's my mum,' his partner's daughter chimed in, no doubt worried that she might be read as my girlfriend. I smiled through the awkwardness and we moved through to the drinks reception.

My feeling of isolation grew as the evening went on. White guests approached me, seeking fellow fish out of water. Uncles were amazed to see me eating so proficiently with my hands and, upon discovering I spoke Punjabi, accosted me to shame their kids, for surely if this white man could speak the language, what was their excuse? One uncle even whipped out his phone for me to record a video message, his flash blinding me. I tried to convince myself I was having a good time, that the attention was fun, that I was entertaining and being a good guest, but I didn't want to be performing tonight. I had come here wanting to be enveloped by the familiar. I had come seeking escape, but I felt more trapped than ever.

Then the dhol kicked in. The sound cut through the air and wrapped itself around my soul. There it was: home. I saw the spark in my dad's eye. It had found him too. We made our way to the dance floor and we let loose.

The beauty of bhangra, I find, is the simplicity of the dance. Both the eldest elder and the youngest child can contribute a verse. The bend of the knee can be slight or profound, the twist of the hand, gentle or extreme. All lend equal weight to the great performance. And like all great folk dances, there are spontaneous moments where pairs and groups come together and transform the jubilant atmosphere into a synchronous triumph of celebration. Moments of unity where everything that isn't immediate is forgotten. And I was in the thick of it. A child once more. I locked eyes with my dad and I could see he was back there too. And then, lost in the beat, I spun around and my world collapsed.

A young Punjabi girl was sitting at a table, her legs not quite reaching the floor, while her small hands rubbed nervously at her dress. Her eyes were wide, staring, her confusion equalled only by her fascination. Staring. At me. My curiosity became realisation, my body felt heavy and the music seemed to fade. She couldn't fathom what I was. A bhangra-dancing white man. I saw the thoughts swirl in her mind. To her, I was alien.

I now had a choice to make: build a labyrinth and hide her away, or accept that I could no longer avoid the path I needed to walk.

The choice hung over me for several days after the wedding and I found expression for my conflict by penning a short story, inspired by my recent discovery of the works of sci-fi writer, Robert Sheckley.

He belonged to two worlds yet felt suspended in the void that separated them. Exclusion drew attention, it was exciting and had always appealed to Narj's sensibilities. But for the first time in his life, he found himself craving the anonymity of being among his people. But no such people existed. Narj was exhausted. He had never felt so acutely self-aware and he longed for the ignorance of his youth. He felt paradoxically present yet absent.

I emailed a copy of this short story, titled *Alienation*, to my mum, with the caveat that it was 'a kind of thought experiment'. When I visited her a week later, I was excited to hear her thoughts and then horrified to discover how upset she was. 'I remember being really shocked,' my mum recalls, 'because I hadn't thought that bringing you up with both cultures would have given you a problem. I felt like I'd had a door slammed in my face. I felt like I'd made a massive mistake somehow. Even now it makes me ...' My mum chokes up as the memory rushes back into the present.

My mum and dad, along with Grandad and BG, had

created a perfect little world in Leicester, where being a white Punjabi was totally normal. But aged 24, I was venturing out into society, interacting with a world organised by categories, borders and binaries. I felt entirely alone. But I was on the right path. In initiating the conversation with my mum, by writing 'a conflict had sparked within Narj and he feared there was no resolution to be found', I had stepped out and approached the first threshold.

'Man pack and wolf pack have cast me out,' said Mowgli. 'Now I will hunt alone in the jungle.'[5]

Darkness stretched before me. Veiled from view were books I needed to read, conversations I needed to have and experiences I'd never imagined. I stepped into the wilderness. The adventure had begun.

2

MY NAME IS JASSA AHLUWALIA AND I HAVE IMPERIAL NOSTALGIA

We escape the trauma of the history we happen to be living through by entering the mythic time of the history we didn't.

PETER MITCHELL, *IMPERIAL NOSTALGIA*

WHEN I SAT down to read Rudyard Kipling's *Kim* in 2015, I felt guilty and conflicted. This was the man who coined the term 'white man's burden', a writer who 'has been variously labelled a colonialist, a jingoist, a racist, an anti-Semite, a misogynist [and] a right-wing imperialist warmonger'.[1] To even countenance reading *Kim* felt like a transgression. But I was drawn to it nonetheless. I'd heard that it was the story of a little white boy who lived on the streets of Punjab. I nervously opened up this forbidden text and, to my horror and delight, found myself transported back to my childhood.

I had turned to Kipling because I felt I had nowhere else to look. I was seeking a past in which to root myself and so turned to the creator of my beloved Mowgli. After all, I had visited Delhi zoo as a child, seen Bagheera and Shere Khan in real life, and was taught that their stories had been penned by a white British man who lived in Lahore and spoke the language. I had grown up with a strong sense of belonging in Leicester, but I had no white Punjabi contemporaries at school and tales of the Raj felt confusingly familiar. And though in 2015, aged 24, I was aware that *The Jungle Book* had its fair share of critics (academics like John A. McClure have labelled it an imperial allegory, describing Mowgli as 'behaving towards the beasts as the British do to the Indians'), when I got to the end of 'Tiger! Tiger!', I saw no imperial conqueror, but a young boy, much like myself, grappling with belonging and identity:

> These two things fight together in me as the snakes
> fight in the spring. The water comes out of my eyes;
> yet I laugh while it falls. Why? I am two Mowglis
> … my heart is heavy with the things that I do not
> understand.[2]

My heart was also heavy. I longed to understand. And as I began to read *Kim*, I found comfort in the familiar. Never had I read anything that spoke to me so directly:

> Though he spoke the vernacular by preference, and
> his mother-tongue in a clipped uncertain sing-song;
> though he consorted on terms of perfect equality with
> the small boys of the bazar; Kim was white.[3]

Here was me. The Jassa who spent summers in India, played cricket in the gullies and forgot how to speak English. Kim's mother had 'died of cholera in Ferozepore', the city only an hour away by car from Uncle Jagir's house in Moga. And his holiday escape from St Xavier's School in Lucknow echoed my dad's childhood jailbreaks from St Joseph's Convent School in Bathinda.

As I read that Kim 'turned now and again from his king-of-the-castle game with little Chota Lal, and Abdullah ... to make a rude remark to the native policeman', I remembered how I would affectionately taunt one of my grandad's younger brothers by calling him '*gadhā* uncle', 'donkey uncle', on account of his wild beard and countenance. 'The big Punjabi grinned tolerantly: he knew Kim of old.'⁴ This line, minus the implicit racial hierarchy, could just have easily described my uncle and me.

Forever curious and in search of adventure, Kim becomes a disciple to a Tibetan monk who is on a quest for Enlightenment. Recognising this as an opportunity for subterfuge, an Afghan horse trader who moonlights as a British secret agent enlists Kim to carry a message to an Englishman in a city they'll be passing through. As a street-smart chameleon who relishes 'the game for its own sake' Kim soon finds himself being schooled in espionage and, under the guise of the monk's attendant, becomes increasingly embroiled in the machinations of the Great Game – the imperial rivalry between Britain and Russia.

It is a rip-roaring tale. Even Edward Said, author of *Orientalism*, one of the founding texts of postcolonial studies, writes that, '*Kim* is a work of great aesthetic merit; it cannot be dismissed simply as the racist imagining of one fairly disturbed and ultra-reactionary imperialist.'[5]

When I reached the end, I was deeply moved. The climax of Kim's quest leaves him physically and emotionally spent and he recuperates in the care of an elderly woman, whom he meets earlier in his travels. When he wakes after a day and half of 'sleep that soaked like rain after drought', he contemplates his being and 'felt, though he could not put it into words, that his soul was out of gear with its surroundings—a cog-wheel unconnected with any machinery.'[6]

> 'I am Kim. I am Kim. And what is Kim?' His soul repeated it again and again.
>
> He did not want to cry,—had never felt less like crying in his life,—but of a sudden easy, stupid tears trickled down his nose, and with an almost audible click he felt the wheels of his being lock up anew on the world without.[7]

I cried with Kim, aghast that I was having such a sincere emotional response to an explicitly colonial text. The sudden realisation of one's place in the world was all that I desired and Kim appeared to have succeeded. But as I flicked through the final pages, my tears dried up. I saw now why Kipling had earned his reputation: Kim had discovered his true calling was not to be 'Little Friend of all the World', as he was once known on the streets of Lahore, but as a British spy, an agent of the hierarchies that kept India in British hands. This was the function of the colonial hybrid: to act as an intermediary and preserve the established order.

I wanted to ignore this. I wanted to forget the racist descriptions I'd encountered along the way. I desperately wanted to read Kipling's work as an impassioned critique of the injustice of having to choose a single identity, with his fervour for empire rooted exclusively in the rich hybridity it precipitated. I remembered now how much I hated the ending of Disney's *The Jungle Book* as a child.

Reminiscing about their victory over Shere Khan, the animated Baloo and Mowgli find themselves with Bagheera at the edge of the Man-Village. 'Nobody is ever going to come between us,' says Baloo as they hug. And then a girl is heard singing 'My Own Home' and Mowgli becomes enthralled. Baloo cautions but Bagheera encourages. He wanders off, doe eyed, following his seductress towards manhood. 'Mowgli is where he belongs now,' says Bagheera.[8]

This was the truth of it. According to Kipling, fluid childhood must lead to fixed and bordered adulthood. But this wasn't the answer I wanted. I didn't want to become a 'sahib' and choose white over brown. If this was the conclusion, why was I so enamoured with these tales?

I was no doubt latching on to the emotional currents underpinning Kipling's work: Mowgli and Kim are both young boys separated from their birth parents. This had also been Kipling's experience when, aged five and fifteen weeks, he left India for schooling in England. On a much smaller scale, I had left my parents in Coventry to attend school in the care of Grandad and BG in Leicester. And while I never suffered the beatings that Kipling did, I would wail uncontrollably when my mum dropped me off, cry myself to sleep and wet the bed. But beyond these thematic resonances, I've come to understand that Kipling, like me, was grappling with the uncertainties of early adulthood and finding solace in his Indian youth.

Kipling left India in 1889 to advance his career as a writer and took his 'first steps toward assuming the mantle of the bard of empire'[9] with his 1891 poem 'The English Flag'. In 1892, he married Carrie Balestier and they moved to the United States. When she fell pregnant that year, memories of his boyhood surfaced and inspired thoughts of a 'Thibetan lama and Kim o' the Rishti', alongside visions of the Indian jungle and 'a wolf boy'.[10] When he became a father on the night of 29 December 1892, the overwhelming joy of beholding his 'first beloved' tapped into the wellspring of his childhood and *The Jungle Book* sprang to life. He inscribed a first edition with: 'This book belongs to Josephine Kipling for whom it was written by her father, May 1894.'[11] When Josephine died of pneumonia in March 1899, aged six, he was devastated. He had already begun to retreat into writing *Kim* as a way of coping with the death of his uncle and his sister's mental health crises in 1898, but his efforts took on a renewed focus in the wake of losing 'The daughter that was all to him!'[12] India and his childhood were a lost paradise into which he could escape. In reading *Kim*, I was attempting to do the same. Unable to make sense of my mixed heritage in the present day, I sought out a fictitious antecedent, an imaginary past where all was well and the world made sense.

I came in search of an answer, but left having learnt a lesson: I was not Mowgli, I was not Kim, I was Jassa, and I still didn't know who that was.

White Mughals

> To Jassa,
> Happy 25th!
> Enjoy William Dalrymple's
> writing. He brings
> India to life!
> all my love Mummy
>
> xxxx

I stared in disbelief at the title as I pulled the book out of the gift bag. *White Mughals*. I had heard of the author, William Dalrymple – his account of living in Delhi, *City of Djinns*, had made a deep impression on both my parents and they'd briefly entertained moving there themselves during the nineties – but I had never read his work. I was familiar with the Mughals though, the imperial dynasty that had ruled vast swathes of the Indian subcontinent from 1526 to 1857.

The year I was born, Channel 4 released a six-part series called *The Great Moghuls* and my dad had watched every episode, recorded them onto VHS, taken notes and given a talk on Mughal landmarks to a group of teachers in Leamington Spa, who were travelling to India for the first time. My memories of roaming India's tourist hotspots are replete with my dad regaling me with the histories of emperors Babur, Humayun, Akbar, Jahangir, Shah Jahan and Aurangzeb. But I had never heard of 'white Mughals'. The title seemed to reach into my soul. I flipped the book over and read the blurb.

This was the story of James Achilles Kirkpatrick, the East India Company representative at the court of the Nizam of Hyderabad, who, in 1798, fell in love with Mughal princess, Khair un-Nissa, converted to Islam and became a double agent, working against the British. An incredible tale to be sure, but what really captivated me was the claim that this story was not an anomaly. Their tragic tale, it seemed, represented a forgotten past of intermarriage and cultural fluidity where British men came of age immersed in Indian customs.

This was the history that predated Kipling and the Raj: the Victorian generation who, as Dalrymple observes, 'succeeded in colonising not only India but also, more permanently, our imaginations, to the exclusion of all other images of the Indo-British encounter'. And then came the assurance I'd been craving, the final line of the book's introduction: 'This unlikely group of expatriates provides a timely reminder that it is indeed very possible – and has always been possible – to reconcile the two worlds.'[13]

Late 18th-century India felt immediately familiar. Not because of cultural harmony – the tragedy of James Kirkpatrick and Khair un-Nissa is that they fell in love at a time when ethnic divides were increasingly being policed – but because of family conflict. Khair was a Sayyeda, a member of the endogamous Muslim community that traces its lineage to the Prophet Muhammed (peace be upon him), and her chastity was of paramount concern to many in her family. So, when her relationship with Kirkpatrick, and subsequent pregnancy, became the talk of Hyderabad, her grandfather was driven into a 'phrenzy at the indignity offered to the honour of his family by such proceedings, and had declared his intention of proceeding to the Mecca Masjid (the principle mosque of the city)'[14] to incite the Muslims of the Deccan to rise up against the British.

My grandad had reacted with similar invective, albeit more parochially, when my aunty converted and married a Punjabi Muslim in 1996, and he banned them from visiting the house. BG found herself caught in the crossfire and I bore witness to her tears of distress as she bewailed the religious divide cleaving our family. In much the same way, Sharaf un-Nissa, Khair's mother and matchmaker, mourned for the time 'before the distinctions introduced by Musa [Moses], Isa [Jesus] and Mohamed were known to the world'.[15] I was not alone, it seemed, in longing for an idyllic past.

Within the opening pages of *White Mughals*, my Indo-European origins began to reveal themselves. It all began with the Portuguese, who arrived in India 28 years before the Mughals and just over a hundred years before the East India Company. In the aftermath of Afonso de Albuquerque's conquest of Goa in 1510, he ordered his men to marry the widows of the city's massacred Muslim defenders, before forcibly converting them to Christianity. As brutal as this episode was, it didn't take long for India to assimilate its latest intruder. By 1560, pluralism was thriving – prompting a visiting Jesuit to declare that 'the Inquisition is more necessary in these parts than anywhere else, since all the Christians here live together with the Muslims, the Jews and the Hindus'[16] – and hybridity followed. In 1585, it was decreed that only Indo-Portuguese of Brahminical ancestry could train as Roman Catholic priests. 'The Portuguese in India, and their Indo-Portuguese descendants, did not leave one culture to inhabit another' writes Dalrymple, 'so much as live in both at the same time.'[17]

During my 2014 trip to Mumbai, I got a literal taste for the lasting legacy of this fusion. One afternoon, after wandering Juhu beach between meetings, I went in search of a bite to eat and found myself in a no-frills restaurant. Despite the bright sunshine, it was dark inside, the heat kept at bay by brown tinted windows. Through the gloom, I scoured the menu in search of something local and unfamiliar.

Until I'd arrived in Mumbai, I hadn't realised quite how Punjabi my tastes were. I'd relied on room service for my first few days in the city and as I got to know my waiter, he confessed he had expected to meet a sardar, a turbaned Sikh man. 'Because of my name?' I asked. 'No, sir.' He chuckled. 'Because of the food!' I had no idea that my love of aloo praunthe and dhal makhani could be so revealing.

Back in the restaurant off Juhu beach, a quick google on the WiFi told me that 'pav bhaji' was a local speciality. And it was on the menu. Perfect. I placed my order. I had no idea what to expect but I certainly hadn't anticipated a buttered bread roll that looked like it had been plucked out of my primary school memories – this was, as we say in Leicester, a cob. The mixed veg curry accompanying it looked more familiar, but I was utterly bewildered by the batch baked bap. It looked so foreign and out of place. Thankfully, there was no one around to watch me awkwardly experiment with how to eat it. Did I fill the roll? Tear it into chunks like a roti? What on earth was this?

Pav bhaji is, in the words of *Masala Lab* author Krish Ashok, 'the least Indian, most globalised and most Indian of dishes'.[18] The pav, the bread roll, pronounced and sometimes written pao, is simply the Portuguese word for bread, *pão*. The colonisers brought their leavened baking style with them and the name stuck. The bhaji, the mixed veg curry, is even more historically rich. Apart from the spices, none of the ingredients are from India. Tomatoes, chillies and peppers came from Mexico via Portugal. Likewise, the Peruvian native, the potato, first came to India's shores on Dutch and Portuguese ships and, to this day, is known in both Marathi and Gujarati by the Portuguese word *batata*. The humble tuber became an Indian staple after the British cultivated them at scale in the north, during the 18th century, where it became known as the aloo, a Sanskrit word for 'edible root'.[19]

It blows my mind to contemplate the fact that Guru Nanak, who died in 1539, never ate aloo gobi or aloo gajar; both cauliflowers and carrots were also British imports. But to say that either dish is not truly Indian would be absurd. Potato stuffed samosas are as quintessentially Punjabi as the pav bhaji is a Mumbai classic. The acculturation of food followed a tradition that stretched back to the earliest days of Indian civilisation, when the Indo-Aryans began to accommodate local deities as avatars of their gods, giving rise to the Hindu pantheon.[20] Before the East India Company established dominance in the subcontinent, the English authorities remained wary of India's apparent ability to absorb and reshape its invaders.

Through interactions with the Ottoman Empire, the concept of 'turning Turk' had become well established in the English imagination and when the first English treaty with the Mughal Empire was inked in 1616, point eight of the document insisted that 'English fugitives were to be delivered up' to the East India Company trading post.[21] The clause was little heeded though and, in the 1670s, it came to light that the Mughals were operating a covert recruitment network in Bombay. Many early Brits in India came from the margins of society, had no loyalty to the London elite who had shipped them off and were in awe of both Mughal opulence and the tolerant grandeur of the Deccan sultanates.

It's also worth noting just how young and impressionable Company administrators were when they first came ashore. As the trading company morphed into a colonial government, anyone joining the civil service had to do so before their 16th birthday. And coming of age in India inevitably meant sex with Indian women: 'young men attach themselves to the women of this country; and acquire a liking, or taste, for their society and customs, which soon supersedes every other attraction,' wrote one observer.[22] For those who leant into Hindu culture, this included vegetarianism, while many were enticed by the wonders of shampoo and regular bathing, practices derided as 'effeminate' back in London. ('Shampoo! Indian!' as Sanjeev Bhaskar's Mr Everything Comes From

India might say. A word my grandad always delighted in telling me originated from the Hindi word for massage: *champna*. Shampoo being an anglicisation of the imperative, *champo*, meaning 'press!')

One in three of the Bengal Wills, dated 1780 to 1785, contains a bequest to Indian partners or mixed heritage children, and Urdu poets began to forgo Muslim protagonists in favour of star-crossed Hindu girls and English men. This by no means meant that these were all loving and equal relationships. While some *bibis* (wives) inherited vast estates, others received only a passing mention beneath instructions for the care of dogs. Coercion, trafficking and abuse were also rife; indeed, letters and legal rulings show that many men came to India in order to satisfy their perversions. But insofar as the bedroom was a liminal space over the course of the 18th century, the urban hubs of British power became more insular as the Company came into the ascendancy and Mughal power began to wane. Theatres, churches and growing prosperity in Bombay, Madras and Calcutta served to stem defections to Indian courts, whose wealth was diminishing in the face of British rapacity. Away from these Presidency towns, however, rich hybridities continued to flourish.

David Ochterlony arrived in India as an 18-year-old cadet in 1777, rose through the ranks of the Company's Bengal army and took to the battlefield against the Marathas during the 1803 Battle of Delhi. [23] In the wake of victory, he was appointed resident of the city. His role was to represent British interests, which he did, but his appearance and lifestyle was anything but. He preferred Indian fashion, encouraged

41

the use of his Mughal title, Nasir-ud-Daula (defender of the state) and was rumoured to take promenades around the walls of the Red Fort every evening, followed by his 13 concubines, each atop their own elephant.

Dublin-born Charles Stuart, who also arrived in India as a teen cadet in the same year as Ochterlony, similarly travelled the countryside with his Indian wife, followed by 'a cavalcade of children's carriages "and a palkee load of little babies"'.[24] His obituary in the *Asiatic Journal* attests to his hybrid life, for he 'had studied the language, manners and customs of the natives of this country with so much enthusiasm, that his intimacy with them, and his toleration of, or rather apparent conformity to their ideas and prejudices, obtained for him the name *Hindoo* Stuart'. And he was highly critical of Christian missionaries:

> I would repose the Hindoo system on the broad basis
> of its own merits; convinced, that, on the enlarged
> principles of moral reasoning, it little needs the
> meliorating hand of Christian dispensations, to render
> its votaries, a sufficiently correct and moral people, for
> all the useful purposes of civilized society.[25]

In 1813, late in his military career, Stuart found himself being severely reprimanded for publishing new Regimental Orders after he took command of the 4th Native Infantry. Sepoys of the first battalion had been complaining about their uniforms and the lack of consideration given to religious observances; Stuart saw fit to 'obviate all possible discontent by due forbearance on this score', but swiftly found himself suspended and transferred.[26] The adjutant-general, on behalf of the commander-in-chief, condemned Stuart for acting with the 'highest imprudence and indiscretion of which a commanding officer of a native corps could be guilty'.[27] He died in Calcutta in 1828, buried in the city's Great Christian Burial Ground, beneath a domed tomb, carved to resemble a mandir.

It was with these characters in mind that I would later discover a book called *The Rajah From Tipperary* on my grandad's bookshelf, a chronicle of the life of George Thomas. This particular Irishman boarded a British man-o'-war in Bristol in the early 1780s and upon reaching Madras deserted his ship and European rule. He formed and became the leader of the 'Irish Pindaris', a mercenary group 'of many races and religions ... identified by their being detached from any settled home, territory or fixed alliance'[28] before finding service under Begum Samru in 1787. Thought to have developed her ruthless aptitude for survival as a young nautch girl, this warrior queen honed her talents as the wife of mercenary Walter Reinhardt, 'a butcher from Leipzig' and 'one of the most vicious and despicable adventurers that the turmoil of the century had the misfortune to spew forth'.[29] In the wake of his death by fever in Agra, the begum petitioned Mughal emperor Shah Alam II – who had dubbed her Zeb un-Nissa: 'ornament of womankind' – and was awarded all rights of succession, rising to become ruler of the principality of Sardhana. She took Thomas as her lover and they proved to be something of a power couple before betrayal and conflict drove them apart. Thomas would later end up a ruler himself, establishing a kingdom in Haryana, building a fort, minting his own coins and forgetting how to speak English.

Just as the fictitious paradise of Kim's Lahore had seduced me, I once again found myself romanticising the colonial era. *Perhaps this was the time and place in which I belonged?* I wondered. Walking the streets around my flat in East London, the streets that had once thronged with the comings and goings of empire and India, I listened to the soundtrack of *Midnight in Paris*, wishing I could slip through the cracks of time like Owen Wilson and visit what I imagined to be my own golden age. I knew that empire was nothing to be celebrated, but I couldn't help being drawn to these stories. I wanted to promenade with Ochterlony, celebrate Diwali with Hindoo Stuart and swashbuckle with Jehazi Sahib, as George Thomas was known. It was easy to be disabused of my attachment to Kim and Mowgli, imaginary children who ultimately reject fluidity. But the white Mughals were real people who, I imagined, could have easily comprehended a white Punjabi such as myself. Once again, struggling to make sense of my present, I turned my gaze towards the past. How could I inhabit this world? I longed to bring these characters to life on stage or screen.

*

Visiting my dad over the Christmas holidays, I flicked through a copy of the latest programme from Leicester's Curve Theatre and an image caught my eye: a sepia-toned photo of a brown man, in military uniform, wearing a tall turban, emblazoned with the title *Wipers*. The play, by Ishy Din – 'inspired by the real life story of Khuddadad Khan, the first South Asian soldier to be awarded a Victoria Cross for his extraordinary bravery at the First Battle of Ypres' – wasn't set to open until April 2016.[30] I had no idea if there was a suitable role for me. And the time period was firmly the age of Kipling, not the white Mughals. But I sensed an opportunity. As I geared up for my final night shoot on *Peaky Blinders*, I pinged off a tweet to director Suba Das: 'Mr Das! As a half Punjabi Leicester boy I'd love to grab a coffee. Fascinated by #Wipers.' I followed up with an email:

> I've been grappling with my identity as an adult - sparked by a recent experience at an Indian wedding - often finding myself straddling two worlds that both feel equally me. I'm discovering that I have a strange affinity with the history of British India and my personal reading has increasingly been focused on the history of empire, essentially tracing my earliest origins.

In the New Year, I found myself nervously climbing the stairs at the American Church on Tottenham Court Road and auditioning for the role of Second Lieutenant Thomas Dixon-Wright. A couple of months later, I began rehearsals in Leicester and was overjoyed to find myself stepping back in time alongside three actors of Punjabi heritage: Waleed Akhtar, Sartaj Garewal and Simon Rivers. In their company, hunkered down in a French barn in 1914, cooking dhal in our mess tins, I got a taste of what it was like to live as my full self.

It was made clear to us from the off that the play was still undergoing rewrites and revisions. This was somewhat normal for a new play, but *Wipers* proved to be a more fluid experience than most. As a cast, we had considerable input, essentially devising many scenes, and I was able to inject large amounts of my own history and research. Whereas it had never occurred to me to suggest a mixed background for Rocky in *Some Girls*, and although Thomas was not mixed, I grasped the opportunity to bring personal specificity to the role in whatever ways I could. In a rehearsal studio in Leicester, surrounded by supportive brown faces, I felt safe and confident to do so:

THOMAS: The only elephant I've ever seen was a small carved one my father bought for my mother, when they were first courting, from an India display ... at an Empire exhibition. Incredible little thing. They said that a native was carving it in front of their eyes ... I thought it was a toy and managed to break its tusks ... my father was not best pleased.

The anecdote of the carved elephant was entirely my own; my mum had bought it from a Thai importer in Leamington Spa as a gift for my dad. He still has it, one tusk forever lost. Thomas was initially written as someone quite ignorant of the subcontinent. In an early draft, teen recruit Ayub Khan schools him in the history of 1876, when Queen Victoria was declared Empress of India. I didn't want to dilute the impact of Ayub's anti-colonial dialogue in any way – it was incredibly refreshing – but I felt that it would be more interesting, more nuanced and true to the time, if India existed in the background of Thomas's life somehow, as it had done in Britain for over 200 years at this point. I'd read about the Colonial and Indian Exhibition of 1886, held in South Kensington, and offered it up in rehearsal.

As deeply rewarding as this experience was, there were also brief moments where I was reminded I wasn't fully congruent. One lunchtime as we headed into Leicester to get some food, I was relishing being able to joke and banter as a Punjabi among Punjabis. We were all at some point or another testing the barriers of acceptability. During rehearsals, I had learnt the phrase *muth maar*, slang for masturbation, and I don't recall what I proffered, but I remember the response: 'You're not brown enough to make that joke.' It was said in jest, and I smiled along, but it cut deep.

Once the play opened and we began meeting audiences, and despite our names and faces being on the posters, I frequently found myself being mistaken for Simon. Born Amardip Singh Nahal, he adopted Simon Rivers to get work. In an interview with BBC Asian Network later that year, he shared, 'I don't tend to get a lot of Asian roles … Or if I do, they're always with a twist: the fish out of water, or the mixed race [one], or the one who doesn't really wanna, you know, be part of the culture.'[31] For him, as for me, *Wipers* was a welcome opportunity to connect with his Punjabi heritage.

Even before I spoke to Simon Rivers about all of this,

I absolutely knew why he had adopted his stage name. It was a sad reality of the business. I'd done work experience as a teen at ICM London, a leading talent agency, and the founder, Duncan Heath, had suggested I get the mole on my nose removed and give some thought to my professional name. The mole got zapped on my eighteenth birthday, but I considered my name my superpower: it stuck in people's minds. Plus, it was the only 'visible' bit of me that was Punjabi. So being approached and assumed to be Simon on account of my whiteness was galling.

These were minor niggles though. The joy of sharing the stage was unparalleled and I had dog tags made up as press night gifts, punched with our tour dates and a line from the play, 'We eat together, we fight together, we die together.' The night Grandad and BG attended, my co-stars treated them like royalty. They slipped in and out of Punjabi as they spoke, and BG affectionately embraced Waleed and pinched his cheeks to make sure he was okay; she'd felt sorry for him on account of the bullying his character had endured. I watched the scene unfold in the Curve foyer, my two worlds effortlessly becoming one.

I'd assumed that this would be the experience to prompt new and profound insight, the bolt of lightning that would illuminate my path through the jungle. But I was wrong. The play could never do that. The tour would come to an end and I'd have to face reality, and the present, once more. A reality and a present in which Grandad and BG were both becoming visibly old and frail. How would I cope when their seats were empty? I longed to know.

The work of a lifetime

I began rereading *His Dark Materials* in 2015, after it was announced that the BBC was planning a big-budget adaptation of the full trilogy. I'd devoured the books in my early teens and had been so impressed with *Northern Lights* that I'd lent it to a girl I had a crush on at school. Much to my dismay, a romance never blossomed. And, most tragically, I never got the book back.

My memories of the book were of magic, darkness and secrets. All the events had made sense, but the mysteries had never fully revealed themselves to me. I knew that 'Dust' was central to the story, but I'd never really grasped what it was. I hadn't cared to dwell on what it meant that Lyra had a dæmon, called Pantalaimon, which was a physical manifestation of her innermost self in the form of an animal. The fact that he could shapeshift, but would eventually choose to settle when she grew up, felt entirely natural.

Revisiting the book as an adult, I marvelled at its complexity and depths. Pullman's 'Dust' is elementary particles of awareness and I now began to see how the whole trilogy was essentially a treatise on consciousness. By the time I was doing *Wipers* in Leicester, I was deep into the third and final instalment, *The Amber Spyglass*. My primary reason for reading the books had been to figure out which roles I might be able to audition for, so I was caught totally unawares when the angel Xaphania swoops down on page 519.

"Why –" Lyra began, and found her voice weak and trembling – "why can't I read the alethiometer anymore? Why can't I even do that? That was the one thing I could do really well, and it's just not there anymore – it just vanished as if it had never come …"

"You read it by grace," said Xaphania, looking at her, "and you can regain it by work."

Lying in my childhood bedroom in Leicester, I continued slowly and turned the page carefully and deliberately.

"How long will that take?"

"A lifetime."

"That long …"

"But your reading will be even better then, after a lifetime of thought and effort, because it will come from conscious understanding. Grace attained like that is deeper and fuller than grace that comes freely, and furthermore, once you've gained it, it will never leave you."

"You mean a *full* lifetime, don't you?" Lyra whispered. "A whole long life? Not … not just … a few years …"

"Yes, I do," said the angel.

My mind shone with blinding clarity: my alethiometer, my golden compass, was Punjabi – my heritage. Just as I had once been able to speak and traverse the two worlds of my being with effortless ease, Lyra had passed between numerous realities, guided by her intuitive ability to read her alethiometer. What lay before us both was a choice: grieve our lost innocence or begin the work of life. The language that had once so easily replaced my mother tongue now required study. The culture that felt innate in my youth demanded inquiry. Whatever grief I'd felt in India was now suddenly replaced with excitement. My misguided belief that I could make my world whole again by reaching back through time began to dissolve. I no longer needed to cling to my childhood or a romanticised past, I realised. I didn't need Mowgli, or Kim or the white Mughals. Yes, they had all deepened my understanding of the history that had led to my present, but it was my future that truly demanded my attention. I had to look inwards and ahead; the answers I sought would not be found by looking backwards.

I didn't spend much time in 2016 dwelling on my nostalgia. The rush of seeing through the illusion was potent and I raced headlong through the jungle. But in 2023, writing this book, I paused to reflect. The tears I had cried in India were born of real grief over the loss of my fluid childhood and fear of my elders' inevitable death. I had a sense that through Lyra I had overcome this pain, but I hadn't stopped to examine the process or how it might connect to the nostalgia that had been on display all around me ever since: 'Make America Great Again'; *Stranger Things*; Instagram accounts fetishising the Windows 95 startup sound; Captain Tom, invoked as a kind of living Spitfire, walking laps of his garden in the face of a virulent invader, while the Queen channelled Vera Lynn and assured the nation that 'we will meet again'.

Staring at my notes, uninspired, I did what I knew I shouldn't: I opened Twitter. The first tweet to greet me was from *Ten Thousand Posts*, a favourite podcast about how 'everything is posting', announcing their latest episode, 'A little Nostalgia, as a Treat ft. Peter Mitchell'. I couldn't believe my luck. Mitchell's book *Imperial Nostalgia: How the British Conquered Themselves* was on my reading list, but I'd put it off while I was assembling a timeline of my relationship with empire. I stopped what I was doing, started listening and was immediately rewarded.

'We escape the trauma of the history we happen to be living through by entering the mythic time of the history we didn't,' Mitchell writes. Central to his exploration of nostalgia is the act of mourning and how attachment to that which has been lost – be it empire, a loved one or one's childhood – can become a pathological obsession. Citing the work of Svetlana Boym, he elucidates that nostalgia began its life as a mental health diagnosis, first coined in 1688 by Swiss doctor Johannes Hofer as a union of two Greek words: *nostos*, 'home', and *algos*, 'pain'.[32] Discovering that the word 'nostalgia' was essentially Greek for 'homesickness' made reassuring sense. Home was what I'd been searching for in Mowgli's jungle, in the streets of Kim's Lahore and in the divans of the white Mughals. Mitchell goes on to make a compelling case for imperial nostalgia being an intense grief brought about by the impossibility of return. It manifests as a refusal to meaningfully connect past with present, curtailing any ability to imagine a better future. Instead, the past must be monumentalised, the future can never again be as great, and the present exists only as a realm of sorrow, in which the remaining vestiges of the lost world must be guarded or recreated. 'You can't say anything more!' 'What this generation needs is a war!' 'How dare these lefty woke snowflake students criticise my national newspaper column!' 'I'll chain myself to Nelson!' The imperial nostalgic moves through time, facing backwards, misty eyed and viewing those who dare to dissent as 'both hysterical weaklings and puritanical bullies'.[33]

Fizzing with the thrill of seeing my nebulous feelings expressed as rigorously researched legible thoughts, I reached out to Peter Mitchell via Hussein Kesvani, one of the hosts of *Ten Thousand Posts*. I desperately wanted to talk to him about something he called the 'Imperial Wonder Boy', both a literary trope and a mythologised historical figure, described in his book as someone:

> at home anywhere except home, a madcap cultural intercessor and inveterate dresser-up who nonetheless embodies the natural supremacy of his race and class; scholar, diplomat, soldier, secret agent; incalculable mystery and shrewd self-promoter; immensely worldly-wise and queerly innocent; both improbable historical reality and carefully tended myth.[34]

This felt familiar. Very familiar. These were the kinds of historical and literary characters I'd been drawn to: David Ochterlony, 'Hindoo' Stuart, George Thomas, Kim. What was their power? Mitchell had the answer.

One of the functions of the Imperial Wonder Boy, he explains, is the nostalgic escape he offers us 'from our own experience of historical time into a brighter, warmer history in which contradictions are resolved, the stakes are clear, and everybody knows how it ends.'[35] Such is Kim, Kipling's turn-of-the-century creation, whose India betrays no whiff of the independence movement that had been growing during his lifetime. The 1857 uprising of Indian sepoys features only as the distant memory of an 'an old, withered man, who had served the Government in the days of the Mutiny' and the novel ends, as we've seen, with Kim resolved to his 'natural supremacy'.[36] [37] '*Kim* is this kind of fantasy of fully achieved cosmopolitanism,' says Peter, 'but all this fluidity falls back to being in the service of white supremacy. But he's also not posh. And he's Irish. He's both an example of and a counterpoint to the Imperial Wonder Boy. In the same way that Kipling writes a weird counterpoint to the claims of his era, of British imperialism, while explicitly endorsing it at the same time.'

Over the course of our Zoom, I came to a realisation, and I offered up a theory: was the Imperial Wonder Boy perhaps a stunted classical hero? They leave the familiar and venture into the unknown – as all heroes must – but they do not undergo a true transformation and return. This is not to downplay the fact that this fictional figure lent real-world legitimacy to colonial racism and brutality. But in a mythological sense, the Imperial Wonder Boy never learns to trust the Force or master control of the Matrix. Instead, they wander back the way they came, carrying not Promethean fire, but wearing a necklace bought at a bazaar. Instead of saving the world, they assume their roles as sahibs, deliver after-dinner speeches, and run for the leadership of the Conservative party.

The reason Lyra unlocked what Kim hadn't dawned on me. She, too, embodied the trappings of the Imperial Wonder Boy. Just as we meet the chameleon orphan Kim fighting for dominance atop a cannon on the streets of Lahore, we encounter orphan Lyra slinging mud at the Gyptians in Oxford, equally at home with the college masters and kitchen staff. They begin their journeys as innocents, engaged in mock battles that echo the great forces shaping their worlds: worlds they do not yet grasp. Kim the Irish son of a dead colonial soldier; Lyra the ward of an Oxfordian scholar-adventurer. But then they diverge. Lyra continues on the path of the hero, while Kim turns back. He remains childlike and learns to accept his role as a colonial administrator. Lyra, on the other hand, grows up, experiences romantic love and vanquishes the Authority. She could perhaps be described as an Anti-Authoritarian Wonder Girl. Kim exemplifies how, after leaving India in 1889, Kipling 'for the rest of his life … lived in his art on the memories of his early Indian years'.[38] Kim is a nostalgic creation who exists in a timeless, unchanging India. Conversely, Lyra embodies maturation and the pursuit of knowledge in a multiverse that is left, and leaves her, fundamentally altered. I began wanting to be Kim, pining for my fluid childhood, but by 2016 I had become Lyra, studying the characters of the Punjabi alphabet as she does the symbols of her alethiometer. I would never escape to a lost paradise, but perhaps I could build one. I had been shown the way beyond nostalgia, I began the pursuit of wisdom.

Embracing ambiguity

Rereading *His Dark Materials* left me amazed that I'd ever understood any of it as a teen. There was so much complex detail that I'd clearly glossed over or simply accepted as part of the fantasy. For example, the technology behind the lodestone resonator, a device used by the diminutive Gallivespians to communicate across vast distances and worlds, was described as quantum entanglement.

Seeing 'quantum entanglement' on the page of what is ostensibly a young adult novel, my schoolboy curiosity was sparked. I folded the page and made a note to return to it. Back at my dad's in late 2016, I had the radio on and was mesmerised by an excerpt from Carlo Rovelli's *Reality Is Not What It Seems*, featured on *Book of the Week* on Radio 4. 'In the world described by quantum mechanics there is no reality except in the *relations* between physical systems. It isn't things that enter into relations but, rather, relations that ground the notion of "thing".'[39] Late that night, I fired up my laptop, opened YouTube and went in search of more. What I found was a documentary by physicist Brian Greene, called *The Fabric of the Cosmos*.

Here, I discovered that Pullman's Gallivespians were talking about a very real magic. Quantum entanglement, something Einstein famously dismissed as 'spooky action at a distance', describes 'how two subatomic particles can be intimately linked to each other even if separated by billions of light-years of space.'[40] Or as the Gallivespian Tialys explains to Lyra, with a dash of artistic licence, 'It means that two particles can exist that only have properties in common, so that whatever happens to one happens to the other at the same moment, no matter how far apart they are.'[41]

I felt like this fundamental physics applied to me. I lived with two worlds entangled inside of me, my sense of self existing in a fuzzy state of uncertainty. My journey into the jungle was about finding clarity. I was here to answer the question, *who am I?* And I expected a definitive answer. But physics was suggesting that some of the fundamental behaviours of the universe were not uniquely predictable. And nothing made this clearer to me than the double-slit experiment.

Imagine a blank white canvas and a barrier a few metres in front of it with two horizontal slits. If you were to fire paintballs at the canvas, you would create a pattern of two stripes corresponding with the two slits. (And if your aim was a bit wonky, you'd get paint on the barrier.) But if you were to replace your paintballs with electrons and shrink the whole setup down to the quantum realm, the pattern you would create would look entirely different. There would be a series of stripes all over the canvas. Even directly behind the solid bits of the barrier in places no paintball could reach.

This, scientists realised, indicated the existence of probability waves. Electrons only became recognisable as particles, with a fixed position, when they were observed. Until then, nothing was set. And this struck a chord with me, I knew what it felt like to be a particle.

Until I am observed, I exist in a state of possibility, went my thinking. *Within myself I am all things, all the time, able to pass through the world effortlessly as a wave of being. But my Punjabiness, my Englishness, my qualities as a brother, son, actor, writer, only form when I'm seen by others or when I try to find the defined box I imagine I'm searching for. Perhaps there is nothing definitive about my nature. Perhaps the very things I'm trying to escape – uncertainty, confusion and ambiguity – are in fact the reality I need to embrace.*

Or to use Carlo Rovelli's phrasing, perhaps there wasn't a 'me' that entered into relations but, rather, relations that grounded the notion of 'me'.

*

I have always been Jassa Singh Ahluwalia. But my birth certificate has my first name recorded as Jasvinder. This, I was told, was at the insistence of my grandad who felt I needed to have a proper, traditional, Sikh Punjabi name. When I was born, my parents hadn't settled on what to call me. In light of my whiteness, they knew they wanted my name to connect me to my Punjabi roots, but they also wanted to keep it short. Jassa was the perfect fit. My namesake, Jassa Singh Ahluwalia, was a celebrated 18th-century Sikh military commander and founder of the Ahluwalia misl, one of a confederacy of sovereign states that were later united under Maharaja Ranjit Singh to form what is commonly known as the Sikh Empire. But my grandad, perhaps confusing traditional with typical, managed to get Jasvinder over the line on the official document. My parents reasoned that this wouldn't matter much; it kept my grandad happy and they'd only ever call me Jassa. They never suspected my legal name might kill me.

In mid-August, 2016, I awoke in the dead of night to a stabbing pain in my gut. I'd just spent the weekend in Brighton with my flatmate, Christian. We'd marvelled at the orientalist Pavilion, the sun and salt water had cleared up my eczema-prone skin and we'd enjoyed some seafood. *Perhaps it was a dodgy prawn?* I thought to myself. I dragged myself out of bed, doubled over in pain, trying to control my breathing.

The Royal London Hospital was only a stone's throw away from where I was living at the time. But walking was out of the question. I called an Uber and stumbled half asleep to the A&E reception desk, giving my name between gasps. A long wait ensued before a doctor took me aside and began lubricating a gloved finger. He'd clocked from my admission form that I was an actor and – I assume to break the ice – asked, 'So what would I have seen you in?' Trying my best to ignore his probing, I explained that I'd recently appeared in *Peaky Blinders*. He seemed dissatisfied; he'd heard of the show but hadn't seen it. Plus, his examination was inconclusive. I was told I'd need a scan. In the meantime, I'd be held overnight and was given a much-needed dose of morphine.

I was moved to a ward and the drugs dulled the pain enough for me to get some sleep. By the time I stirred the next day, though, I could sense something was wrong. My condition hadn't deteriorated – not yet anyway – but it was late in the morning and nobody had come to check on me. Bizarrely though, I could hear my name.

'Jasvinder Ahluwalia. He was brought to this ward, where

is he?' 'Are you sure?' 'We haven't seen him.' The staff were becoming increasingly frustrated with each other. I began to hear the swish of curtains being pulled back and forth: *Swish!* 'Jasvinder? No.' *Swish!* 'Jasvinder? No.' They got to my bay. I was so weak and tired, I could barely move; my consciousness and my body felt entirely separated. But I felt relieved that the system had caught up with me. *Swish!* 'Jasvinder?' The South Asian doctor looked me in the eye. 'No.' He closed the curtain and moved on.

Panic. What had just happened? Was I invisible? Was the morphine playing tricks on me? *Swish!* 'Jasvinder?' The doctor continued his search next door. Before my existential crisis gathered too much momentum, I mustered all the energy I could and croaked out, 'I'm here!' My curtain was pulled back again and the doctor stared at me, confused. 'Jasvinder? Jasvinder Singh Ahluwalia?' he asked, disbelieving. I lifted a weak hand to point to the whiteboard above me, my name clearly written out in block capitals. 'We've been looking for you.' It felt like an accusation, as if I'd somehow been hiding from them. 'We were looking for an Indian.'

I didn't have the energy to explain my backstory: the pain in my gut was back with a vengeance. My appendix was about to rupture and what should have been routine surgery became a lifesaving operation, though I came close to missing my slot on the table. The porter who had been charged with rolling me down to theatre flat out refused to move my bed. He was adamant that there had been a clerical error: there was just no way my face corresponded to the name on his clipboard. My surgery had been delayed several times at this point due to higher priority casualties coming through A&E and I'd not eaten since the night before. I didn't know what to do. So I shouted at him in Punjabi, letting off a string of expletives that he thankfully couldn't understand. Hearing the commotion, a nurse came over and confirmed that I was indeed who I claimed to be. The porter chuckled about the confusion as he wheeled me off, but I was seething. Bed-bound and emotionally exhausted, I felt robbed of my most basic dignity, my name, rendering me invisible and powerless.

I woke up with a drainage tube plugged into my lower abdomen and my recovery was painful and slow, a particular low point being when I shat myself while desperately trying to urinate through the pain of a UTI I'd picked up. It was a grim experience. But that feeling of invisibility remains the most painful memory of all. When I was finally discharged, I shuffled out of the ward determined to find a way to assert my identity in the world.

*

My name, Jassa, has always been somewhat ambiguous to those who aren't familiar with Punjabi history or know my family background. Combined with my face, people, usually white, often take wild and confident guesses: Danish, Norwegian, Dutch, Swedish maybe? But if I meet a Punjabi uncle or aunty, they often repeat my name back to me, draw out the syllables, and, upon learning my full name, give me an examining stare to see if I'm worthy of such a storied title. I had always enjoyed this. Both the anonymity and the recognition. My parents couldn't have picked a better name. And now I wanted it to be my only name. The name on my passport, the name on my health records, the name that could, like a quantum particle, be both specific and enigmatic.

I entered 2017 finding out how to put together an official change of name declaration with which I could update my legal documents. I thought it would require going to some sort of Ministry of Names and paying a fee, but it turned out to be a remarkably simple and free process. I found the wording online, added my personal details, along with those of two witnesses, and printed it off. I was worried it was all a bit too easy, so I'd formatted the text using the most old-fashioned looking font I could find and loaded my printer with heavy parchment paper. This made it all feel more official somehow. I knew it was a stupid flourish, but at least I'd be less likely to misplace the originals.

BY THIS DEED OF CHANGE OF NAME made by myself the undersigned Jassa Singh Ahluwalia of [my address at the time] formerly known as Jasvinder Singh Ahluwalia, a British Citizen under section 37(1) of the British Nationality Act 1981

HEREBY DECLARE AS FOLLOWS:

I. I ABSOLUTELY and entirely renounce, relinquish and abandon the use of my said former name Jasvinder Singh Ahluwalia and assume, adopt and determine to take and use from the date hereof the name of Jassa Singh Ahluwalia in substitution for my former name of Jasvinder Singh Ahluwalia

…

SIGNED AS A DEED THIS 13TH DAY OF FEBRUARY IN THE YEAR 2017

A few signatures over dinner and that was it. A small flick of the pen, a quantum leap on my journey. For though nothing around me had really changed, I was on a new course. What I was truly absolutely and entirely renouncing, relinquishing and abandoning was my pursuit of certainty. What I was henceforth assuming, adopting and determining to take and use was ambiguity.

3

HALF-CASTING

Pictures shall not infer that low forms of sex
relationship are the accepted or common thing ...
Miscegenation (sex relationships between the white
and black races) is forbidden.

THE MOTION PICTURE PRODUCTION CODE OF 1930

IN MARCH 2017, I walked the short distance from
Richmond station to the Orange Tree Theatre. I assured
myself that I needn't be nervous. I had met both the director
and the casting director as a duo before and I had come
close to working with them. The room was going to be
friendly and supportive. But I was anxious. The role I had
been asked to prepare was 'Pete – an enslaved man on the
plantation ... traditional Louisiana accent. Melodrama/
parody style!' Was my racist parody of an enslaved Black man
going to pass muster?

The play, *An Octoroon*, by Branden Jacobs-Jenkins, was
critically acclaimed when it premiered Off-Broadway in 2014
and the *New York Times* would go on to rank it among the best

American plays 'since "Angels in America"'.[1] I had also read the full script. I knew that what was being asked of me had immense artistic merit, but I feared, irrationally, that it was all a big set-up: that as soon as I opened my mouth, I would be both laughed at and condemned. 'Mr. Jacobs-Jenkins is all about that unease; the subject is discomfiting, and he intends to make it more so' wrote the *New York Times'* Jesse Green.

Race is a social construct – not a biological reality, but a fiction made real through consensus – and Jacobs-Jenkins deploys blackface, whiteface and redface to tear this story apart and excoriate racial stereotypes. Newly committed to my own racial ambiguity, I replied to my agent's email to confess that 'this is both terrifying and hugely exciting'. But as I neared the entrance to the theatre, a little voice in my head whispered, *You're not the right kind of mixed race.*

The script dictates that Pete is 'played by [the] same actor playing ASSISTANT' and Assistant is to be 'played by an Indigenous American actor/actress, a mixed race actor, a South Asian actor/actress, or one who can pass as Native American'. The ethnicities are 'listed in order of preference'. When I'd first seen this breakdown, I was overjoyed. A request for someone mixed race and South Asian – I was perfect! And then a moment later: doubt. Was I perfect? It was all very well me embracing my ambiguity, but there was nothing ambiguous about my appearance. And appearance was what the play and the world of acting revolves around. Appearance is what you list on your CV. Appearance is what casting directors use to find talent. What you actually are is second to what gatekeepers perceive you to be. And despite knowing that the creative team knew me and would only have asked me to come in if I had a real shot, my doubt sunk its claws into me.

I did a good audition. But I didn't own it. I was deferential. I was so grateful to be auditioning for an explicitly 'mixed race' role, so thankful for the chance to read for a play that subverted racial thinking, that I didn't put my stamp on it. In the room, I gave it everything I had, but I'd left a crucial part of myself at the door: my conviction.

I didn't get the part and, as I anticipated, a brilliant actor who 'appeared' more mixed was chosen. Would things be different if I were to audition now? I have no idea if I'd get the job, but that's not what matters. The difference would be that I would claim the role with my full self. I wouldn't be doffing my cap and seeking permission. I'd be walking into the room knowing that my mixedness, my whiteness and my unseen brownness were my power, my unique angle that would serve only to enhance Jacobs-Jenkins' bizarre and beautiful anti-racist vitriol. But in 2017, I still respected the social construct of race enough to think of myself as 'not the right kind of mixed'. Why?

At the time of my audition, I didn't have the clarity of mind to know that that was the question I needed to be asking. When it came to the history of race, I was resigned to my story being on the periphery, unaware that the confidence I sought would never be found from the sidelines. Plus, my challenges felt entirely modern: I was a white-presenting mixed British Indian trying to make it as an actor in the age of Netflix. I felt like an anomaly. I felt alone in my experience.

I had no idea that I was in fact part of a history that had been playing out since the birth of Hollywood, a history rooted in the very emergence of race.

2017: A lonely year

In early 2017, in an attempt to feel less isolated, I was in the thick of learning Punjabi. Or, more specifically, Gurmukhi, the script used to read and write Punjabi in present-day India. If I could become literate, my thinking went, I would be granting myself access to a whole new kind of belonging. If I could read literature, poetry and scripture, I would be able to connect with my heritage, directly and personally, and discover what lay beyond the realm of loved ones.

In the Sikh tradition, a Gurmukh is one who is 'guru facing' or, to put it another way, is accepting of the ultimate wisdom. The first appearance of the word Gurmukh in the Guru Granth Sahib can be translated as: 'By facing the guru, you become aware of the unheard cosmic sound within you, you become aware that it is divine, and you realise that it is merged in all.' Gurmukhi, then, is the script of the guru facing, the wisdom seekers, and those who seek are known as Sikhs, ਸਿੱਖਣਾ (sikhna) being the verb 'to learn'. It was developed from earlier scripts in use in northern India and standardised by Guru Nanak's successor, Guru Angad, who lived during the first half of the 16th century. Thus, Gurmukhi became the dominant script for Sikh Punjabis, while Shahmukhi, the same Nastaliq script used for Urdu, remains the standard for Punjabi in Pakistan. (The two epigraphs of this book, the first from the Guru Granth Sahib and the second by Sufi poet Bulleh Shah, are both written in Punjabi but the former uses the Gurmukhi script, while the latter uses Shahmukhi.)

It can be difficult for those of us who have grown up with alphabets and languages being one and the same thing to grasp the idea of a particular script being just one medium for writing a language. But just as you can use the English alphabet to phonetically write another language (like Chinese pinyin or Romanised Hindi), the reverse is also true; you can write English words phonetically using other scripts, including Gurmukhi. BG used to do it all the time. Once I could start to read basic words, I realised that her shopping lists, though written in Gurmukhi, were all English words. Reading 'ਕੈਰਟ' out loud produced the sound 'cai-rut', though when she spoke, she would only ever refer to ਗਾਜਰ (gajar), the Punjabi word for carrot. Similarly, my mum, having learnt Gurmukhi while dating my dad, impressed family in India by reading from a local newspaper. She was adamant she couldn't understand any of it, but they insisted she must know at least one of the words – she recited it out loud several times before it dawned on her that she was saying 'camera'.

I had learnt the first few characters of Gurmukhi as a child and made a video for Instagram parodying the experience while I was in Chandigarh for my TEDx talk in 2020. I passed a camel near Sukhna Lake and was transported back to the rote learning of my infancy: ūṛā – ūṭh. ūṛā (ੳ) is the first letter of the Punjabi alphabet. ūṭh (ਊਠ) is the Punjabi word for camel. Just as English speaking kids are drilled with the phrase 'a is for apple', I was made to repeat 'ūṛā – ūṭh' ad infinitum. This way of learning the language is incredibly inefficient and it's no wonder many of us never got past the first few letters. Punjabi cannot be properly learnt by simply memorising the characters because the vowel sounds are not individual letters. Instead, the consonants are all modified by vowel notations. For example, put two curved dashes beneath the equivalent of an H, and 'huh' (ਹ) becomes 'hoo' (ਹੂ). It's an elegant system. Once you get the hang of it, you can be reading Punjabi in no time and, unlike English, there are no alternative pronunciations to confuse you.

I learnt all of this via YouTube. In the run-up to Christmas 2016, I found BaruSahibHP, the YouTube channel of The Kalgidhar Society, and the title of one of their videos caught my eye: 'Learn Gurmukhi (Punjabi) in 5 days'. Having repeated ūṛā – ūṭh for an eternity with little progress, I was sceptical, but over the course of a week I set aside 40 minutes each day, watched each video and followed along with the lessons in my notebook. To my astonishment, by the weekend, I was reading Gurmukhi. Slowly and clumsily, but I was no longer illiterate. I wondered if this was how Lyra might feel, turning the hands of her alethiometer, examining the symbols and discerning a meaning for the first time since her childhood. A whole new world now opened up, and I felt a warm wave of inclusion wash over me. Reading allowed me to better imagine myself as a member of a Punjabi community that existed beyond time and my immediate surroundings. I started using Punjabi dictionaries and Google Translate to expand my vocabulary. And I discovered that I now had a whole new way of spending meaningful time with Grandad and BG.

Over time, my grandad's usual habit of reading the newspaper cover-to-cover was being replaced by a more overt interest in spiritual matters. The *Observer* became a well-thumbed gutka (a small book containing selected Sikh scripture) and his visits to hospital became more frequent. Keen to engage with his intellect, to keep his mind active, I would find Punjabi children's stories online, written in Gurmukhi, and read them with him. He would correct me, explain the meanings of unfamiliar words and he'd digress into anecdotes. My progress brought him great joy and I cherished the intimacy. With each sentence we read, I felt my grip on my past loosen; a future in which my Punjabi got better, not worse, now seemed entirely possible. And when reading alone, my isolation felt more tolerable.

This was my main concern during the first half of 2017: fending off an increasingly crippling sense of isolation, while trying to get my stalling acting career back on track. Looking back, I see now that my mental health was spiralling. The demands of the industry were taking their toll on me. And the gatekeeping and the crap pay felt increasingly pronounced, not least because one of the few jobs I did manage to land that year was a minor supporting role in *Slaughterhouse Rulez*, a film predicated on class hierarchy and generational wealth. Having breakfast with Michael Sheen and fanboying over the fact that he had early access to *La Belle Sauvage*, Philip Pullman's prequel to *His Dark Materials*, briefly put a smile on my face. But no amount of rubbing shoulders with stars could change the fact that I was scraping by financially, watching my uni mates complete their masters, start well-paid jobs and move into lovely modern flats with their partners.

During the shoot, I remember being asked by one particularly flush cast member why I was worrying about the cost of dinner since we all had per diems. Where they saw fun tokens, I saw rent – my total income for 2017 to 2018 was £11,883. I was single, lonely and struggling to pay mates' rates to stay in a flat that an actor friend had just bought after starring in a hit TV show.

On set, cliques developed quickly. Everyone was perfectly civil – I even shared a moment of profound recognition with mixed British-Japanese actor and author Hanako Footman – but I never felt included. The only real friendships I forged were with my two Black co-stars, Alhaji Fofana and Cory Chambers, bonding in our trailers over our shared immigrant family histories. I spoke about Partition and Indian–Pakistani rivalry, and Cory, whose heritage is Jamaican, and Alhaji, whose family hails from Sierra Leone, clued me in on the playground hilarities that ensued during their school days when Black Jamaicans discovered they were not exclusively Caribbean (and therefore cool) but were also African, and how African kids would try and pass themselves off as Jamaican for clout. Their company and conversation kept me smiling. With them, I felt like I belonged. I'd felt a similar ease of being with John Boyega and David Gyasi when filming *The Whale*, revelling in the similarities I shared with their respective Nigerian and Ghanaian roots.

Two days after I started work on *Slaughterhouse Rulez*, my

grandad died. It was a Wednesday. I'd found out on Saturday night that he'd gone into hospital and on Sunday evening he'd been resuscitated. I informed the producers on Monday morning and they kindly dropped me from the scene I was in and put me on a train to Leicester as soon as possible. I arrived at the hospital just after 3pm and before I saw Grandad, I saw BG, sat by his side, dressed in white. It was a stark look for a woman who always opted for a colourful salwar kameez, and a clear sign that she had accepted what was happening, white being the colour of mourning in the Dharmic traditions.

I'd seen Grandad's decline first-hand, noticing how he would sometimes use his partial deafness to cover for bouts of forgetfulness. Reading Punjabi together, he would tire quickly and need to rest. When he died on 9 August, I was fortunate enough to be by his side, holding his hand. And though the sadness was immense, I didn't feel loss. This perhaps seems strange given that my year thus far had been defined by a creeping isolation, but the magnitude of the moment seemed to awaken something in me. I felt that I was being offered a great opportunity: the chance to step up and carry the torch.

Once I'd seen Grandad's coffin enter the flames, I reminded myself that I had *chosen* the life of an artist with the freedom won by his hard work, and I got myself a bar job. As I mopped the floor at Genesis Cinema for £7.90 an hour, I thought of Grandad arriving in the UK. Finding work befitting his training as a teacher had proved difficult in 1965, but he was determined to succeed. He had worked as a foundry labourer, then a railway porter, before finding better pay with the Post Office, where he was told he needed six months' delivery experience before he could be considered for promotion. Keen to avoid being out in the winter weather, he persuaded his supervisor to let him take his tests early and by Christmas he had a job in the sorting office, a job he did for four years, allowing him to buy his first house and support the family.

As I approached Christmas over 50 years later, I didn't dare entertain dreams of homeownership, but the routine, social interaction and dash of creativity involved with mixing cocktails was keeping my anxiety and loneliness at bay. I had turned 27 in September and moved into a six-person houseshare a couple of days later, treating myself to a small leather armchair as a birthday indulgence. I squeezed this 'occasional chair' into the corner of my new room and it invited me to start reading again. *La Belle Sauvage* was, of course, top of my Christmas wish list, but in second place was *The Tartan Turban*, by John Keay.

The book had featured in the *Guardian* as one of William Dalrymple's top reads of 2017 and was described as being 'about the allegedly half-Aztec, half-Scottish mercenary Alexander Gardner' who reached the pinnacle of his career serving the Sikh Empire. In a photograph taken around 1863–64, he can be seen reclining in a tartan suit, sporting a matching turban embellished with an egret plume. In the new year, I ordered myself a copy and, to quote the subtitle, went 'in search of Alexander Gardner'. I was once again finding comfort by escaping into history, but I was no longer doing so with nostalgic longing. Perhaps I could learn something from Gardner, a man of mixed origins, born in America, who made

Punjab his home. I had signed my tenancy agreement with my newly minted legal name, but I still hadn't found home.

Half-breeds from a land that's torn

John Keay's account begins with a 32-year-old 'half-Kashmiri' woman going in search of her origins. I was immediately hooked. Helena Haughton Campbell Botha (née Gardner) was Alexander Gardner's daughter and in the spring of 1898, she arrived in Srinagar, where she was born and lived as an infant, in search of her deceased father's fortune, estimated at around £1m in cash, plus jewels and treasure worth tenfold more. She was, as Keay puts it, of 'exotic parentage' and her mother was known only as 'Bibi Kali', suggesting she was of Hindu ancestry. But, and this is entirely my own conjecture, this name may also have been a description. As well as referring to the goddess, 'Kali' can mean dark or black, and she wouldn't have been the first 'native wife' to have been described as such.

I'd glossed over it at the time – it didn't fit the image of the romantic past I was wanting to imagine and escape to – but I'd come across 'The Dark Girl' in *White Mughals*. She was one of James Kirkpatrick's early mistresses, 'perhaps of Tamil or Telugu origin', and vanishes from his correspondence once he's introduced to Khair un-Nissa. I'd also done my best to ignore the fact that Khair 'was twelve when she met thirty-five-year-old Kirkpatrick, thirteen when she became pregnant with his child, and fourteen when they married'.[2] Prior to this reputed love story unfolding, Kirkpatrick had fathered a son with 'The Dark Girl', referred to as the 'Hindustani boy', and showed such little interest in his fate that his own father 'wrote to admonish him'. The child died from a fever in his English grandfather's arms and his mother may well have suffered a similar fate. What we can be sure of is that 'she received no legacy or any mention at all in James's will'.[3]

During the age of the white Mughals, class was paramount. Khair un-Nissa was a Mughal aristocrat who deserved love; 'The Dark Girl' was a lowly mistress whose name, like Helena's mother, was not even recorded. The fact that her skin tone was noted though, says a lot. Colour prejudice was a precursor to race being turned into a 'scientific' idea over the course of the 19th century, with concepts of 'racial hygiene' that would develop into the eugenics movement. But even before 'scientific racism' had been fully formed, mixed heritage children started to be considered a problem.

Much of the literature I have read on the history of race concerns itself, rightly, with white supremacy, the subjugation of the Global Majority, antisemitism and anti-Blackness. The transatlantic slave trade, colonialism, genocide and segregation were all justified by the socially constructed belief that humans were not in fact one people, but distinct races. But in much of this literature, mixed heritage people feature as footnotes and asides. I have come to believe that this is because the mixed experience has, for a long time, been considered a fringe interest. It seems to require too much explanation and therefore distracts from the broader sweep of race history. As such, mixed people rarely take centre stage and only get a passing mention in even the most celebrated texts. I remember reading *To Kill a Mockingbird* as a young teen and coming across a brief aside from Jem to Scout, which seared itself into my memory. Mixed kids are 'real sad' he tells his sister. 'They're just in-betweens, don't belong anywhere.'[4]

I loved Scout and Jem, but I wanted to read more about *these* kids, *their* stories. In 2018, just as I had explained in my Ismail self-tape three years earlier, I still felt 'in-between'.

Mixed children are central to the emergence of race. You can't have concepts of purity or racial hygiene without attendant notions of impurity and contamination. If you're trying to construct a world around strict racial division, the very existence of mixed heritage kids poses a threat. As Sita Balani puts it in *Deadly and Slick*, the mixed heritage person 'is where the *work* of upholding racial regimes becomes visible'.[5] Over the course of the late 18th century and beyond, the creation of a boundary between Europeans and their mixed heritage descendants became more and more visible in India and would ultimately lead to Anglo-Indians becoming a separate community, indeed the only community specifically defined in the Constitution of India. Whereas 'Scheduled Castes' and 'Scheduled Tribes' are simply listed by name, Article 366 reads:

(2) "an Anglo-Indian" means a person whose father or any of whose other male progenitors in the male line is or was of European descent but who is domiciled within the territory of India and is or was born within such territory of parents habitually resident therein and not established there for temporary purposes only.

This definition was deemed as important as, and sits alongside, such broad terms as 'clause', 'debt' and 'taxation'.

In 2018, I didn't know this definition existed. It was simply one of two terms I'd come across that I felt might apply to me and offer me belonging. The other was Eurasian, which I had first encountered in between bouts of gunning down zombies in Mallorca in 2014.

The ReZort was billed as *Jurassic Park* meets *28 Days Later*. In a world in which the zombie apocalypse is recent history, a luxury island resort acts as both a holiday destination and a zombie safari park, all against the backdrop of a growing refugee crisis. Zombie movie enthusiasts loved it but, sadly, this potent bag of timely ingredients didn't quite add up to the mainstream breakout hit we had hoped for. Nevertheless, I had a great time.

My co-star, Kevin Shen, was fast becoming, and remains, a close friend. His infectious energy had landed him the role of our overly enthusiastic safari leader and during our downtime we got to talking about representation on screen. He opened my eyes to the racist stereotype of the desexualised East Asian man, and I shared with him my nascent anxieties around my unseen mixed heritage identity. With this in mind, Kevin gifted me a copy of a play that he'd recently starred in.

Yellow Face, by David Henry Hwang, is, in his own words, 'a kind of unreliable memoir'.[6] Kevin starred as David in the National Theatre's production alongside soon-to-be household name, Gemma Chan. And though key elements of the play are fictitious, the events of the opening were painfully real: the 1990 casting controversy surrounding *Miss Saigon*.

I grew up loving *Miss Saigon*. My dad had taken my mum to see it for her birthday in the mid-nineties during its original West End run. The cast recording was one of a small selection of musical soundtracks we had on CD and I listened to it endlessly as my passion for musical theatre and performing emerged in earnest during my teens. I was too young to really grasp the story, summed up in *Yellow Face* as: 'A Vietnamese prostitute falls in love with some white soldier and kills herself so her baby can come to America.' But I was gripped by its emotion. As I grew older and began to learn the songs, one track became something of a personal anthem.

> I never thought one day I'd plead
> For half-breeds from a land that's torn
> But then I saw a camp for children
> Whose crime was being born
>
> They're called Bui-Doi[7]

This song – 'Bui Doi' – was the first time I'd come across a specific label for mixed heritage kids. I felt a profound connection and in my late teens I often found myself belting it out when I was home alone. I didn't understand the emotion that rose up in me. But it felt good. It made me want to cry, but also smile. So it came as an unwelcome shock to discover that this musical was the subject of protest and criticism on account of its orientalism, racism and misogyny. I knew Jonathan Pryce had been in the original cast – known to me in my teens as 'the old guy from *Pirates of the Caribbean*' – but I had absolutely no idea that the role he had originated was a mixed Vietnamese French pimp. Pryce taped his eyes, darkened his skin and was awarded an Olivier for his efforts. This is where *Yellow Face* begins. With actor B.D. Wong calling David to tell him about the Broadway transfer:

> BD: Jonathan Pryce is playing an Asian pimp.
> DHH: Yeah, Roz Chao saw it there. Said his eyes are all taped up and everything. That would never happen here.
> BD: They're bringing the show to Broadway.
> DHH: I know. But this is America – they're not gonna cast a white guy here.
> BD: They have.
> DHH: You're sure the actor's white? Maybe he's mixed race. Nowadays, it's so hard to tell. He could have a Caucasian father, so his last name wouldn't sound Asian or maybe he's one of those Korean adoptees, or–
> BD: David, it's Jonathan Pryce.[8]

This is the central premise of *Yellow Face*, a mock-documentary play about David Henry Hwang, in the wake of leading protests against the casting of Pryce in *Miss Saigon*, mistakenly casting the character Marcus, a white actor, in an Asian role. Instead of admitting his error, in fear of ridicule, David passes Marcus off as mixed. But events begin to spiral out of control when Marcus embraces his new ethnic identity and becomes a leading light in the Asian American community, overshadowing David.

I ripped through the play between shooting at the undead. But I was too young, naive and full of myself to really understand it. When the play eventually reveals that Marcus, the white actor, is a fictitious creation woven into real life events, David confesses why he created him: 'To take words like "Asian" and "American," like "race" and "nation," mess them up so bad no one has any idea what they even mean anymore. Cuz that was Dad's dream: a world where he could be Jimmy Stewart. And a white guy — can even be an Asian.'[9]

If I had truly absorbed what I was reading in 2014, I might have arrived at a way of understanding myself and the world a lot sooner. As it was, the only thing that stuck in my head was the word 'Eurasian'. That was how Marcus is (falsely) described throughout. A label that allowed him, despite his appearance, to be welcomed into the Asian American community. I wanted what Marcus had. And unlike him, I was real and actually mixed!

The play's central theme passed me by and I became convinced that I just needed to find the right label. Marcus was Eurasian. The orphans of *Miss Saigon* had *bụi đời*. (Though, in keeping with the musical's lax approach to authenticity, I've since learnt that this refers to street children in general and has no connotations of mixed identity.)[10] What one or two words could sum me up? What moniker could give me home?

Changing my name and committing to ambiguity was all

well and good, but it didn't offer belonging. And no amount of reading seemed to be helping me either. Perhaps I needed to write instead? Perhaps I needed to create 'the right kind of mixed' for myself. In 2018, I poured myself into a script. I wrote a half-hour TV pilot and submitted it to the BBC Writersroom with the logline: 'A young man of Anglo-Indian heritage grapples with his identity and relationships.'

*

Anglo-Indian was the closest term I had encountered that felt like me. I say 'closest' because it has multiple meanings. Rudyard Kipling was described as Anglo-Indian. As was the singer and Las Vegas headliner Engelbert Humperdinck, who was born in Madras and lived down the road from me in Leicester. So an Anglo-Indian was a white person who was born in India? Yes. But Engelbert did look kind of Indian. His website states that he is of 'German and Welsh ethnic descent' but some sources suggest his mother may have had Anglo-Indian heritage, in the mixed heritage sense of the term. Given that Madras had one of the biggest mixed populations in the early 1900s and The Hump was born in 1936, that would make sense. It may also explain why a prominent contemporary is reported to have referred to him using the P-word when he was establishing his pop career during the 1960s.

Anglo-Indian is a messy term that has evolved over time, something comedian Russell Peters (who I had always assumed was Punjabi) grapples with in his memoir *Call Me Russell*:

Both of my parents are Anglo-Indian. Both of their parents were Anglo-Indian, and before that one of their greatgrandfathers or great-great-grandfathers was British, Welsh, Scottish or Irish – one of those ishes. That's what it is to be an Anglo-Indian. Somewhere in your genes is a British father and an Indian mother. Anglo-Indians, or AI's, mixed with the British when they occupied India. That's why my name is Russell Peters instead of something you'd be more likely to expect for a guy who looks like me, both of whose parents were born in India. Anglo-Indians come in all shades – from blond-haired and blue-eyed to dark-skinned with very traditional "Indian" features.[11]

The first historical reference to Anglo-Indians I'd encountered was in *White Mughals*, in which Dalrymple explains how 'in 1786 an order was passed banning Anglo-Indian orphans of British soldiers from travelling to England to be educated' and how later in 1791 'an order was issued that no one with an Indian parent could be employed by the civil, military or marine branches of the Company.'[12] These measures were brought in by Governor General Lord Cornwallis, who arrived in India still smarting from his defeat in America at the hands of George Washington. Cornwallis believed an educated and militarily trained class of people with ties to the land needed to be marginalised so as to secure British dominion and avoid another 'Declaration of Independence'.

The Haitian Revolution, in which enslaved Black people declared their freedom and defeated French colonial powers, had also begun in 1791. This major blow to white supremacy prompted Viscount Valentia, who travelled in India between 1802 and 1806, to write that:

> The most rapidly accumulating evil of Bengal is the increase of half-caste children … In every country where this intermediate caste has been permitted to rise, it has ultimately tended to its ruin. Spanish-America and San Domingo [Haiti] are examples of this fact. Their increase in India is beyond calculation: and though possibly there may be nothing to fear from the sloth of the Hindus, and the rapidly declining consequence of Musalmans, yet it may be justly apprehended that this tribe may hereafter become too powerful for control … With numbers in their favour, with a close relationship to the natives, and without an equal proportion of the pusillanimity and indolence which is natural to them, what may not in future time be dreaded from them![13]

The Haitian Revolution did not prompt the crackdown on Anglo-Indians. But race, white supremacy and colonial power were becoming inextricably intertwined through the 19th century. 'My children are uncommonly fair,' wrote David Ochterlony in around 1803, 'but if educated [in India] in the European manner they will in spite of complexion labour under all the disadvantages of being known as the NATURAL DAUGHTERS OF OCHTERLONY BY A NATIVE WOMAN – In that one sentence is compressed all that ill nature and illiberality can convey.'[14] It's important to note the influence of class here. Had Ochterlony's fair-skinned children been legitimate, as opposed to 'natural born', they would have been in a better position.

Nevertheless, these accounts make clear that mixed heritage people were growing to be considered a threat to the imperial project in India. In a world in which race was fast becoming central to social hierarchy, those who could traverse boundaries, with rare exceptions, could no longer be tolerated. And the very fact that they might have a meaningful connection to the land was why they were to be treated with suspicion. By 1886, a War Office file reveals that there was opposition to any attempt to:

> Enlist any Eurasian or other 'man of colour' … in the name of all that is dear to us let us keep our British Regiments strictly British … [Once] we begin to fill our ranks with alien races, our downfall must soon follow.[15]

I felt a sense of kinship with these historical Anglo-Indians. I too had felt like my heritage was leaving me on the fringes of my chosen field. In 2015, Channel 4's *Indian Summers*, a Raj-era period drama, felt like the perfect project for me, brimming with Anglo-Indian intrigue. But the first I had heard of it was the cast announcement. Trawling through the faces I couldn't help but feel I wasn't white enough to play the colonisers, brown enough to play the colonised or 'exotic' enough to be mixed. ('Exotic' being the adjective favoured by journalist Simon Button to describe Amber Rose Revah's 'good looks' in a profile piece for the *Express*, a trope Natalie Morris explores in detail in a chapter titled 'Exoticisation, Fetishisation and Othering' in her book *Mixed/Other*.)[16] That said, the casting of Revah, an actor of Polish Jewish and Kenyan Indian ancestry, in the mixed heritage role of Leena Prasad, was a rare and refreshing diversification of what 'mixed race' looked like on screen. Even though her appearance did little to challenge notions of 'mixed' equating to intermediate skin tones (as Russell Peters says, 'Anglo-Indians come in all shades'), it was a refreshing change from 'mixed race' being a synonym for 'light-skinned Black'.

Another instance of feeling sidelined had come in late 2016 when I bumped into Meera Syal in the car park at Ealing Studios. I was there shooting Andy Serkis' *Planet of the Apes: The Last Frontier*, an experimental narrative video game, playing a white American teen. Meera was there for a meeting about a TV film that was in the offing, *The Boy with the Topknot*, based on the best-selling memoir by Sathnam Sanghera. Meera, aware of my heritage, encouraged me to get seen by the casting director. I emailed my agent enthusiastically, but I tempered my hopes:

> I realise there may not be a specific role suitable for me but would it be possible to get a general [meeting] perhaps while I'm on site? I don't think the perfect Punjabi role is ever going to come along until I write it but I'd love to connect more with people involved in bringing these stories to life.

I bought the book and was instantly in fits of laughter and then tears. I took to Twitter:

> Me: Just started reading @Sathnam's #TheBoy
> WithTheTopknot. I ache from laughing. I never had
> a topknot but I see me and my family in every page.
> Sathnam: Very nice to hear. Thankyou.
> Me: No, thank YOU! I'm just gutted I can't help
> bring it to life on screen. It's inspiring me to better
> articulate my own identity.

It was all so familiar, the same even. Both the trivial and the profound. Penguin bars for dessert after roti and sabji – that was my childhood. Hushed up family mental health struggles – snap. I went in for a general meeting but there was no role for me. When casting was nearing completion in 2017, I discovered that a friend was going in for a chemistry read for the white female lead. I was so excited for her, and fuming with impotent rage that she had a shot when I didn't. I did get the chance to make a contribution during the film's post-production though; I was part of the ensemble hired to record the background voices. I was hired because I was a good deal, I could cover both the English-speaking and Punjabi scenes.

Come 2018, the script I submitted to BBC Writersroom was my attempt at writing the perfect mixed role I longed for. From the total of 3,845 scripts submitted that year, mine made it into the 137 that received a full read and script report:

Jassa is a strong central character with whom we immediately engage … Whilst Jassa's internal struggle is unique and compelling, the story itself does feel a little slight … this piece may benefit from an additional sub plot; something that enriches Jassa's journey whilst allowing us an even greater insight into his unique world … At the moment whilst we really engage with Jassa and enjoy spending time with him, I'm not sure his emotional motivations are quite coming across … All in all, an enjoyable and thought provoking read.

My close friend and fellow writer Cristian Solimeno was slightly more incisive with his feedback. We spoke on the phone after he'd read it and he asked, very seriously, if I was okay. I tried to reassure him, but he wasn't having it. 'You sound depressed, dude.'

My loneliness and despair was all over the page. And despite messaging my on/off not-girlfriend in mid-2017 and sharing that I was suffering from 'a bout of depression, I think' after I'd spent the morning 'sat on my bed crying', I was yet to seek out the help I needed.

It's painful to look back at the younger me. I want to reach out, give him a hug and let him know that he was never alone. It would be another five years, with this book well underway, before I'd really grasp that I had always been the right kind of mixed. I just hadn't yet found my history.

Mixed history

In 2022, with my TEDx talk having clocked up over 100,000 views on YouTube, and my BBC One documentary – *Am I English?* – having aired that April, I was invited to give a talk to the City of London's Ethnicity and Race Staff Network as part of South Asian Heritage Month. To my astonishment, the event was titled #BothNotHalf. I was giving the keynote and my fellow guest speaker, Ciara Garcha, an Oxford history student, was giving a presentation on her own mixed heritage and research into mixed histories. When she put her title slide up on the projector, I couldn't quite believe what I was seeing: *Both Not Half: South Asian Heritage Month 2022*. This was the first time I'd seen anyone else use the phrase in something approaching an academic setting. It felt wonderful that those three words had the potential to be bigger than me. And then Ciara began her talk, and I was captivated.

She began by sharing her full name – Ciara Rose Aman Garcha – and explaining how it perfectly encapsulated her identity. A blend of Irish (Ciara) from her maternal grandfather, English (Rose) from her maternal grandmother, and Punjabi (Aman Garcha) from her father. Just as my parents had known that my name would be a crucial link to my heritage, Ciara shared, 'When I was younger, I hated my name, I wanted a "normal" one. But as I grew up, that changed. Being mixed, I felt that nothing was entirely mine, but my name ensured I could claim ownership of my identity.' I listened, enthralled, as she explained how her Irish and Punjabi grandfathers had both settled in the West Midlands within two years of each other during the 1960s and how, though their stories were 'worlds apart', they both worked as bus drivers and both faced discrimination in the form of 'No Blacks, No Irish' policies. As a result, her Punjabi grandfather used to frequent his local Irish pub, one of the few places he was welcome. Ciara's mixed heritage began to take shape long before her parents had even met.

I was already fully engrossed, but when Ciara began to talk about her research, I strained my neck to see her slides. She was arguing that mixed heritage people are not a modern phenomenon. I knew this, of course, but I had never heard this statement made so explicitly, and I had never come across these images. Up on the screen were what she described as Spanish 'casta paintings'.

'This distinct genre of Spanish-American art generally depicted an interracial family,' explained Ciara, 'consisting of two parents of different racial backgrounds and one or two of their mixed offspring. The labels or captions describe the mixing shown in each image: listing the castes of the two parents and the caste that resulted from the specific union.'

The extent to which these images and names were actually used on a day-to-day basis in 18th-century New Spain (Mexico) is much debated, but 'where casta labels were used, local variants arose and different labels were often used interchangeably, highlighting the fluidity even of this seemingly detailed and rigid system.'[17] Seeing them made me feel strangely emotional, for though their existence literally made visible the work of upholding racial regimes, I felt comforted and seen. In Ciara's presentation, mixed people were centre stage.

A 1725 painting by José de Ibarra is titled 'De Castizo

y Española, Español', which translates as 'from a Castizo man [the offspring of a mixed European-Native American and a Spaniard] and a Spanish woman, a Spaniard'. The child depicted has been sufficiently whitened to be deemed Spanish. But whereas the paintings show that Indigenous Americans could be sufficiently whitened, they also show that Black heritage cannot be 'overcome', echoing the 'One-drop Rule' that operated in the US.

When we look at how different mixed children were classified during this period of history, the intent of the ruling class becomes remarkably apparent. The Spanish were keen to expand their numbers by mixing with and whitening the Indigenous Americans to establish a 'white Spanish' colonial elite, whereas the US government sought to perpetuate enslavement. White masters didn't have to buy enslaved Black people if they could breed enslaved mixed children through rape. Conversely, US authorities readily recognised those of mixed European-Native American ancestry as white so as to weaken Indigenous claims to the land. These blood-quantum laws, created by white settlers, used fractional language to assess Native American legitimacy. Their legacy is still felt, enforced, perversely, by Native Americans themselves. 'My tribe requires that members be at least one-eighth Jamestown S'Klallam by blood. Because I am exactly one-eighth, unless I have kids with another citizen, my kids will be ineligible to join,' wrote Leah Myers in a June 2023 article for *The Atlantic*.[18]

These differing approaches to categorising mixed children are known as hypodescent and hyperdescent. Hypodescent being the practice of assigning mixed children to a subordinate racial group in a given power context (such as the 'one-drop rule'), while hyperdescent categorises mixed children according to the part of their racial heritage that is seen as socially dominant. One of the most distressing recent examples of hyperdescent policy in action is the case of the Stolen Generations in Australia. The 1886 Half-Caste Act allowed the forcible removal of mixed children from their parents right up until 1967, with some controls persisting into the early 1970s, with the aim of socially engineering a white society. This testimony by Millicent D. gives a sense of the generational trauma:

At the age of four, I was taken away from my family and placed in Sister Kate's Home – Western Australia where I was kept as a ward of the state until I was eighteen years old. I was forbidden to see any of my family or know of their whereabouts ... They said it was very degrading to belong to an Aboriginal family and that I should be ashamed of myself, I was inferior ... My daughter was born [in 1962] ... I was so happy, I had a beautiful baby girl of my own who I could love and cherish and have with me always. But my dreams were soon crushed: the bastards took her from me and said she would be fostered out until I was old enough to look after her ... My baby was taken away from me just as I was from my mother ... In desperation I rang the King Edward Memorial Hospital. They said there was no record of me ever giving birth or of my daughter Toni.[19]

Only after Millicent received an enquiry from the South Australian welfare authorities in January 1996 was she finally reunited with her daughter. On 30 October 2009, the Aboriginal and Torres Strait Islander Healing Foundation was established to address the ongoing 'trauma that was caused by colonisation and actions like the forced removal of children'.[20] Hopes for more systemic progress suffered a painful setback in October 2023, when Australians voted in a referendum to reject a proposal to recognise Aboriginal people in the country's constitution.

The separation of mixed children from their parents had a precedent in colonial India. Christopher Hawes, author of *Poor Relations: The Making of A Eurasian Community in British India 1773–1833*, explained in an interview with Glenn D'Cruz that:

> In the early days of the community, if you were born Eurasian the odds on chance were that you would be taken from your Indian mother as early as possible and sent out to an orphanage because that was official policy. You would stay in that orphanage and if you were a lower class Eurasian, the son of a soldier, you would actually go back into the army as a bandsman, and you would marry the daughter of a British soldier. So, you would be completely institutionalised from the very beginning. If you were middle class, and shall we say, the son of an officer by an Indian woman, you would go to the orphanage but, of course, a higher class orphanage for sons and

daughters of officers and you could get a clerical
job in a government office, or you might become
an apothecary, an engineer, or a surveyor or indigo
farmer ... I don't know what it must have been like
to never have been brought up in a family situation –
it is almost impossible to envisage.[21]

In *Anglo-India and the End of Empire*, historian Uther
Charlton-Stevens (himself the son of an Anglo-Indian father)
writes that this approach to childrearing explains why 'the
bulk of what became the Anglo-Indian community were
so profoundly culturally oriented towards Britain, and so
effectively deracinated from Indian society and culture.'[22]

My own separation from my parents was only ever
temporary, but encountering these histories, I feel a deep
affinity with their suffering and isolation. And just as Anglo-
Indian children were effectively made British, I suppose, in a
way, I was made Punjabi through growing up with Grandad
and BG.

As distressing as much of this history is, and as with Ciara's
talk, discovering Uther Charlton-Stevens' work proved to
be profoundly comforting. I wished I'd encountered his
book earlier, but it was only published in September 2022.
Histories that centre mixed people remain painfully hard to
find. If they were more readily available, I'd have perhaps
discovered sooner that my search for community and a name
as a mixed person was far from a new endeavour.

Recognition and erasure

In 1684, during the early days of the British colonial project, the East India Company issued a directive imploring its officials in Madras to provide for 'such soldiers as are single men' by 'prudently [inducing] them to marry 'Gentoos', in imitation of *ye dutch politicks*, and raise from them a stock of Protestant mestizees'.[23] It would have perhaps been more accurate to call it Portuguese 'politicks', but since the Iberians were Catholic, that wouldn't do. Doubling down on this stated intent, on 8 April 1687 the Company's directors issued another despatch: 'The marriage of our soldiers to the native women of Fort St. George, formerly recommended by you, is a matter of such consequence to posterity, that we shall be content to encourage it with some expense, and have been thinking for the future to appoint a [gold] pagoda to be paid to the mother of any child that shall hereafter be born of any such future marriage, on the day the child is christened.'[24]

By the end of the 18th century, such incentives were not necessary. British men were regularly finding wives from among the mixed community. 'Between 1783 and 1820,' writes Charlton-Stevens, 'the Lower Orphan School in Calcutta allowed private soldiers "of good character and able to support a wife" to choose a bride from among "the Cinderellas of the establishment" on a single brief visual inspection.' The officers and other higher ranking men took their pick of the mixed daughters of similarly high status parents at debutante-style balls until the 1830s.[25]

A gender divide emerged. It became entirely possible for light-skin women to marry up, improve their social status and become absorbed into whiteness, 'the young men, on the other hand … linger out existence as clerks … forming alliances with girls of their own hue, and thus perpetuat[e] … a race of poor, puny mortals discarded by the very nations whence they sprung.'[26]

Fast forward to the late 19th century and mixed women also found themselves discarded. They could not compete with the 'fishing fleet' – white women arriving from Britain via steamship, care of the newly inaugurated Suez Canal, in search of husbands. Their arrival heralded the age of the 'memsahib'.

When I speak to Uther Charlton-Stevens about all of this, he's keen to point out that it is crucial to remember that, 'even at its high-water mark, circa 1880–1920, colonial British racism remained fundamentally class-inflected.' Memsahibs were the wives and fiancés of the elite, the title being a blend of 'ma'am' and 'sahib'. In her 2011 PhD thesis, Valerie Anderson explains that:

> The presence of 'fishing fleet' women was an irrelevance to common British soldiers who belonged, like Indians, effectively to another race. Amongst the permanently poorer European men who might have wanted a European wife choice was severely limited by the policies of Company and Crown to keep working-class European settlement to a minimum.[27]

The mixed of British India had once occupied privileged positions within the Company and were sought-after brides. But as the 1800s wore on, they suffered social and economic decline. In response, an increasingly endogamous community with a political voice began to take shape. And that community needed a name.

'I think the term Eurasians, suggested by Mr. Ricketts, in his excellent little Address, written some months ago, is the most comprehensive that can be established,' wrote one A.H. in *The Calcutta Journal*, 6 November 1821. 'It is a compound formed from Europe and Asia, and will apply more or less, to the children of Europeans of all nations born in India. My father having been a German, I do not see, how I can, without tacitly disavowing my origin, call myself an Indo-Briton, an Asiatic-Briton, or even an Anglo-Asiatic.'[28] But not everyone agreed: 'Why, Sir, am I not an *Indian*? With that name I am content. All the rest is a matter of pedigree …'[29]

When the Company used the term 'Half Caste' in an official order in 1827, the debate grew more heated. (Discovering that this term was considered 'highly insulting and intolerable' almost two hundred years ago makes it even more alarming that I still occasionally hear it used uncritically today.)[30] In response to a petition, the governor of Madras decided 'Indo-Briton' was preferable to 'Eurasian' as it encouraged descendants of all European persuasions to 'consider themselves a branch of the great venerable British oak'. But identity cannot be so easily ascribed. The petitioners, unreceptive to being grafted, sought to organise 'a general meeting' to be 'convened by advertisement' so as to reach 'a final settlement' on the matter.[31] This proposal was dismissed and debates raged on.

As the century unfolded, 'Eurasian' emerged as the most prevalent term in common usage. But coupled with rising white supremacy and the proliferation of racial stereotypes in literature, it soon acquired a pejorative meaning akin to 'half-caste'. From the 1880s onwards, mixed community leaders sought a new appellation and set their sights on 'Anglo-Indian', a term long associated with colonial Brits. Uther Charlton-Stevens contends that this demand 'could be seen as yet another strategy to break down the dividing lines that colonial British society had sought to erect against the mixed, and to blur the boundaries between them and the unmixed'.[32]

This blurring became official when 'Anglo-Indian' was included for the first time on the 1911 census as the 'official designation of the mixed race, instead of Eurasian, their former designation, which was very unpopular amongst them'.[33] That same year, on 19 February, a mixed heritage Anglo-Indian girl was born in Bombay. She would grow up to become the first person of Asian descent to be nominated for an Academy Award, but her groundbreaking achievement would go unnoticed – Merle Oberon insisted she was white.

*

On the 24 January 2023, *The Hollywood Reporter* tweeted, 'Michelle Yeoh has made history as the first person who identifies as Asian to ever be nominated for best actress at the #Oscars.'[34] Rooted in anti-woke sentiment, many were quick to criticise the use of 'identifies as'. Perhaps with this in mind, when *Variety* tweeted a few hours later, they opted for:

> Michelle Yeoh is the second Asian woman nominated for Lead Actress — after Merle Oberon, from 1935's "The Dark Angel" — but the first Asian woman who publicly identifies as such to be nominated. Oberon's heritage wasn't known until after her death.[35]

Similarly, when Black actor Jodie Turner-Smith took to TV screens in October 2020 as Anne Boleyn, she was following in Merle Oberon's footsteps; her breakout role had been as the Tudor queen in the 1933 film, *The Private Life of Henry VIII*.

Merle Oberon went to 'extraordinarily painful lengths to be accepted as a white woman'.[36] She began working on her RP accent as a teen in Bombay and lightened 'her skin with bleach creams loaded with ammoniated mercury'.[37] A *Guardian* article by Andrew Lawrence, written in the lead-up to the 2023 Academy Awards, explains Oberon's journey to the UK and stardom:

> Those who didn't dump her outright after discovering her race helped sponsor her moves from India to France and England, where she worked for a time as a club hostess under the name Queenie O'Brien. When she became romantically involved with the Hungarian-born British director Alexander Korda, Oberon's acting career clicked into high gear.[38]

Korda's production company, London Films, worked with Oberon to construct a sufficiently white backstory to enable her to achieve stardom in a racist society. Estelle Merle O'Brien Thompson became Merle Oberon, a Tasmanian-born colonial Brit whose birth records had perished in a fire. And while Oberon passed as white, her darker-skinned mother Charlotte – actually her biological grandmother, though it's unclear if Merle Oberon was aware of this herself – was passed off as a servant.

Oberon doted on Charlotte, paid for everything and surrounded her with friends who showed her great affection. After she tragically died at the age of 54, Charlotte was buried in 'an unmarked grave' after 'several cemeteries rejected [her] on the grounds that she was Indian'.

It was common practice in the early days of Hollywood for the 'Big Five' studios to give their actors fake biographies in order to cultivate stars. Margarita Carmen Cansino, of Spanish and Irish American ancestry, was catapulted to fame as the white glamour icon Rita Hayworth. And there was an 'unwritten rule that no star could have a Jewish name'.[39] But there were also many written rules. The Hays Code stipulated in section II of 'Particular Applications' that: 'The sanctity of the institution of marriage and the home shall be upheld. Pictures shall not infer that low forms of sex relationship are the accepted or common thing.' Number 6 on the list: 'Miscegenation (sex relationships between the white and black races) is forbidden.'[40] Had Oberon's true heritage been public knowledge, her 1934 kiss with Douglas Fairbanks in *The*

Scarlet Pimpernel would have been scandalous. The British Board of Film Censors were similarly averse to romance that transgressed racial boundaries and forbade Anna May Wong, Hollywood's first Asian-American star, from kissing English actor John Longden in the 1930 film *The Road to Dishonour*:

> He may sit at her feet; sing her a love song; kiss her hand; clasp her in his arms; but on no account must he kiss her lips.[41]

Were Wong a white girl in yellow face however, the kiss would have been perfectly acceptable. Interracial romance had to be confined to the realm of fiction and fantasy; authenticity was too great a threat to societies built on racial hierarchy. During the 1960s, interracial kisses on TV shows, like *Star Trek* in the US and *Emergency Ward 10* in the UK, were viewed as historic moments (though given the complex history of race on screen, neither can be said to be 'firsts', not least because Gordon Heath played the titular role in a 1955 BBC production of *Othello*, in which he kissed Rosemary Harris.)[42][43] And to this day, I frequently meet Black women who comment on how refreshing it was for them as teens, watching *Some Girls*, to see Adelayo Adedayo and me kissing as loved-up Viva and Rocky, a dark-skinned Black girl and a white boy. Progress has been painfully slow.

Back in the early days of Hollywood, Vivien Leigh didn't have to work quite as hard as Merle Oberon to pass as white.

She was born in Darjeeling to a British father and a fair-skinned mixed heritage mother. Her mother was not white enough, however, to prevent her father from having to 'resign from the Bengal Club' when they got married.[44] Her 1940 Best Actress win for *Gone with the Wind* arguably makes her, not Michelle Yeoh, 'the first person of Asian descent to *win* an Academy Award'.[45]

For Anglo-Indians who couldn't easily pass as white Brits or Americans, other forms of whiteness provided a pathway to fame. William Henry Pratt, the son of two Anglo-Indian parents, is best known as Boris Karloff. He has two stars on the Hollywood Walk of Fame and *Empire* magazine ranked his 1931 performance as Frankenstein's monster the sixth-greatest horror movie character of all time. Discovering his ancestry strongly resonated with me: I too have courted Slavic ancestry, having played Russian in both the BBC's *Peaky Blinders* and TNT's *Legends*.

Anna Kashfi is a notable exception in the Hollywood trend towards whiteness. Born Joan O'Callaghan in Chakradharpur, 'there was, undoubtedly, "Indian blood" in both [her parents]',[46] though they themselves claimed to be white. Kashfi, however, leant into her appearance and was announced to Hollywood in 1955 as an 'exotic 19-year-old actress from India by way of London and Paris'.[47] When she married Marlon Brando in 1957, she wore a 'pink gold-embroidered sari'.[48] The very next day, her suppressed Anglo-Indian heritage became the focus of sensational press columns after her mother told reporters, 'There is no Indian blood in my family or my husband's family.'[49] In 2015, *The Hollywood*

Reporter led with: 'Anna Kashfi, an alluring and ethnically ambiguous actress who was the first wife of Marlon Brando, has died. She was 80.'

When I speak to Uther Charlton-Stevens about Kashfi, he makes an incisive observation: 'The fact that producers wanted to depict her as Indian to me highlights that Hollywood is very much thinking in binary terms. You can be one thing or the other.' Kashfi was too brown to pass as white and was therefore packaged as a 'safely exotic' (as I myself was once described) Orientalist other, rumoured to be an Indian princess. 'They preferred that she be Indian rather than mixed,' Uther continues. 'They can tolerate the idea of somebody being Indian but the idea that somebody could be mixed is less easy to explain, which speaks to your whole issue of wanting to be recognised as both.'

Career advancement in Hollywood came from hiding mixedness. This rang true with me. Away from specific roles and scripts that I was drawn to, I had always, instinctively, kept quiet about my heritage. As discussed earlier, my Indian ancestry was my personal life. I had held on to my name, but Jassa Ahluwalia was just ambiguous enough to keep me professionally white.

Krishna Pandit Bhanji on the other hand, had to change his name. Not strictly Anglo-Indian in the historical sense, but born to a Kenyan Gujarati father and English mother in 1943, his prolific career only got off the ground after changing his name to Ben Kingsley. 'I had one audition as Krishna Bhanji and they said, "Beautiful audition but we don't quite know how to place you in our forthcoming season." I changed my name, crossed the road, and they said when can you start?'[50]

For a long time, Sir Ben was my only reference point as an actor of mixed South Asian and English ancestry. His heritage and immense talent has made him one of the most versatile actors of all time and, looking at his career I felt hopeful that I too might be able to emulate his range and success. Though none of his most famous roles are mixed, whenever I met other actors, he was my go-to for explaining my background. When I was shooting *The Whale* in 2013, I met an ostensibly white actor who, like me, had a South Asian grandfather. Sitting across from each other on a minibus in Malta, I gleefully launched into my Ben Kingsley spiel. Ferdinand Kingsley smiled and nodded along, before affectionately replying, 'Yeah … He's my dad.' I felt like a total arse.

In late 2018, I was ignorant of Anglo-Indian history and entirely unaware of the overlap with the birth of Hollywood. As I saw it, Sir Ben was a curious outlier, the exception not the rule. I had no idea that both he and I were part of a long history of mixed heritage South Asians striving for success on screen. All I could think about was that voice in my head that told me I was the wrong kind of mixed. I felt deeply confused about what to do with my Punjabi identity and it occurred to me that it was entirely possible that had my first agent implored me to change my name, I would've done so. Perhaps my career would look very different now. But as 2019 began, I was no longer content to quietly pass as white. It was not enough to be credited as Jassa Ahluwalia.

The loneliness was becoming unbearable. I resolved to assert my Punjabi heritage. And I wanted to see mixed people on screen, not as ethnically ambiguous shapeshifters, but as mixed people. Being a chameleon is part of the joy of being an actor, but I wanted to play with my true colours.

4
BOTH NOT HALF

The races of mankind will never again be able to go back to their citadels of high-walled exclusiveness.

RABINDRANATH TAGORE, *THE RELIGION OF MAN*

ON MONDAY 7 January 2019, the first Monday of the year, I cycled the hour-long journey home from my side hustle as a personal assistant, had a shower and began making some dhal. It was a cold, dark winter's evening and the simmering lentils – a warming pot of spiced goodness, brimming with childhood familiarity – were steaming up the windows of my poorly ventilated kitchen. The joys of Christmas had passed, the New Year had been toasted and reality was returning. A reality in which, aged 28, I was still living in a six-person houseshare.

I needed some extra protein to get me through the week. Being the vegan-dabbling millennial that I am, I pulled some Quorn Vegan Pieces out of the freezer. 'Deliciously Versatile' the packet claimed. Just as I was about to cut it open, I chuckled to myself, imagining the ire of an old Punjabi uncle, my grandad perhaps, outraged by the inclusion of such an unorthodox ingredient.

Unusually, I had the kitchen to myself, so I improvised a scene in Punjabi and shot a few angles. It was all incredibly lo-fi. The lighting was awful, my hair was still damp from the shower, I was in my dressing gown and I didn't think to add subtitles. While I fried up a tarka – a mix of spices, onions and garlic – I stitched the 23 seconds together on my phone. It made me laugh, but I ran it by my sister Ramanique just in case. 'So funny! Post!' came her reply. I uploaded the skit to Instagram and Twitter and sat down to eat. I had no idea that I had just set in motion a series of events that would lead to me hosting an awards ceremony at Wembley, giving a TEDx talk in India, broadcasting on national radio and, ultimately, writing this book.

Going viral

I went to bed that night not long after 10pm without paying much attention to my phone. I didn't have any social media notifications turned on and my primary concern was making sure I had enough sleep to get through the next day. My boss at the time was Jane MacQuitty, *The Times'* wine critic – a wonderful woman, with a heart of gold, whose passion for drinks was matched only by her disdain for technology.

When I arrived at Jane's home office the following morning, the video was getting a lot of attention on Twitter. More attention than anything I'd ever posted. Around 9:45am, BBC Asian Network presenter Noreen Khan retweeted it to her then 114k followers. Sanjeev Bhaskar and Sathnam Sanghera followed suit. Eshaan Akbar had also retweeted and by 11am we were arranging to meet for a coffee. Before it had even hit midday the video had topped 10,000 views. Similar madness was unfolding over on Instagram, with one person suggesting I was lip syncing. 'WHY IS HIS PUNJABI BETTER THAN BOTH OF OURS I FEEL OFFENDED' wrote a young woman, tagging her friend. 'Remember Rocky from Some Girls? This is him. Hahahahahhaha im really dead,' commented another. 'When a gora speaks better Punjabi than you lmao.' 'So confused.' And then one comment made me stop scrolling: 'This guy has better punjabi than both of us and he's only half punjabi.'

Only. Half. I stared at those words. The intent behind the comment was in no way malicious, but it hurt. I felt diminished. I felt like I was being robbed of something essential to me. And as I stared at my screen, realisation dawned. '#bothnothalf' I replied. 'Oh sorry my bad,' came her gracious response.

I felt like I was suddenly in a different world. Everything was the same, but it all made more sense somehow.

*

As unexpected and unplanned as the skit was, it didn't come from nowhere. I had been craving something I could point to and say, 'Look! I really am Punjabi!' and I had role models to inspire me.

Guz Khan shot to fame in 2015, a Birmingham school teacher whose alter ego, Mobeen, called on viewers to boycott

Jurassic World because of a scene about 'pakis'. His hysterical outrage and disbelief, both at the existence of the Pakisaurus and the oblivious use of the racial slur, became a viral hit and launched Khan's comedy and acting career. (The film actually refers to the Pachycephalosaurus, but 'pachys' doesn't sound any less offensive.) I'd also been bingeing content by Canadian comedian Jasmeet Singh Raina, better known by his YouTube moniker JusReign. His hilarious and incisive 'Desi parents and …' series from 2016 was some of the most relatable comedy I'd seen since *Goodness Gracious Me*. It was through exposure to these comedians that for the first time in my adult life I felt connected to my contemporaries in the global South Asian diaspora. In every outrageous caricature and scenario, I recognised my family and myself. It felt like they were granting me permission to belong. I had no pretensions of becoming a comedian or a YouTuber, but I recognised the potential that a few seconds of video had to open doors. I wanted to be among them. I wanted to push back and take control of my identity and my narrative as a mixed heritage artist. My Quorn-dhal video was a shot across the bow, an impromptu attempt to raise my flag and proudly declare who I was. The only problem was, I hadn't given any thought to what I would do if it worked.

My Instagram follower count was shooting up and I was feeling the weight of expectation to repeat my success. I felt like I was being dragged along, terrified to let go, a suffocating feeling that only intensified over the coming weeks.

A fortnight after posting my video, I was at the National Army Museum in Chelsea. I was attending the launch of

Turbans and Tales, a photo book documenting a three-year portraiture project that explored Sikh identity. The venue seemed an odd choice at first, but I soon learnt that the museum was the repository of collections from the British Indian Army, the military force founded in 1858 in the wake of the Indian Uprising. (The 1857 Uprising was a violent rebellion by Indian soldiers against their colonisers, attempting to re-establish the authority of the last Mughal emperor, Bahadur Shah Zafar. Depending on your political perspective it is known variously as the Indian Mutiny, the Sepoy Revolt and the First War of Independence.) Sikhs, designated a 'martial race' by their Victorian overlords, supported the British in crushing the rebellion and were recruited in their droves. As such, the National Army Museum has become a sort of unofficial home for various Sikh and Punjabi heritage events. Overseeing its impressive archive was curator Jasdeep Singh, who had invited me that evening as an excuse for us to meet; a mutual friend had connected us via email back in 2018 on account of our shared passion for tabla.

I knew Jasdeep wore a turban, but in a hall filling up with Sikhs that didn't help much. I glanced around, trying not to feel too out of place. I didn't recognise anyone but as my gaze lingered on various faces, I started to notice something odd. People were looking back at me, and quite a few weren't looking at me like I was white. That sounds weird, I know. But for most of my adult life, whenever I've been in a predominantly non-white environment, I feel it. The assumption that I'm an outsider is somehow tangible. I'd always found this particularly painful because I often feel most at ease in South Asian settings. I was once out for dinner with a turban-wearing friend and as we entered the restaurant, we passed another Sikh. The two men shared a nod of mutual recognition. 'Do you know him?' I asked. 'No, just a Singh, innit,' he replied. The Singh nod, I'd never had that. I longed for it.

As the event kicked off, Jasdeep emerged from the crowd and started to introduce me to other guests. Immediately, people started telling me how hilarious they'd found my video – as if I'd been making them for years – and, amazingly, how #BothNotHalf had resonated with their experiences as British South Asians. I was inundated by tales of people's mixed heritage nieces and nephews, jokes were being cracked in Punjabi and my phone was filling up with contacts. Among them was Magic Singh and *Britain's Got Talent* dancing sensation Madhu Singh. Magic and his wife Pavan (of Pavan Henna fame) were telling me about this incredible new app called TikTok (Magic had amassed over one million followers) and Madhu was pitching ideas for future skits and collaborations. I was deeply and thoroughly overwhelmed. Never before had my Punjabi identity been known, without need for explanation, outside of my family. After several years of feeling isolated and alone, the sense of belonging, of being seen, was intense. My eyes glistened. I was also panicking. What was my next video going to be? How could I harness this breakthrough? What the hell was TikTok?

I turned to my journal and through my writing a question emerged: what did I want to achieve?

I spent several months working through various ideas,

talking to friends, family and mentors. I put out the occasional video when the feeling took me, but I simply couldn't figure out what I wanted to say. I wanted to share my story, but what was my story? Did I actually know? Sure, I'd lived through the various events of my life, but I hadn't actually sat down and mapped how those disparate moments were all connected, how they all coalesced to make me, me. 'When I feel confused about something, I write about it until I turn into the person who shows up on paper: a person who is plausibly trustworthy, intuitive, and clear,' writes Jia Tolentino in the introduction to *Trick Mirror*. I opened up a blank document. Who would I become?

TEDxChandigarh

By early November 2019, I had a 4,000-word personal essay and a sense of purpose. I had also just been asked to host the BritAsia TV Punjabi Music Awards at Wembley Arena. While I brushed up on the hits of Sidhu Moosewala, I began emailing my writing to journalists, hoping to find an outlet that would publish it.

Sathnam Sanghera was the first to get back to me: 'To me it feels like the first draft of something bigger. A book on race? But books take forever. And there's a lot to be said for getting it out.' Despite being a successful author and becoming an informal mentor to me, Sathnam has tried to put me off writing this book at every stage. He warned me, correctly, that it would be a torturous process.

In the build-up to hosting at Wembley, I was doing what

any self-promoting and self-absorbed performer does: posting relentlessly on social media and scouring my replies. I tapped on a DM and froze with unexpected delight:

> pritika.mehta
> Dear Jassa, I deeply admire your personality and the way you personify diversity in the 21st century. As a licensee from TED Talks, I am honoured to extend you an invitation to be a speaker at TEDxChandigarh. I strongly believe that your talk can create magic and inspire millions of people worldwide.

Creating magic and inspiring millions seemed like a tall order. But the timing was perfect. My unpublished essay was a ready-made talk. I couldn't believe my luck. But I needed a sponsor. The organisers could cover everything in India, but I had to cover my flight, and I didn't have £800 to spare. After coming off stage at Wembley, having MC'd a wild evening of Punjabi music and big personalities – a fight almost broke out backstage after an artist's entourage took issue with Paul Chowdhry's trademark acerbic humour – I managed to grab a few minutes with BritAsiaTV CEO Tony Shergill. As Mickey Singh was being mobbed in the hotel lobby, I gave Tony an elevator pitch. Within a couple of weeks, we had a deal. I was all set. And then it almost all fell apart.

The TEDx event in Chandigarh was scheduled for 12 January 2020. The fourth series of *Unforgotten* was due to start filming on the 13th. My role only required a few days of filming and, given that the overall shoot ran until mid-April,

I figured there wouldn't be any issues; I'd never been needed on day one before. But there's a first time for everything and suddenly I was facing an impossible choice: do the TEDx talk or shoot *Unforgotten*. 'If you are considering pulling out that is going to go down very badly,' cautioned my agent's assistant. 'Regrettably we do need to let them know in the next hour or so.'

It was 20 December, offices were closing down for the Christmas holidays and I felt utterly helpless. A TEDx talk, in India, was simply too perfect an opportunity to miss. But *Unforgotten* was a £12k payday: there was no way I could turn it down.

Looking back, I'd like to think I would've pulled out of the shoot, with the certainty that my TEDx talk would be the most important thing I'd do in 2020, knowing that it would lead to some of the most rewarding work I've ever done. But the reality is I was worried about my rent. My turnover for 2019–20 was £23,000. There was no way I could turn down over half my annual earnings. I was saved, thankfully, by a generous last-minute intervention by Sanjeev Bhaskar, Nicola Walker and our showrunner, Chris Lang. Without them, my TEDx talk would never have happened.

I spent my Christmas holiday streamlining my 4,000 words into a 17-minute talk and committing it to memory. In the New Year I'd be off to Chandigarh, the state capital of Punjab, a city that also serves as the capital of the neighbouring state of Haryana – a 'both not half' city.

*

Thursday 9 January 2019

Currently sat on a plane to India. Feels preposterous
to be flying all this way for two nights. All feels
quite surreal. I have no idea how this trip is going
to affect me, but it can't not, surely. As absurd as
this trip feels, so much of today, once I'd arrived at
Heathrow, felt right. An ease. Things were 'intensely
themselves' (a beautiful phrase I've just come across in
The Secret Commonwealth). From the chirpy security
guy, to being offered a free banana from Pret, to the
excitement of the couple en route to Goa in Premium,
recognising and saying hi to Henning Wehn (so tall)
on the jet bridge, saying hello to the Sikh couple
and the Singh who recognised me as I made my way
to my seat. The plane is filled with familiar smells,
tupperware is out, babies are crying. All so familiar.
India feels trapped behind a hazy veil of memory and
emotion. I can't wait to feel its reality. Like returning
to an old school.

My last visit had been in 2014, the trip that had reduced me
to fearful tears. 'Who am I?' I was still working on the answer.
But the question no longer scared me. I felt awakened, ready
to begin a new chapter of my relationship with the literal land
of my father. And as soon as I stepped off the plane in Delhi,
the 'hazy veil' started to lift.

The first thing I did, while I waited for my connecting
flight to Chandigarh, was find the nearest street food outlet
and order a fat stack of aloo praunthe – buttery potato-stuffed

flatbreads, eaten with yogurt. I was consciously recreating the ritual of my childhood summer holidays. The interminably long car journeys from Delhi airport to my uncle's house in Punjab would be punctuated by a pit stop at a roadside dhaba where we'd get our first taste of India: aloo praunthe – the ultimate comfort food.

On this occasion, the comfort wasn't just culinary. I was halfway through my meal when the chef stepped out from behind the counter to ask me how it was. 'Excellent,' I replied. He shone with pride and then, after a slightly awkward pause, 'You're Punjabi aren't you?' I beamed and nodded, my mouth full. Though I was a bit confused. I'd only spoken in Punjabi with his colleague on the till and even then, very briefly. I doubted he'd heard enough to deduce my origins. I wondered if he'd perhaps seen one of my videos, but something in the tone of his voice said no. 'I saw the way you were eating, I knew you had to be.' I grinned so hard I almost forgot to swallow.

*

As soon as I arrived in Chandigarh, I felt like I was preparing for a play. My press night nerves were building, and not least because of our esteemed venue: the Tagore Theatre.

Rabindranath Tagore (1861–1941) was a Bengali poly-math. A poet, playwright, painter and essayist, he won the 1913 Nobel Prize in Literature, becoming the first Indian (and first non-European) to receive the award. A black-and-white photo of this intellectual giant loomed large in the foyer of the theatre. I was unfamiliar with his work, but I knew his name and his mystery intimidated me. Had I been more familiar with his writing, I may have found comfort and inspiration:

> The races of mankind will never again be able to go back to their citadels of high-walled exclusiveness. They are to-day exposed to one another, physically and intellectually. The shells, which have so long given them full security within their individual enclosures have been broken, and by no artificial process can they be mended again. So we have to accept this fact, even though we have not yet fully adapted our minds to this changed environment of publicity, even though through it we may have to run all the risks entailed by the wider expansion of life's freedom.[1]

Chaperoning me to the theatre was student and TEDx volunteer Abhishek Chauhan. He'd greeted me at the airport on Friday and we'd become best buds. After my rehearsal on Saturday, we'd gone for a walk around Sukhna Lake, where a bird had pooped on my head. Abhishek kindly sacrificed his handkerchief and cleaned me up, before we swung by his favourite microbrewery for a beer. I'd never seen this side of India: the contemporary, the urban, the hipster, the youthful. My memories were full of farms, villages and elders. I was forging a new story, with Abhishek guiding me. By the time he came to pick me up on Sunday, we had a solid rapport, prompting him to sincerely (and unhelpfully) point out that

I seemed tense. He wanted to chat, but I needed to focus on my breathing. I hadn't felt nerves like this before.

After an interminably long delay, countless trips to the bathroom and a lot of pacing up and down the corridor, I found myself mic'd up and waiting in the wings. The red circle was in front of me. The auditorium was packed. I stepped into the light. And I began:

When I was fifteen years old, I had an argument
with a street vendor. I'd been to India many times
before, but this was my first time visiting the Wagah
Border. I was excited. I'd heard stories about the wild
leg kicking ceremony, I'd been practising … But I
was also tired. It had been a long, hot day, and as our
rickshaw pulled up amongst the crowd, a young man
rushed over, clutching bottles of water.

'Water, water, cold water!'

I already had a bottle of water, I showed him, smiled a
courteous 'no thank you'.

'Ah, but this is cold water, sir! Ice cold: feel!'

He thrust the bottle of water into my hand. He was
right, it was freezing. But I had a slight headache
coming on and I really just needed a moment to
myself. So, being an Englishman, I defaulted to what
I know best: awkward politeness.

'No thank you. Sorry, I have plenty of water. I don't need anything. Sorry, sorry, thank you.'

'Sir, lots of people. Very hot. You will need *more* water!'

I was impressed by his persistence but still, 'No, thank you.'

'Best price!'

The crowd was starting to swell.

'One litre, two litre—'

I snapped.

'*Oh shad deh yaar, mera sir part dha pya! Kini vari mein kya, mere kul paani hai! Kisi hor nu thang kar!*'

My Punjabi tirade – 'leave it dude, my head is killing me, I've said it so many times, I've got water, go bother someone else' – prompted raucous applause. The sound hit my chest as a wave of emotion. I very nearly burst into chest-heaving sobs. This was the same rush of belonging I had felt at the National Army Museum, but on a much grander scale. This wasn't Chelsea, this was Chandigarh. I waited for the whoops and cheers to die down before letting out a laugh to cover the cracks in my voice. I had spent so long focusing on learning my talk that I hadn't given any thought to how it might go down. It was too much to process in the moment, so I took a deep breath, trusting that my rehearsals would keep me on track, and continued.

I concluded by sharing how I had coined #BothNotHalf and reflecting on what it might mean:

Is it merely a hashtag? Or is it something more? For me, it's the distillation of my struggles with my sense of self. The answer to a question I didn't realise I needed to ask. But most importantly, it's not a label – it's an idea.

'Both Not Half' is a non-binary approach to life; an idea that's always existed. It is a rejection of easy distinction and historical prejudice. Whatever our backgrounds – ethnicity, nationality, gender, sexuality, social class – we are each whole individuals whose constituent parts cannot be separated.

Power structures love labels. Labels facilitate division and, ultimately, control. They allow people to whip up tales of 'us and them'. Oversimplified propaganda. Divide and rule. But we can take back our control, our power. By recognising the language of division, in all its forms, and rewriting it into a language of inclusion, we force the world to engage with detail. Instead of simply seeing how we differ from others, we begin to notice how complex we ourselves are.

Instead of seeing divergence, we begin to notice mixes all around us.

The same goes for fashion, food, music, engineering, thinking. So much of our world is defined by what it isn't, as opposed to what it is. But that's another talk.

'Both Not Half' is a rewording and a rewiring of our minds. None of us, nothing, is half anything. Everything, all of us, are both something.

As the applause came, I breathed a sigh of relief. I'd done it. I'd walked the tightrope without a single wobble. The event host, Simarpreet Singh, came on stage to congratulate me and segue into the next talk. Despite us being close in age, his red turban and air of authority reminded me of my grandad. In a photo of this moment, I look like a proud yet bashful child.

I came off stage and was hit by a wave of hunger. But before I could eat, I needed to find my cousin, Rajdeep, and her husband, Japinder, who had been in the audience. They had travelled from their home in Patiala to see me and I only had a few hours before I had to leave for the airport. I wanted to have lunch together. Rajdeep had messaged to say they were in the VIP area and a volunteer walked me over to find them.

Seeing them made everything feel far more real. I had no real memories of Rajdeep, but she had plenty of me as a child (she's my dad's first cousin) and her presence bridged my past and present. She presented me with a phulkari, a traditional Punjabi embroidered shawl, and we hugged and beamed with familial pride. And then the audience broke for lunch and all hope of having a meaningful conversation vanished.

As the VIP area filled up, I was approached by countless individuals keen to share how much my story had resonated with them. Not just people in interfaith marriages, but also those with parents from different corners of India, as well as Indians who now lived abroad. I marvelled at the numerous different ways in which people saw themselves reflected. The idea that Both Not Half could go beyond 'race' was no longer theoretical; I saw the glow in people's eyes as they told me they no longer felt fractured and fractional, but whole and multiple.

Then it got too much. I was getting mobbed. This was unlike anything I'd ever experienced; a cautionary insight into what real fame looked like. I couldn't move for phones clamouring for selfies and I still hadn't eaten. I spotted Abhishek across the room and he, in turn, clocked my panic and came to the rescue. He put his arm around me like a personal bodyguard, employed his colleagues to part the crowd and whisked me backstage. Rajdeep and Japinder followed shortly after.

Eating lunch out of takeaway boxes in a dressing room, within smelling distance of the toilets, was not quite what I'd imagined for our family meal, but it had its own peculiar charm. And we were soon joined by my dear friend Suresh, who lived a few doors down from Uncle Jagir in Moga. He had been visiting friends in Barnala for Lohri celebrations the previous day and had extended his trip to see me for a couple of hours.

'I'll be back in April,' I assured them, totally unaware that a pandemic was imminent.

Lockdown

I landed back at Heathrow, went home, had a shower, jumped in the car that *Unforgotten* had sent for me and was in makeup by 3.40pm. A couple of weeks later, I attended the Dunhill pre-BAFTA Filmmakers Party – a swanky black-tie affair thronging with veritable stars. I'd attended the previous year and had used it as an excuse to film a sketch, but I'd struggled to make any meaningful connections with fellow guests. These events look incredibly fun and glamorous in the photos, but the reality is much more akin to an episode of *BoJack Horseman*. This year, with renewed confidence off the back of my TEDx talk, I was determined to have a more grounded experience.

Not long after arriving and having my photos taken, I spotted Malachi Kirby, one of the most genuine and sincere people I've ever met in the business. We've never worked together, but our paths had crossed at various events and we'd developed a mutual respect and professional friendship. Over drinks, I told him all about #BothNotHalf and my trip to India, and he shared that he was working on his debut play *Level Up* with the Bush Theatre. Before we were done talking, someone came to drag Malachi away. 'We're doing a big BAME photo!' they said. I grinned broadly as I watched Black, brown and mixed actors jostle into position. The energy was that of a big Indian family at a tourist attraction. I loved it. And I felt heartbroken: I knew I couldn't get involved.

I gave Malachi a smile and a nod so as to say 'catch you later', but he wasn't having it. 'Come on.' He said it so casually, as if there was no doubt in his mind, but his look told me he knew exactly what this meant to me. He took me by the arm and we crouched down near the front. I recounted this story in my BBC documentary *Am I English?* and the emotion of the memory caught me off guard. Fighting back the tears I explained, 'It felt like such a big moment, that Malachi really got how I was feeling in that moment, I felt like I belonged there, but I also knew that to volunteer myself to be in that photo would just raise so many questions. Somebody even did shout out 'Random white guy!' And then somebody next to me shouted out 'he's mixed!' That felt so good. It felt *so* good.

Once the photo appeared online a few days later, I dropped Malachi a text: 'Hi Malachi, just want to say a huge thank you again for encouraging me to get involved with this photo. I know it seems trivial but this whole last year has been about articulating my mixed heritage to myself and others. In short, I felt seen and it felt wonderful.'

I had to resist the urge to write more. I could have easily effused about how intensely validated I felt in that moment. It was one thing for me to have a sense of my own identity, but for that to be accepted and celebrated by another was something else entirely. The boost it gave me was unprecedented. I was no longer alone. Were such an event to happen today, I would assuredly step into the frame. I would of course expect questions, but I would be able to answer them with confidence.

Attending Vinay Patel's Brown Christmas in 2023, a South Asian-led festive party for freelance creatives, someone asked me in the toilets how I'd come to be in attendance. 'Because I'm brown,' I told him. I only dropped some Punjabi after giving him sufficient time to stew in confusion at the urinal. I'm no longer afraid of the friction that comes with asserting my true self.

'You are most definitely seen and appreciated,' came Malachi's reply. I felt more ready than ever for the year ahead.

I had a final day on *Unforgotten* scheduled for 19 March. But just a couple of days before, I received an email 'declaring an event of force majeure'. Production was to be suspended 'with immediate effect'. I never got to film my final scene, the ensuing lockdowns forced me to cancel my spring trip to India, and it became unclear if my TEDx talk would ever make it online.

I had been told that it would be uploaded to the TEDx YouTube channel by mid-March, but as spring became summer it was still nowhere to be seen. The joy of Chandigarh faded into a sad, aching frustration. I had banked on using the talk as a calling card, a way to open doors and create opportunity, but all I could do was wait. I filled my days with reading, wrote an article for *Burnt Roti* about enmeshment trauma in South Asian families and was commissioned by Rifco Theatre to write a spoken word piece, exploring the British Asian experience of lockdown. My inspiration: Uncle Jagir, and how my sister had woken me up on 31 March to tell me he had died from an early morning heart attack.

I heard the news through tears

Fuelled by fears
We'd buried when we booked our flights
Their day in India began with mourning
While we lay asleep
In our locked down night

My grandad's brother had died
The pyre was already burning
It was all just so, unexpected
Would it have been easier
I wonder
If he'd been infected?

Natural causes seem crueller
In these unnatural times
Rites of passage blocked
By social distance
And grounded airlines

ਆਪ ਸਭ ਨੂੰ ਸਤਿ ਸ੍ਰੀ ਅਕਾਲ
ਆਪ ਸਭ ਨੂੰ...
[Greetings to you all]
[To you all …]

When only words can touch
Language has new meaning
But how do we share
our joy, our grief?
When those for whom we care

are far and speak
A speech we only half learnt
When birth and death
Were not our burdens
to bear
I didn't have the words to share
How I felt.

Rare terms, now common usage
Quarantine, pandemic
Inequity, systemic
How to begin my Punjabi condolence
When I've only ever expressed
Material moments

ਪਾਬੰਦੀਆਂ, ਖਿਆਲਾਂ, ਕਿਰਪਾ ਅਤੇ ਉਦਾਸ
ਸੁੱਖ ਦੁੱਖ ਅਤੇ ਹੁਕਮਿ,
ਸੰਤੋਖ ਅਤੇ ਪਿਆਰ
['Restrictions', 'thoughts', 'grace' and 'sad',]
['Joy', 'pain' and 'divine order']
['Contentment' and 'love']

I needed new words
To nourish old bonds
The elders we cling to
Are guardians soon gone
We fear their death
As a loss of our past
But when the time comes

We can fight or run
Search for new meaning
Or else, succumb

Were we self isolated, before we locked down?
Shut off from our past
Afraid of our crown
Embarrassed by a tongue
That doesn't feel our own
Heavy is the head
But we don't wear it alone
To be self sovereign is simply to be
We can stay at home
And still be free.

The past has gone,
New futures await.
Swim with the river
There's freedom in fate.

The death of Uncle Jagir was a huge moment for my immediate family. He was our anchor to India. I remember struggling to say goodbye at the security checkpoint at Amritsar airport in 2006, not knowing when, or if, I'd see him again. I remember going back for a second hug. And I remember how walking away from him seemed harder than the usual ritual of watching him fade from view out of the back window of a car.

Uncle Jagir, the embodiment of my Indian childhood,

had died. And yet I felt more rooted than ever.

This book

With little fanfare, I woke up on 14 August to discover my talk was finally online. The first few comments were a bit disheartening: 'Sorry, but a bit boooring.' And, 'You can deny science and call yourself one human race and ignore miscegenation health pitfalls but science will prevail.' Yikes. But the positivity soon began to drown them out. The most rewarding comments were the likes of: 'Something my boy will want to hear about as he's starting his journey'; 'My nephew as well. Sending this to my brother and his wife'; 'I sent the link to my kids immediately after watching'.

One of the first people I sent the link to was Sathnam Sanghera. I was fishing for a retweet and he kindly obliged, before messaging to say, 'BTW, if you ever plan to write a book, gimme a shout. Am working with a literary agency to boost their bame clients.' My reply: 'Oh cool! Thank you so much. Well, I would absolutely love to turn the ideas of #BothNotHalf into a book. Would that be the sort of thing they had in mind? This TEDx thing is going to be my covering letter for everything now 😄'

Turns out, yes. That was exactly what they had in mind. Sathnam introduced me to literary agent Hattie Grünewald and I was confused when she started talking about what 'we' would do to get my book published. For some reason, I was convinced our Zoom meeting was just about giving me some advice. I didn't know the first thing about writing a book.

I barely knew the difference between an agent and a publisher. But here I was, being offered representation!

Here was the opportunity I'd been craving. The kind of opportunity I'd subconsciously been reaching for when I posted my first skit. The reason I'd written the talk. The reason I'd moved heaven and earth to ensure I could make it to Chandigarh. A door was opening and I needed to step through. But I had some concerns. The agency, The Blair Partnership, is best known for representing J.K. Rowling and I strongly disagreed with her public interventions on trans rights. I knew that I would want to write about #BothNotHalf in the context of queer politics and I was worried this might be met with resistance. I arranged another Zoom call and Hattie assured me that her job was to represent *me*, not edit or censor. And a quick glance at her social media – 'Views my own. Trans liberation now.' – gave me confidence.

I share all this behind-the-scenes not because I've run out of things to say, but because the process of actually writing this book has been integral to my journey. I struggled for over a year, limping along, trying to find my way. I was terrified. I couldn't finish a single chapter. How on earth was I going to manage a whole book? The growing success of my TEDx talk and my subsequent BBC documentary did little to give me confidence. If anything, they piled on the pressure. The heartfelt messages I was receiving convinced me I needed to nail it. I needed to come up with answers, not just for myself, but for everyone. I eventually admitted defeat and sent off a rambling thirteen thousand words to Hattie. There was no real conclusion, but I didn't know what else to do. I needed feedback. And after a fraught weekend, I turned to my journal.

Tuesday 22 March 2022

The last few days have been pretty punishing. I committed to sending Hattie a finished draft of my sample chapter last week and unleashed my deep seated insecurities about my ability and worthiness as a writer. Felt deeply depressed for about 48–72 hours and have finally referred myself via the NHS for some therapy. Have my assessment call on the 30th. Had some personal breakthroughs though, I think. Amrit [singer-songwriter Amrit Kaur, my housemate at the time] floored me slightly on Friday night by questioning whether the book is a vanity project. There was some truth in it, and it hurt. What I've come to understand over the weekend is that I've been treating the book as a way of proving something to myself, making it so hard for myself so as to make any achievement incontrovertible proof that I deserve a seat at the table. I've articulated Both Not Half but I'm still desperately trying to prove who I am. I'm reaching for an ideal when what I need is already to hand: my experiences. I'm waiting for feedback from Hattie but I'm already preparing to block off time to give this my all. I know what I want to say and I feel like I'm just figuring out how to say it. I need to approach it with the same passion I had for my TEDx talk. And I need to stop seeing this book as my

ticket to intellectual/academic acceptance. These past
few days I've really confronted the relief I felt when
I dropped out of uni. The sudden loss of pressure
because now I couldn't fail. I've always doubted if I
could've completed my degree. My perfectionism runs
deep. Attending Sharan's book launch on Thursday
[*Burning My Roti*, by Sharan Dhaliwal], surrounded
by so many amazing titles by writers of the Global
Majority, I should've felt inspired. Instead my mind
was telling me 'all these people have done it, why are
you finding it so hard, why can't you?' Toxic as fuck.
I booked my therapy assessment the next day.

The NHS arranged a six-week course of cognitive behavioural
therapy, which had its merits, but it was only when I invested
in some private psychotherapy that I came to understand my
tendency towards 'rescuing'.

At the heart of the psychology of a rescuer is the desire
to be needed. They offer help in order to make others
dependent on them and so ensure that they themselves won't
be abandoned. I had articulated #BothNotHalf for myself
but I was still craving validation and belonging. I felt I would
only get that, and so find peace, if I authored 'The Definitive
Book' on mixed experience. I had set myself an impossible
task and, in failing, was forced to stare my insecurities in the
face. I wasn't conscious of it at the time, but in attempting
to 'fix' others through my writing, I was really trying to 'fix'
myself. It would take writing this book for me to shake off
the idea that so many of us with mixed identity carry: that

we are puzzles to be solved. We are not jigsaws missing pieces or stray tiles who do not fit into the bigger picture. We are people who exist, whole and multiple. There is nothing to fix.

*

Selling the book proved trickier than any of us expected. A TEDx talk, a BBC documentary and a tight pitch felt like more than enough. And though many publishers were keen to meet with me, offers were in short supply. I shared my frustrations with Sathnam: 'Sadly a lot of publishers dropped out because they couldn't get it past their money people. Basically a lot of them already had a 'mixed' book on their list and god forbid there be more than one voice or perspective …'

Part of the curse of underrepresentation is that when opportunities do arise, competition is fierce. Until a particular 'niche' has a proven track record of profitability, there's only one seat at the table, if at all. I've had to check my own tendency towards competition on several occasions and focus on celebrating my peers, like Laila Woozeer, who I met at the launch of their fabulously lyrical memoir, *Not Quite White*. We've since become good friends and have spoken at length about how the industry makes so many marginalised voices feel like they're in competition, despite the fact that people like to read multiple books on the same topic. In our case it feels particularly bizarre, given that the mixed population is the fastest growing demographic in the UK – there will be interested readers for years to come.

We've also discussed how our experiences have differed quite wildly when it comes to responses from the public. Laila is frequently interrogated about their experience of being mixed and prompted to dwell on their trauma over their joy. Whereas with me, people tend to gloss over my story entirely and offer up their own. Even when they don't have mixed ethnic heritage, people love to share how #BothNotHalf resonates with them, due to class or geographic origins. I can't help but feel that my appearance as a white man is helping me out here. I look like 'the default' we so frequently see on film and TV and through which so many of us are used to understanding the world. I invite you to consider if my writing would feel different to you if I was a woman, or trans, or Black, or all of those things. Be honest. Would I feel less relatable? Would it be on me to make myself more palatable to you? Or would it be on you to question your prejudices and expand your horizons?

Despite the disappointing response from publishers, the company I really wanted – Bonnier Books UK – came through. They're the reason you're reading this. My meeting with Susannah Otter was one of the few meetings where I didn't have to explain why this book was necessary or different. She simply got it and was more interested in discussing how to ensure this book found its audience. I was gutted when Susannah announced her move to a different publishing house after my first edit, but I had equal confidence in her assistant who stepped up, Lucy Tirahan, herself of mixed English-Indian heritage. She was familiar with 'Both Not Half' before my proposal had landed on her desk. I'd found my home.

What follows is what happened next. When I started

writing this book, I thought I knew the ending. I thought 'Both Not Half' was the answer and all I needed to do was pose the question. But as I began putting words to paper, something started to happen. The bigger picture I'd hinted at during the final moments of my TEDx talk started to come into vision. 'Both Not Half' hadn't simply changed my relationship with my mixed heritage identity, it was fundamentally changing how I saw the world.

5

USEFUL FICTIONS, DANGEROUS NARRATIVES

Nations themselves are narrations. The power to narrate, or to block other narratives from forming and emerging, is very important to culture and imperialism, and constitutes one of the main connections between them.

EDWARD SAID, *CULTURE AND IMPERIALISM*

MY NATIONAL IDENTITY crisis began in earnest in January 2016. 'Please could you send a 100 word biography.' I was in the midst of rehearsals for a play when I received this email from the production team. My profile was destined to feature in the programme. But I had a problem. I no longer knew how to describe myself. Was I English? British? British-Asian? For most of my life, I'd not actually given much thought to my national identity. It was only now, as a young adult, awakened to the conflicts of my mixed identity and confronted with having to biographise myself, that I began to give it serious thought. But did it even matter? Perhaps I was worrying over nothing. Perhaps I could simply omit my nationality.

I looked up a few Wikipedia entries to see what the form was: Sir Ian Murray McKellen is an English stage and film actor; Dame Judith Olivia Dench is a British actress; Gurinder Chadha is a British film director of Indian origin. I expanded to sports: David Robert Joseph Beckham is an English former professional footballer; Sachin Ramesh Tendulkar is an Indian former international cricketer. Then music: Robyn Rihanna Fenty is a Barbadian singer. We are defined by our work and nationality is our go-to adjective. It was a standard, a part of reality it seemed, that I didn't feel I could deviate from.

I was born and grew up in England, avidly tracking the national football team on my wall chart during World Cups, so I guess I felt somewhat English. But we were Team GB at the Olympics and my passport declared me a 'British Citizen', so I also felt British. Thanks to its adoption by far-right groups like the English Defence League, I never grew particularly fond of the Saint George's Cross. But, being too young to remember it as a banner of the National Front – a fascist, racist and often violent political party active during the 1970s – I embraced the Union Jack. In my early 20s, I bought a hand-painted Union Jack T-shirt in Camden from a woman with a limited command of English. I loved it so much that I even wore it for my *Ripper Street* self-tape in 2013. I didn't realise it at the time but looking back, I was pretty comfortable with my dual British-English identity. Indeed, research by Opinium in 2020 shows that most

English, Welsh and Scottish people identify equally with both their British and national identities.

So maybe either English or British would do for my biography? Perhaps, but it felt incomplete. What about that other term that had been a feature of my upbringing, British Asian? My grandad used to get the 'Asia Edition' of our local paper, the *Leicester Mercury*. I would listen to BBC Asian Network. The British Asian Trust was founded in 2007 by prominent South Asian-origin business leaders and King Charles III (then Prince of Wales). But it didn't sit right. British Asian had always been a descriptor that best suited my dad, never me. It's always felt to me like a way of saying, 'I might look Asian, but I am British. I might be brown, but I do belong here.' The uncomfortable implication being that Britishness equates to whiteness. Plus, British Asian has come to feel dated as more of us become aware of the fact that it's a label that does not reflect the full extent of Asia and excludes the UK's East and South East Asian populations.

I mulled over my options and eventually settled on 'British Indian'. And then five days later I sent a follow-up email: 'Could I please change "British Indian" to "Anglo-Indian"? Subtle distinction that I've been grappling with.' It was an imperfect, outmoded choice, and I was yet to discover the full extent of Anglo-Indian history, but it would work for now. I wanted to be seen. After all, was national identity not an intimate part of one's personal identity?

Later that year, I saw headlines about an interview actor Riz Ahmed had done while promoting the HBO series *The Night Of.* During his appearance on *The Late Show with*

Stephen Colbert, Ahmed was asked about his heritage. 'When I was growing up, I felt like I had to qualify it and say I'm British-Pakistani but now I feel like, in this day and age,' he gestures to himself, 'this is what British looks like.' The audience burst into applause. The clip has almost 3 million views on YouTube.

At the time, I didn't get it. Or rather, I understood it – it felt powerful – but I didn't feel like it applied to me. For a visibly brown man to claim British as his national identity, free of any qualifier, felt deeply meaningful. But for me, it felt like I was erasing a part of myself. My existential angst began to spiral, not helped by the fact that I had just moved out of my uni flatshare. My ex-flatmates were moving on to the next stages of their lives. I, on the other hand, an actor and drop-out, found myself crashing in a spare room in East London on a fold-out sofa. I self-medicated on podcasts and lectures, wandering around the Olympic Village. And then one clear winter's day, I made a discovery that blew my mind.

[15:27, 30/11/2016] Jassa: Arend, I've just finished listening to a lecture on the creation of national identity and I want to chat about it so bad. I feel like a great deal of modern day social anxiety is born out of a belief that national identity is a natural and unchangeable law.

It was Arend's spare room that I was crashing in. A German who grew up in Scotland, before studying music at Oxford, Arend and I spent many evenings over *Abendbrot* boring his then boyfriend, now husband, Josh, pondering the nature of identity. I cherished these conversations. They made me feel less alone, a nightly reminder that it was okay to ask questions and seek help. A space in which to share and explore. So now, discovery in hand, I couldn't contain my excitement. I still remember bounding down Logan Close, headphones in, sun on my face, feeling like I'd just unearthed a powerful ancient artefact. The cloud of confusion I'd been living under began to fade.

The lecture I'd been listening to explained that national identity was an invention of the 18th and 19th centuries, filling the void left by the breakdown of traditional communities and religious ties in the wake of industrialisation. It is for this reason that Johann Sebastian Bach is regarded as a *German* composer, despite being born in 1685 in the Ernestine duchy, ruled by the House of Wettin, and dying in 1750, over a hundred years before the German Empire came into existence. This is not to say that German cultural identity did not exist during Bach's time, but he was only elevated to the status of national hero after his works were rediscovered during the early 19th century. The Industrial Revolution pioneered new forms of manufacturing, both on factory floors and in people's imaginations.

I felt liberated. So much so that it became a key point in my TEDx talk: 'I realised national identities were a construct – a construct I didn't need.' When journalist Tim Walker shared the talk with his followers on Twitter he quoted that specific line. I dropped him a text to say thank you. And to make a confession.

[12:13, 17/08/2020] Jassa: … you've quoted the
one line I'm having doubts about! I'm wondering if
national identities of sorts are necessary …

The doubts had crept in not long after I'd flown back from
giving the talk in India, when the pandemic struck. With
Brexit soon to come into force and with covid raging, I
couldn't shake the feeling that I cared about England. I cared
about Britain. I cared deeply about my fellow citizens and
the future of our nation. When I leant out of my flat window
to 'Clap for Our Carers' for the first time, I was struck by
a sense of national unity I'd never felt before. Over the
coming weeks, pots and pans were introduced. Two of my
wooden spatulas were sacrificed to the cause. I got to know
my neighbours. Ian from downstairs revealed he was the
proud owner of an antique, hand-operated rotary fire bell.
Our local chorus grew louder by the week. And across the
country local expressions took on culturally specific flavours;
in Birmingham, the female bhangra troop Eternal Taal took
to the streets with their dhols, in Scotland, bagpipes blasted.
It was all unexpectedly emotional. Though sadly short-lived.

I was tempted to ignore my doubts. Rejecting national
identity had freed me to articulate #BothNotHalf and reconcile
my British citizenship with my Indian heritage. I finally felt at
ease. Plus, the only public figures embracing nationhood as a
vehicle for meaning seemed to be members of the Conservative
government and their cheerleaders, bent on stoking cultural
divides, repelling refugees and advocating for a hard Brexit.
GB News was announced in September 2020 with overt

Union Jack branding and a clear 'anti-woke' agenda. I had no great desire to join the 'flag shagging' ranks. But I also knew I had to follow my gut. Something about this whole national identity thing felt wrong. So, just as I had looked to history to understand and move beyond my imperial nostalgia, I decided I needed to revisit the origins of national identity. My sweeping rejection on the TEDx red circle was based on a single half-hour lecture at a time when I was looking for easy answers. Perhaps I had missed something.

A brief history of nationalism

If you zoom out far enough, it becomes obvious that national identities are not some sort of primordial truth. For 2.5 million years our hunter-gatherer ancestors roamed freely as part of small, tight-knit communities, living in harmony with the natural world. It's hard to comprehend just how long a period of time that is. It's roughly the time from when Buddha was born circa 563 BC until now, multiplied by a thousand. Human history as hunter-gatherers massively outstrips our time on Earth as beflagged citizens. Settlements only came into being around 11,000 years ago, when the invention of farming allowed people to stay in one place. It was only then, as populations grew, that large-scale cooperation became possible through shared beliefs in things like gods, laws and money. Thus began the age of civilisation.

But when did countries as we now know them become a thing? When did it become the norm for a population to exercise authority over their declared homeland, as defined on a map, in relation to other nations? When and why did it become essential for national identities to exist? And why, if they were invented so recently, do they feel so ancient and immutable?

I began my search for answers by revisiting the conversation I had had with Arend back in 2016:

> [17:08, 30/11/2016] Arend: Hmm. That's a big thing to discuss on WhatsApp. Have you read the Benedict Anderson book I lent you?

I hadn't read the book. It was an intimidating academic tome from the 80s called *Imagined Communities: Reflections on the Origins and Spread of Nationalism*. The title captivated me but the introduction muses on 'the history of Marxism' and 'the *recent* [emphasis added] wars between Vietnam, Cambodia and China'. I found it entirely inaccessible. My friends from university, who actually studied it, confess that they only ever read extracts or commentaries on the key ideas. But, almost five years after first hearing about it, I decided to get myself a copy and hack through the dense text in search of the promised gold within. After looking up various fancy words, translating passages of French (slightly bizarre for a book that devotes a lot of time to the importance of mutual intelligibility) and following up with some digging of my own, I pieced together a brief history of nationalism according to Benedict Anderson.

It seems it all began with Latin. Well, the downfall of Latin. In the mid-1400s, a German craftsman (again, Germany didn't exist yet, but let's not get bogged down) called Johannes Gutenberg pioneered the printing press. (Moveable type was invented in China, and the oldest known printed book in existence was pressed by hand in Korea in 1377.)[1] Up until then, in Europe, books had been laboriously handwritten. They were rare and expensive. They were also in Latin, the language of the church and power. So, too, were the first printed books. But by the late 1500s, with 200 million books coming off the presses of Europe, booksellers were running out of customers. After all, only a small elite understood Latin. Keen to tap into new markets, savvy printers turned to local languages.

But there was a problem. Whereas Latin was unified, with long-established vocabulary, spellings and grammar, local speech varied from region to region. It was not commercially viable to print a handful of books in one dialect of French and then reset the type for the variation up the road. So, printers began to standardise. It wasn't long before unified languages began to emerge from the vast diversity of local tongues. Previously separate communities began to understand each other and so became connected, bound by a shared print language. And as words began to be fixed to the page, languages became fixed in time.

I find it mind-blowing that I can pick up a copy of Jonathan Swift's *Gulliver's Travels*, published in 1726, and make perfect sense of the opening lines:

> My father had a small estate in Nottinghamshire; I
> was the third of five sons. He sent me to Emmanuel
> College in Cambridge at fourteen years old.

But if we go back another few hundred years to 1476 and try and dip into the prologue of Chaucer's *Canterbury Tales*, I find myself lost:

> Whan that Aprille with his shoures sote
> The droghte of Marche hath perced to the rote,
> And bathed every veyne in swich licour.

By slowing the evolution of languages to a snail's pace, printing and books created the illusion of a deep collective past that could be understood, protected and built upon. An exercise that more and more people could participate in as languages became increasingly standardised. This was the linguistic framework from which national consciousness could arise. France emerged as the nation of French, England the nation of English, Portugal the nation of Portuguese. You get the idea. This is why the earliest nations feel as if they emerged from an ancient past. They are rooted in language and since languages have no distinct beginning, instead being passed organically from one generation to the next, the nation itself is imbued with a primordial, familial character. By the 19th century, the heyday of nationalism in Europe, people published books and leaflets about their *fatherlands* in their *mother* tongues, addressing their compatriots as *kinsmen*, brothers and sisters of a shared ancient lineage.

But away from the continent, this framework created conflict. As imperialism swept the globe during the 18th century it became increasingly common for Europeans to be born abroad. With limited connection to their ancestral homelands, colonial outposts became the societies and geographic spaces within which they formed their identities. And a new print innovation validated their sense of separateness: the newspaper. These daily disposable books concerned themselves with the territory in which they were consumed. In doing so, they transformed their readership into 'the public', a community bound by a common print language. And as empires sought to reassert their dominance over these increasingly autonomous colonies, particularly in the Americas, revolutionaries began to publish to their public, through newsprint.

Words soon became action. In America, the Founding Fathers cut themselves off from Britain by declaring independence on 4th July 1776. This, in turn, inspired the French Revolution, beginning in 1789. And during the early 1800s, wars of independence raged throughout Spanish America. Nation states were looming. Even in European countries where the Crown still reigned, people were beginning to claim greater ownership of their societies. Industrialisation had given birth to cities and these rapidly growing metropolises became filled with newspapers, booksellers, theatres and museums, all serving to instruct inhabitants in their national culture. Shared identities were forming and the pressure was on for sovereigns to become national figures.

Language being the framework of national consciousness, this transformation was largely redundant in places like Britain where a single language had come to dominate. English had been the only language of public administration in Wales since 1536; it was only in 1993, with the Welsh

Language Act, that it was established that 'in the course of public business and the administration of justice, so far as is reasonably practicable, the Welsh and English languages are to be treated on the basis of equality'.[2] And English became the official language of Scotland when the three nations united as the Kingdom of Great Britain in 1707.[3] This was a far harder task in places like Russia, where the autocratic Tsar ruled over a vast and diverse territory with little linguistic unity. Following Napoleon's invasion in 1812, proposals to strengthen the empire through promoting a singular Russian nationality began to be discussed. And after nationalist movements in Ukraine and Finland began to look serious, measures such as the compulsory use of Russian in schools came into force.

But this rebranding exercise masked a conflict. Imperialism was about subjugation; nationalism was about self-determination. They were incompatible. This dilemma erupted with violent consequences on the streets of Sarajevo in 1914 when Gavrilo Princip assassinated Archduke Franz Ferdinand of Austria and his wife, Sophie, Duchess of Hohenberg, triggering the outbreak of the First World War. At his trial the 19-year-old declared, 'I am a Yugoslav nationalist, aiming for the unification of all Yugoslavs, and I do not care what form of state, but it must be freed from Austria.' Austria meaning the Austro-Hungarian Empire, to which the assassinated Archduke was heir to the throne.

Thus began the Great War: a war of empires, triggered by a nationalist. The Second World War followed in 1939 and when the guns finally fell silent in 1945, the United Nations was founded, enshrining 'the principle of equal rights and self-determination'. Various empires limped on, but railways, telegrams and growing bilingualism meant that more indigenous peoples than ever before were interacting and developing a national identity. A new revolutionary youth emerged who consciously understood how nation building worked. It was against this backdrop, with nation states fast becoming the new norm, that multilingual, multiethnic citizenships, like India, fought their way into existence.

The second half of the 20th century saw the creation of numerous nation states as colonies declared independence from their colonisers. More recently, South Sudan declared its independence and was internationally recognised as a member of the UN in 2011. The following year, Palestine succeeded at the UN in being upgraded from 'observer entity' to a 'non-member observer State', a de facto recognition of the State of Palestine.[4] Whatever conflicts over sovereignty there are in the world, the framework within which they are all now fought is that of nation states. Nationalism is fuelling Putin's war of aggression and it is nationalism that is inspiring Ukrainian resistance. It is an ideology that can be a dangerous narrative, as embraced by the Nazis and white supremacists to commit atrocities. Or a useful fiction, as employed by Gandhi and anti-colonial revolutionaries to achieve independence for pluralist states. National identities may anchor themselves in a mythic past, but they are not themselves ancient truths, they are dynamic political and cultural innovations, capable of uniting people with a powerful sense of common purpose.

This is what I had failed to appreciate when I first encountered the origins of national identity, the inescapable fact that we live in a world shaped by nationalism. It cannot be avoided. To do so is to bury our heads in the sand while transnational forces – forces unconstrained by international borders, like white supremacy, religious radicalism and corporate greed – weaken our social bonds. Not to mention the harm caused by those who harness exclusionary patriotism to further divisive agendas. Nationalism has become a byword for backward looking, far-right, racist politics, but this reputation obscures its true history: it was born at a time when the world was rapidly changing and identities were evolving. The problem isn't that national identities were invented. The problem is that they stopped evolving.

Living in the past

In 2016, Donald Trump appealed to a bygone era with the rallying call of his presidency: 'Make America Great Again'. In the same year, the Brexiteer slogan 'Let's Take Back Control' envisaged a past in which Britain alone called the shots. In 2018, Prime Minister Narendra Modi assembled a committee of scholars to gather evidence in support of his claim that present day Hindus are 'true Indians' by virtue of direct descent from the nation's earliest inhabitants. In 2021, just under a year before he launched his invasion, Putin published an essay claiming Ukraine's right to exist as an independent country is at odds with Russian history. Similarly, historian Ilan Pappé, in the opening chapter of *Ten Myths About Israel*, explains how the Israeli foreign ministry website paints a 'fabricated picture' of history that obscures the fact that 'Palestine began to develop as a nation long before the arrival of the Zionist movement.'[5]

Appealing to a mythic past to shape the present is a powerful device used by those who fear the rise of representative national cultures. By asserting control over the narrative, ruling elites secure power by offering cheap comfort to the disaffected while simultaneously denying the rest of the population the right to shape their nation's story.

This all made sense to me. But when Trump tried to overturn the 2020 election result, he was slammed by his own vice-president as 'un-American'. An amendment excluding Muslims from seeking asylum in India prompted a 101-day 'organic protest to save [the Indian] Constitution'.[6] In Ukraine, civilians are taking up arms and singing their national anthem into the faces of Russian occupiers. And the Palestinian flag has long been a potent symbol of resistance. Assaults on nationhood are being met with counter-narratives. So why not in Britain? Why have I been so hesitant to reach for a flag when voicing my dissent? And why has it been this way for so long?

In 1941, writer George Orwell observed that, 'England is perhaps the only great country whose intellectuals are ashamed of their own nationality.' He continues:

> In left-wing circles it is always felt that there is
> something slightly disgraceful in being an Englishman
> and that it is a duty to snigger at every English
> institution, from horse racing to suet puddings. It is a
> strange fact, but it is unquestionably true that almost
> any English intellectual would feel more ashamed of

> standing to attention during "God save the King"
> than of stealing from a poor box.[7]

I think I've found an answer. An answer that I hope can empower us to truly 'take back control'. It begins in 1819, at a time when nationalism was reshaping the Americas and France. In St Peter's Field in Manchester, 60,000 protestors had gathered to demand reform of parliamentary representation. The response from the authorities? A cavalry charge that killed 15 people. In a bitter nod to the then recent Battle of Waterloo, the event became known as the Peterloo Massacre. But nothing changed. The 1832 Reform Act failed to extend the right to vote beyond property owners and from 1838 a mass working-class movement swept Britain under the banner of The People's Charter.

The Chartists were unhappy with the dominance of the Whigs in Parliament and had six demands: the right to vote for all men; voting in secret; the abolition of the need for MPs to own property; payment for MPs (to make Parliamentary life more accessible); equally sized constituencies and annual elections. [8] Their petition garnered 1.25 million signatures at a time when the estimated population of England and Wales was just 15 million.[9] It was rejected by Parliament and the ensuing unrest was crushed by the authorities. Undeterred, a second petition was organised in 1842, this time with over 3 million backers. It was again rejected and protestors were arrested. But the movement persisted.

'As demands for reform grew,' writes Billy Bragg in *The Progressive Patriot*, 'the Whigs turned to history to justify their primary position in society. In Charles Babington Macaulay ... they found their greatest propagandist.'[10]

The Whigs couldn't afford to simply put down dissent, they needed to offer these disaffected minds a better story. National consciousness was sparking revolutions across the seas but what if they themselves could become the authors of national identity at home?

Earlier, in 1835, in his role as the president of the Committee on Public Instruction in Bengal, Macaulay set out to create 'a class of persons, Indian in blood and colour, but English in taste, in opinion, in morals and in intellect'.[11] This was colonisation of the mind, a conscious effort to anglicise South Asians and so strengthen the British grip on India. And it worked. Those who spoke English, wore suits and could quote Shakespeare occupied positions of power. After returning to Britain in 1838, Macaulay now turned his hand to fixing on the page what it meant to be English.

While his French counterpart, Jules Michelet, author of *The History of France*, viewed history as the unfolding of the will of the people, Macaulay's motivation was to explain the legitimacy of Whig rule. This isn't an opinion: he was explicit himself. Chapter One of his five-volume *The History of England*, published in 1848, sets out his intention to explain how, thanks to the Glorious Revolution and the Whig ascendancy:

> Our country, from a state of ignominious vassalage,
> rapidly rose to the place of umpire among European
> powers. How her opulence and her martial glory grew

together … how a gigantic commerce gave birth
to a maritime power, compared with which every
other maritime power, ancient or modern, sinks into
insignificance; how Scotland, after ages of enmity, was
at length united to England, not merely by legal bonds,
but by indissoluble ties of interest and affection … how
in Asia, British adventurers founded an empire not less
splendid and more durable than that of Alexander …
the general effect of this chequered narrative will be to
excite thankfulness in all religious minds, and hope in
the breasts of all patriots. For the history of our country
during the last hundred and sixty years is eminently
the history of physical, of moral, and of intellectual
improvement.[12]

This was the origin of the kind of British exceptionalism that
wooed voters during the 2016 Brexit referendum, and it was
no less effective in the mid to late 1800s. Educated imperial
administrators gobbled up the historical justification for their
global dominance. The public, newly literate and hungry for
content, binged on the popular-histories that followed in
Macaulay's wake. And 'anyone rash enough to question it
was condemned as a dangerous radical or a traitor.'[13]

This was history full of heroes and villains, noble patriotic
victors and savage foreign enemies. The British Empire
was unlike anything the world had ever seen. It didn't
matter if you had land and a seat in Parliament, or were
an impoverished labourer, 'we' were all proud Englishmen!
In it together! With a shared, glorious, victorious history. Why

would you make excessive demands of those who had led the way? Do you not love your country? The only 'charter of the land' needed was 'Rule Britannia'.

In the face of a mass working-class movement never before seen, and against the backdrop of the birth of nationalism, the British ruling elite succeeded in clinging to power by defining what it meant to be a patriot. By painting their rise to the top as the beneficent and immutable progress of history, the ongoing and unfolding glorious story of England, the Whigs were able to dismiss their critics as unpatriotic fanatics.[14]

As descendants of a feudal system whose head of state is still a hereditary monarch, progressive movements in Britain have always taken the form of those at the bottom making demands of those at the top. But since it was the establishment who cultivated the definition for Britishness way back in the 1800s, it has become almost impossible for people to demand meaningful change without being accused of hating their country. Whig history is all about journeying from a dark past to a glorious present, it has no space for error or criticism, only deference. It argues that to be British is to look back with pride. But by the turn of the century, the present was less than glorious. As Adam Curtis argues in part five of his BBC series *Can't Get You Out of My Head*, impoverished factory towns were rife with danger, tales of colonial resistance had given birth to racist xenophobia and imperial elites enjoyed unrestrained power and excesses. Macaulay's history offered no salve to urban middle-class anxieties. And so the idyll of the English countryside was born. A place free of smog, foreigners and the establishment. Intellectuals such as Cecil Sharp made it their mission to collect and revive folk traditions and so added a new dimension to British national identity: escapism.

Macaulay and Sharp's legacies converged in September 2020 when the National Trust published a report exploring its links to slavery and colonialism. Despite the organisation being founded in 1895 with the intent that it should 'speak to, and for, everyone',[15] '"Diana from Leicester" … complained that the "majority of members just want to see beautiful houses and gardens, not have others' opinions pushed down their throats".' Meanwhile, a set of parliamentarians styling themselves as the 'Common Sense Group' called for the Trust's public funding to be reviewed. As Peter Mitchell succinctly put it, 'The Trust wants to explore its historic links to slavery, the right wants to preserve an unreal version of the past.'[16]

The governing elite paint inclusive history as a threat to British identity because it's the easiest way for them to retain control of our nation's narrative and so protect their hegemony. They are supported by middle-class conservatives who have no desire to confront the anxieties of their time and prefer the comforts of fantasy. Adding fuel to the fire, economic growth and the increased demand for skilled workers during the post-war period created a higher education boom that changed the very structure of society: people began to ditch national pride in favour of individual identities built around prestigious jobs and personal values ('the sneering metropolitan elite'), devaluing the love of country still cherished by those left behind and so stoking resentment ('flag shaggers'). And with leaders making no effort to update the narrative of the nation to include the Black and brown faces who had helped win the war and rebuild the country, national symbols were easily hijacked by racist movements.

As a result, outside of international sporting events, to be proudly English or British has become culturally and politically divisive. I've had friends tell me that they're ashamed of their national identity, opting instead, as I once did, to view themselves as global citizens. This, in turn, feeds the right's narrative that progressives are an anti-British breed who need to be defended against. We have been left to either champion or reject the static ideas that we have inherited from Macaulay, Sharp and their intellectual descendants, ideas further distorted by the post-war uni boom. There is no unifying process, only a never-ending fight: a culture war. We have been convinced to argue among ourselves on terms set so long ago that we mistake them for reality. It's a distraction that, at its inception, was designed to protect the establishment by curbing the emergence of greater representation. Thankfully, organisations like the National Trust are fighting back. In November 2023, members voted emphatically to reject five candidates endorsed by Restore Trust, the pressure group set up to combat the charity's 'wokeness'.[17] We have been deprived of the right to shape our national identity. This is an affront to our democracy and we must fight back. We must demand change, of ourselves and our leaders.

The disruptive patriot

In mid-2020, as my ideas on national identity were beginning to take shape, I added a Union Jack to my social media bios. My reading had led me to conclude that in order to be part of reshaping national identity, I had to first embrace and identify with it. The emoji was a small act, but it felt like a big step given that only a few months ago I had stood on the TEDx circle in Chandigarh and cast off my national identity. I was nervous. I didn't post about it. In truth, I was scared about the response it might trigger. Earlier that year, some of my tweets had ended up in the *Daily Mail* and *The Times*. My mentions became a hotbed of hate, including one user who, in a series of tweets, posted: 'We know the lead one to blame, @OfficialJassa … Germany 1930s [and] people will not sit quietly for it to happen again. We now know that Jassa is one name on the list to look out for [and] boycott.' Many of my union comrades, who had co-authored the statement that prompted the shitstorm, received far worse.

I noticed that many of those directing their bile in our direction had flags in their usernames and bios. They seemed to believe themselves to be upholding British values and pride. Their banner was the Union Jack. We, on the other hand, were cast as unpatriotic 'McCarthyite' activists.[18] It pissed me off; I had yet to fully understand Britain's history of waving flags in the face of criticism.

A year later, I was better prepared. After hosting an online 'in conversation' with Kavita Puri about *Three Pounds in My Pocket* – her brilliant BBC Radio 4 series, telling the stories of pioneering South Asians who came to Britain from the 1950s onwards – I tweeted about my ignorance:

> In 1976 the racist murder of Gurdip Singh Chaggar in Southall led to a former National Front chairman stating "one down, a million to go". A police officer at the scene said the victim was "just an Asian". This is the history we live with, history I was shocked I didn't know.

In response, someone by the name of Mr Moose posted: 'Go cry somewhere else. The past is the past. Tge [sic] rest of us have moved on, just a shame you lefty bedwetting morons haven't. Just for you. 🇬🇧🇬🇧🇬🇧🇬🇧🇬🇧🇬🇧🇬🇧🇬🇧🇬🇧 🇬🇧🇬🇧🇬🇧🇬🇧🇬🇧🇬🇧🇬🇧🇬🇧🇬🇧🇬🇧🇬🇧🇬🇧🇬🇧🇬🇧🇬🇧🇬🇧🇬🇧 🇬🇧🇬🇧🇬🇧🇬🇧🇬🇧🇬🇧🇬🇧🇬🇧🇬🇧🇬🇧🇬🇧🇬🇧' Thirty-eight Union Jacks, just for me. I wrote back: 'Are the Union flags meant to trigger me? I fly it in my bio. The 1976 racist murder of Gurdip Singh Chaggar is part of our national history. The Southall Youth Movement was founded in response and their anti-racist and anti-fascist values live on; makes me proud to be British. 🇬🇧' Mr Moose never wrote back. I felt empowered. I had found a way to disrupt what it meant to be a patriot.

That said, I was still hesitant to embrace Englishness. While the Scottish and Welsh, in opposition to the dominance of England within the UK, have cultivated separate, modern, progressive identities, being English has become synonymous with being ethnically white. That this is true was evidenced by the MP David Lammy publicly criticising the lack of a

'Black English' option on the 2021 census, while a 2020 interview with actor Rakie Ayola in Black Ballad, written by Chloe Seivwright, a Black writer, begins 'we are both from Wales':

> So after immediately establishing that we are from neighbouring cities, there was a comfortability and connection between us. That's what it means to be Welsh, that unspoken pride and togetherness you feel when in similar company.[19]

In September 2021, it seemed the universe was out to test me. The BBC approached me to make a documentary about English identity. The remit of the half-hour film was that it had to be a personal journey and centre on my connection to the Midlands. Beyond that we were free to do what we wanted. Slightly daunted by the task, I met up with the director, Alex Gower-Jackson, to figure out a plan. After bonding over our mixed identities – he's a Brit of South African origin with ties to Canada – I confessed my reservations about Englishness. Was this because of my mixed heritage? Or was it something deeper? We realised we'd discovered a title for our film: *Am I English?*

Fast forward to the first day of the shoot. We were in my car. Alex had asked me to narrate my drive into Oadby, just outside of Leicester, the town where I grew up and where my dad still lives. As I tried to speak, I was ambushed by overwhelming emotion. The roads were no longer dull tarmac but streets steeped in memory. There was my primary school, where Grandad taught, and this was the route I walked home with BG. Here was the pub I had my first drink in on my 18th birthday and there was the pool where I learnt to swim. I pointed out all the changes and when they had occurred. I eased off the accelerator: the speed cameras were new. I had left Leicester to pursue my career in London and had thought I'd built an identity based on my values in the capital. But sitting in my car, and later walking through Leicester's city centre, it hit me that I was connected to this place more powerfully than I had ever realised.

As our shoot progressed, I discovered my strength of connection to place wasn't reserved for my childhood hangouts. Taking advantage of our BBC credentials, we arranged for me and my mum to visit the Rotunda, an iconic cylindrical high-rise built in 1962 that was designed by my grandpa, her dad, James A. Roberts. I used to travel to the city once a month during my early teens to attend classes at the Birmingham Royal Ballet, but I'd never actually visited the Rotunda. My mum would point it out as we passed over Spaghetti Junction. She would tell me about my grandpa's penthouse offices; his unrealised plans for a revolving restaurant and a weather indicator, designed to look like a candlewick; and how as a child she used to launch paper aeroplanes across the city from the top floor windows. But the building itself always stood at arm's length, like a slightly distant family member, much like my grandpa was.

I'd been sharing the progress of our shoot on Instagram that day and my inbox had been filling up with people's connections to Birmingham and the Rotunda specifically.

It has become an icon. In recognition, the building was granted Grade II listed status in 2000, meaning it is 'of special interest, [and warrants] every effort to preserve it'. One of those tasked with that very duty between 2004 and 2008 was an architect who used to meet his girlfriend, now wife, at the bus stop outside the Rotunda. I only learnt his name on the day we were shooting. On camera, I turned the final page of the coffee table book commemorating the refurbishment and found myself staring at a portrait of Davinder Bansal, a turban-wearing Sikh. That feeling of intense emotion hit again. Here was a landmark, built by my white English grandfather in the sixties, refurbished by a British Sikh in the noughties, an intimate reflection of my own identity, serving as a locus for belonging for a whole city.

Through doing the documentary, I discovered my strength of connection to place. To Leicester, to Birmingham, to the Midlands and, ultimately, to England. It made me realise that to be a patriot is to be someone who inspires belonging. Perhaps with sufficient devolution of power we wouldn't need to look beyond our city or our region. For all I have argued, I am not wedded to the nation state. But so long as the major decisions that affect our lives happen at that level, we must strive for national community.

By the final day of filming, a photoshoot for BBC iPlayer, I felt comfortable enough, excited even, to drape myself in the St George's Cross, claim it as my own, and declare myself English.

The journey also served to invigorate my longing to disrupt the meaning of British patriotism. The only contributor in the film who isn't one of my family members is journalist and author Sathnam Sanghera. He seemed to get the journey I was on, plus we were both Punjabi Sikhs from the Midlands working in the media.

Our filming location was the historic Punjab restaurant in Covent Garden, where photos and memorabilia honouring Punjabi and Sikh history line the walls. We sat down beneath a portrait of Welsh Elvis impersonator, Peter Singh ('I don't smoke dope, I don't like bourbon, all I want to do is shake my turban') and tucked into some samosas and kali dhal. In relation to my personal struggle, he shared his insight that, 'We are, as a nation, we are British Asian … The problem is, the dominant narrative of my lifetime, and probably yours too, in the media, has been that immigrants arrived here uninvited with no connection to the culture and took advantage of British hospitality. That's why the struggles you're going through feel problematic, when actually, they should feel joyful. They're just a reflection of your home nation's history.'

I want more of us to share in the joy of shaping nationhood. National identity is an essential feature of any nation state. It is the identity of the citizenry, a powerful tool that we ignore at our peril. For too long those of us fighting for social progress in Britain have been afraid of embracing our national symbols because of the narrow history attributed to them: the racism, the far right, the atrocities of empire, our 'world-beating' exceptionalism. But we can change those meanings and create new ones, confidently interrogating what has gone before while pioneering a vision for the future. In the words of Billy Bragg, the English are 'The People of the Hyphen'.[20] Anglo-Saxon is a hyphenated word, reflecting the fact that the Kingdom of England emerged out of a melting pot of migrants (Saxons, Angles and Jutes) and Celtic Britons. To be English is to be mixed. The Empire makes that even truer of British identity. Donning the flag was a reclamation of an aspect of who I am. I didn't need to choose between British and English. I could be, and disrupt, both.

National identity has always been, and always will be, a political project. We must now demand that the project be democratised. We all must have a say in what it means to be a patriot. Indeed, wherever we claim citizenship, it is imperative that our voice be heard in our nation's story.

Defined by diversity

The first step towards being heard is to dispel the myth that national identity is too difficult to pin down in a diverse society. This is a lie that maintains the status quo, built on the assumption that homogeneity is the only way to achieve any sense of unity. Until I articulated #BothNotHalf, it was an idea I bought into myself. National identity is both definable and diverse. We should not think of it as a personal identity, but as a shared, living identity to which we all can contribute. It is that which emerges from the interaction of citizens' civic, cultural and ethnic identities, in the form of shared traditions, culture and language. Ethnic identities are the most closed: you can't decide to join an ethnic group, though mixed relationships and children certainly blur the boundaries. Cultural identities are more open and malleable: languages can be learnt and traditions can be adopted or introduced. Civic identity is open to all citizens. As such, citizenship must be the bedrock of national identity.

I was born a British citizen; my dad became a British citizen. A wealthy American who has made the UK their home can acquire British citizenship, as can a Syrian refugee (though this is not to say that it is equally easy for both to do so). Granted, civic identity alone is not emotive enough to forge a deep sense of unity and belonging, but it must be the foundation from which we build. Relatively homogenous European nations began to emerge at a time when long distance travel was limited and the printing press was displacing regional differences in favour of national similarities. In our modern, highly connected, globalised world it is obvious that national identity must evolve to be defined by diversity and 'exist alongside various subnational identities':

> That is not a problematic idea. There is a large body of sociological and psychological literature on the concept of multiple identities in individuals: We all have and live many identities, including our sexual, professional, linguistic, cultural, religious, ethnic and physical identities. And we constantly arrange and rearrange these according to the contexts and the circumstances.[21]

I'm a son, a brother, an actor, a writer, an Englishman, a Brit, a European, a child of an immigrant, a Sikh, a human, a cishet man, a Punjabi. Just as I described myself as 'both not half', I am all of these identities, not a collection of fractions. As are we all. Identity is malleable and multiple for everyone.

I suspect this is where so much confusion around national identity comes from. How it becomes The Great Undefinable. When you think of national identity as a uniform you either reject or wear at all times, it's impossible to find consensus. There's no way every citizen will ever agree on wearing the same shirt. However, if we think of our national identity as a process – an ever-evolving interaction of our shared civic identity with our personal, cultural and ethnic identities – it becomes less mysterious. It accepts that no individual has the answer and so distributes power among citizens who, building from their equal and shared foundation of citizenship, can weave the national culture with their own distinct threads, whether they are newly naturalised or born in the same town as their British ancestors.

It is of course true that corporate media has disproportionate power when it comes to ramming concepts of nationhood down our throats. As Sita Balani put it to me, 'Do I as an individual British citizen really have the same power to determine what the wider community think of as Englishness as Rupert Murdoch (an Australian-born American citizen) has?' Of course not. But I would suggest that this is not a reason to despair, but a reason to resist, to organise and chip in the cost of a coffee on a monthly basis to alternative media outlets. Don't reject: resist. Because national identity is not a zero-sum game. Things that were once quintessential may fade into obscurity, just as new customs have the potential to become typical.

Fish and chips, a British staple, was a culinary combination pioneered by Joseph Malin, an Eastern European Ashkenazi Jew who set up shop in London's East End around 1860. Bangladeshi migrant restaurateurs created chicken tikka masala, celebrated in 2001 by the then foreign secretary Robin Cook as 'a true British national dish'. Both were introduced by immigrants and one didn't replace the other. In fact, they regularly sit side by side on pub menus. Just like our personal identities, national identities have the capacity for multiplicity, growth and change. Such is the nature of a process. But our ruling elite, so used to being able to wield patriotism to protect their privileged position, don't want you to engage in the process. In fact, they'd rather destroy the very foundations of our nationhood: citizenship.

I am not your loyal subject

When I was 11 years old, I went to my first ever cricket match during the summer holidays. My dad had managed to wangle tickets through work for us to see India vs England at Trent Bridge up the road in Nottingham. At the time, cricket was what I lived for. Three stump holes were a permanent feature in our back lawn and the hedge that ran along one side of the garden was lined with chicken wire to prevent stray balls punching holes through to Grandad and BG's house. My passion for the sport was born in the streets of Punjab – gully cricket, where a wooden board and loose bricks took the place of a wicket – and my hero was Sachin Tendulkar, the greatest batsman of his era and still the only player to have racked up a hundred international centuries. The night before the game in August 2002, I could barely sleep. Sachin Tendulkar was going to be playing. I was beyond excited.

The following morning, we woke up early and got our face paints out. My sister and I had attempted to fashion flags out of fabric off-cuts our mum kept in the house, but our efforts hadn't yielded anything worth waving. Instead, our mum was painting our faces: an English flag on one cheek and an Indian flag on the other. She didn't think anything of it. Nor did we. We were there for the love of the game. To see a legend play. But, unknowingly, we were making something of a statement. We were rejecting the premise of a 'cricket test' that had been devised in 1990, the year I was born, by Conservative MP Norman Tebbit:

> A large proportion of Britain's Asian population fail
> to pass the cricket test. Which side do they cheer for?
> It's an interesting test. Are you still harking back to
> where you came from or where you are?[22]

It wasn't an interesting test. It was a racist test of loyalty that only applied to brown former colonies; white Aussie and Kiwi immigrants were exempt from scrutiny. Some have argued that 'Tebbit's loyalty test is dead'. Indeed, when Pakistan beat India at the Oval in 2017 to win the Champions Trophy, the streets of Birmingham erupted in celebration, with the *Daily Mail* reporting jubilant scenes of Pakistani fans dancing into the night, a police officer joining in with some 'bowled moves' and the presence of an open-top bus emblazoned with the Pakistani flag. But while the world of sport appears to have become more accommodating of multiple identities, the issue of loyalty remains intimately linked to the foundation stone of our nationhood.

In 1995, a boy of around 11 or 12 years of age became a naturalised British citizen. Sadly, he grew up to participate in terrorist activities abroad and was punished by having his British citizenship revoked. In 2018, the Supreme Court ruled in favour of the government's argument that the man, known as Pham, had 'repudiated his obligation of loyalty to the United Kingdom' and it was therefore 'right that, given the facts that he has admitted, he should no longer remain a British citizen'.[23] Good, you might think. Pham was no innocent. What's the issue? The issue is that Pham grew up and became radicalised in the UK, as a British citizen, and should have been prosecuted under treason laws. Why should Vietnam, his supposed birth country, be burdened with him? What gives the UK the right to banish citizens beyond the sea instead of taking responsibility for them? It all feels a bit medieval. And that's because it is. Lady Justice Arden made explicit reference to 'feudal law' when justifying the government's position. As Lord Goldsmith explains in his 2008 report 'Citizenship: Our Common Bond':

The modern day concept of citizenship started in the feudal concept of the allegiance of the subject to the sovereign; and the idea of British citizenship and

the laws which underpin it are themselves fashioned
by Britain's imperial past. The former has led to the
idea that people are "subjects" rather than citizens.[24]

Another case attracted more headlines. In 2019, British-born
Shamima Begum was stripped of her citizenship by the then
home secretary Sajid Javid. She had joined Islamic State as a
schoolgirl in 2015 and lost her fight to be reinstated as a Brit
in February 2021. I personally don't care whether you think
Begum is an evil terrorist, the victim of online grooming or both
– it doesn't matter: depriving anyone of their most basic civic
identity on the basis that they might be eligible for citizenship
elsewhere (in this case Bangladesh, the birth country of her
parents) is a deeply unpatriotic, cowardly, irresponsible and
divisive act. Proponents can try and dress it up in a Union Jack
to pass it off as firm-fisted justice and security all they like. The
fact remains that they are demolishing the foundation stone of
national identity: the equality of citizenship. Their vandalism
means we are left with a hierarchy in which my British
citizenship means less than my mother's. Shared belonging
cannot be built on such crooked foundations.

We must seek to make British citizenship an ironclad
cornerstone of our nationhood. Before 1918, you could only
be stripped of citizenship if you had gained it fraudulently.
Fair enough. But in the thick of the First World War,
with disinformation fuelling hysteria that Germans were
infiltrating all echelons of society, the British Nationality and
Status of Aliens Act was amended to allow naturalised British
citizens to be deprived of their nationality if they showed

themselves 'by act or speech to be disaffected or disloyal to His Majesty'. If you were a British woman, simply marrying an 'alien' was enough for you to lose your nationality; this was only scrapped with the British Nationality Act 1948, a radical bill that entitled all imperial and commonwealth subjects to British citizenship, an early recognition that, thanks to empire, British identity was global and diverse. In 1981, the power to strip nationality was expanded and then in the wake of 9/11, the Nationality, Immigration and Asylum Act 2002 made it possible to banish any Brit with ties abroad. By 2006, it was possible to do so if it was vaguely 'conducive to the public good'. And in 2014, the coalition government inked into law a way around the illegality of making someone stateless, if, as in the case of Shamima Begum, the Home Secretary has grounds to believe the person could acquire another nationality.

Since I began writing this book, the UK has slipped further into this dystopia with the Nationality and Borders Bill, which now makes it possible to deprive someone's citizenship 'without prior notification'.[25] As the Conservative peer Lord Moylan put it in a committee debate that took place in January 2022, 'We have gone, in the space of a century, from an indissoluble bond to a position where an enormous proportion – I cannot calculate it – of British citizens hold their nationality contingently at the discretion of the Home Secretary ... when something as important as nationality and national identity is treated by our own Government like a mere driving licence or library ticket that can be cancelled by administrative fiat, we are all the poorer.'

Britain is encumbered by a medieval attitude, emboldened by memories of imperial dominance that manifests in our present with a 'don't like it, there's the door' mentality. And this feudal mindset persists in our daily lives. Lord Goldsmith's report continues that one of the legal responsibilities of citizenship in the UK is a 'duty of allegiance to the Crown'. Not a duty to fellow citizens: the Crown. Parliament derives its sovereignty from the Crown. Judges swear an oath of 'true allegiance to His Majesty'. We live in a top-down society whose constitutional arrangement promotes loyalty to a monarch, not fellow citizens. We have no document to point to that begins 'We, the people', nothing which clearly and obviously belongs to the citizenry, no principles enshrined in a single easily accessible text that we can wield to curb abuses of power. 'Indeed, it may be said with considerable force that we have no constitution as such at all, merely constitutional conventions,' said Lord Neuberger, the President of the UK Supreme Court in a speech in 2014.

This is a system that benefits those with wealth and power. They are left largely to their own devices, looking to the past, to precedent, for historic answers that suit their present interests. Where there are no answers, or the answers don't fit their agenda, new laws can simply be tailored to suit. After all, parliament is sovereign. Nothing is immutable. And to fill the gap where defined principles might cause them problems, deliberately vague 'British values' are trotted out to justify whatever measures are being introduced – be it the ability to strip citizenship in secret or outlaw disruptive protests of the kind once favoured by the suffragette movement. And of course, 'British values' have the added benefit of casting dissenters as unpatriotic.

In the same way that Putin, Trump, Modi and Netanyahu's politics disgust me, the Nationality and Borders Bill offends me to my core. It lends credence to racists and xenophobes who believe that their 'pure' white Anglo-Saxon heritage makes them 'true' Brits, while trafficked British women and girls are abandoned and left to languish in Syria. It makes me fearful. It makes me rage. The memory of violence and murder at the hands of white ethnonationalists marching under the Union Jack remains strong in minority communities. My dad grew up being told that if the worst did happen, he should do his best to take at least one of his attackers down with him. Throughout his life, my grandfather carried a hockey stick in the boot of his car wherever he went, just in case. And while mourning his death in 2017, my grandmother was the victim of a targeted home invasion robbery; a gang had been targeting South Asian households in search of gold jewellery. The trauma of that event has led to my dad keeping his front door perpetually double locked, with my sister's secondary school hockey stick sat close by the porch.

This fear was articulated with devastating effect by Riz Ahmed in his Oscar-winning short film *The Long Goodbye*, in which preparations for a wedding turn into a state-sanctioned abduction and execution of a Muslim family by paramilitaries wearing the St George's Cross. I was not prepared for its potency. I hadn't realised how much I also felt the threat of ethnonationalist violence hanging in the air. I was paralysed by it, and I still can't watch it without tears of rage welling up. I find the scenes of the women being separated from the men particularly harrowing, a sickening detail that tortured my imagination with the knowledge of the mass rapes perpetrated in Delhi during the 1984 Sikh genocide. The only way I was able to make sense of it was to write. 'Riz just said "it's happening", and I wish I didn't know what he meant, but I did, and I do …' It became a spoken word piece and concludes:

> National identity is a story
> But we got the story wrong
> A misremembered glory
> And now we can't belong
> I don't know how to break up
> Cos I felt single all along
> Riz just said 'it's happening'
> And I don't think he's wrong.

For any true and deeply felt sense of national unity to ever be felt in Britain, for minorities to even begin to feel they have an equal stake in their nation, the powers of citizenship deprivation must be heavily rolled back or, better yet, scrapped. Green life peer Baroness Bennett of Manor Castle made exactly this point in the debate previously mentioned and the Tory peer Lord Moylan voiced his support. In her role as vice chair of the all-party parliamentary group on trafficked Britons in Syria, Baroness Warsi made her thoughts clear in a column for the *Guardian*:

In the wake of the Windrush scandal, the government promised to learn from the failures that led to British citizens being unfairly cast out from their homeland. It must end the dangerous misuse of citizenship-stripping powers, or it is doomed to repeat those failures.[26]

Irrespective of heritage, no one should be more or less of a citizen. This is not a party-political issue, it is a fight to restore the very foundation of our national identity. I refuse to be a loyal subject; I am a British citizen demanding equality for myself and my compatriots.

The fight

Restoring the indissolubility of citizenship is a fundamental struggle that must be won to avoid white supremacy staining our national culture. But it is not the only struggle. Think of what follows as a training montage. This is how we fight.

Raise the flag

The easiest way to begin taking back control of our national culture is to reclaim ownership of our national symbols. Well, easiest in principle. When I turned up to a 'right to strike' rally at Downing Street in January 2023 with a Union Jack, I did get a few funny looks. And I'd be lying if I said I felt totally confident. But there was something powerful and satisfying about raising a national banner in the face of a government hellbent on protecting the super rich at the expense of workers. And I'm not alone in seeking to disrupt. For a long time, BBC 5 Live host Nihal Arthanayake flew five flags in his Twitter name: the Rainbow, the Sri Lankan, the English, the British and the Ukrainian. Empireland author Sathnam Sanghera flies the Union Jack in his bio. Sarah Owen MP flies both the Union Jack and the Malaysian flag, reflecting her mixed heritage. These symbols are not beyond reclamation. When Christian Wakeford defected from the Conservatives to Labour in response to Boris Johnson's partygate scandal, the culture secretary Nadine Dorries tweeted: 'Sadly, @Christian4BuryS has yet to realise that the Union Jack [GB] mask he is wearing to cross the floor to Labour, is not welcome on that side of the house. 👋' It was a weak and feeble retort that revealed just how committed the government is to clinging to power through divide and rule. Raise your voice and raise the flag. It belongs to you.

Love history

True patriotism is rooted in love, not pride. Love is what we feel when we connect with something, flaws and all, and understand it as being intimately connected to us, a part of who we are. We cannot make a list of our loved ones' pros and cons, tot up the bullet points and rank them from good to bad. All we can do is strive to understand each other, and our past. In Britain, we are struggling to shake off Macaulay's legacy of history as a source of pride. A pride used to silence calls for greater representation. The flip side of pride is shame. And neither serve to unite us. Our history is full of such horrors and triumphs. Understanding our place in the world requires us to open ourselves up to these depths. Love demands we ask difficult questions, without judgement, so that we may grow closer to one another. Be curious. Love history.

Glow up

This could be a book unto itself but, deep breath: the UK uses a broken voting system to elect career MPs to an unrestrained Parliament, part composed of an unelected upper house, dominated by the government, checked by a judiciary lacking diversity, all of which is presided over by a hereditary monarch, who doubles as the head of the Church of England. Those who agitate for reform are frequently accused of hating their country, while those who fall foul of the state and find themselves in prison are deprived of their right to vote. Is it any wonder so many of us feel like we don't belong? The Single Transferable Vote, a system created in Britain and advocated by the Electoral Reform Society would be a first step to a better future. Abolishing the Parliamentary private members club, sorry, I mean the House of Lords, should come next. As the Electoral Reform Society website makes clear: 'We're basically alone in Europe for having a fully unelected revising chamber. And no other country in the democratic world has a second chamber bigger than ours.'[27] Not to mention the 26 Lords Spiritual; the only other country that has seats reserved for clerics is Iran. Britain is frequently described as 'the mother of parliaments'; good parents encourage development and growth. We need a glow up.

King Charles the Last

I was quite fond of the Queen. She reminded me of BG and BG loved her too. So maybe there was some transference going on. I felt quite sad when Huw Edwards announced her death, but I was incredulous when I opened my laptop to order some moisturiser on 19 September 2022 and read: 'As a mark of respect, the Boots website will be unavailable between 10:30am & 12:30pm for The Queen's funeral.' Is this the behaviour of a rational nation? Is it right that King Charles, our head of state, is a hereditary monarch who was anointed with holy oil? The royal.uk website states that the 'Sovereign acts as a focus for national identity, unity and pride; gives a sense of stability and continuity'. This may have once been true but our constitutional monarchy feels extremely outdated and defunct. In November 2021, Barbados decided to remove the Queen as head of state. During William and Kate's faltering 2022 Caribbean tour, Jamaica signalled they were going to follow suit and a referendum is scheduled for 2024. Harry and Meghan have stepped away from royal duties, while efforts to rehabilitate the disgraced Prince Andrew continue despite public uproar. How can we grow and evolve when our chief mascot's primary selling point is to remain unchanged? I'm not saying it's unpatriotic to be a monarchist – that would be absurd, monarchy is inarguably a part of our heritage as a nation – but, equally, agitating to cancel the Crown in favour of a people's Head of State should not be considered unpatriotic either. (And no, tourism won't suffer; this is a myth roundly debunked in Graham Smith's *Abolish the Monarchy*.) A year into the reign of King Charles, a YouGov poll found that just 37 % of 18–24-year-olds want to retain the monarchy, while 40% would prefer an elected head of state. For comparison, in 2019, 46% wanted to keep the Royals while only 26% wanted an elected head of state. I suspect (and hope) that it's just a matter of time.

Long live devolution!

Devolution is not a word that stirs the heart. It sounds more like a term you'd write on a flashcard while cramming for an A-level exam. The back would read: 'The transfer of power from central government to local or regional administration.' It ain't sexy. But you know what is? Local people demanding power from our ruling elite. Devolution must become part of our rallying cry for a more representative nation. Starting in the late nineties, the Scottish and Welsh Parliaments and the Northern Irish Assembly were formed and given powers over health, education, transport, aspects of taxation and other policy areas. They all face challenges but the idea that the historic nations of the UK should have power over their domains while working in concert as part of a union greater than the sum of its parts is a dream worth fighting for. England, however, lags behind. By international standards, it has an extremely centralised political system resulting in regional divides unique in the developed world. The Conservatives' 2019 manifesto promised to deliver 'full devolution across England so that every part of our country has the power to shape its own destiny', but they are loath to actually follow through. As the Institute for Public Policy Research puts it:

Since 2014, some powers have been decentralised or delegated to mayors, combined authorities and regional transport bodies, and this has been branded as 'devolution'. Fundamentally, however, the current process is not real devolution – real power has remained with central government, while other important areas of policy have actually become centralised and local government capacity has been cut severely.[28]

Power concedes nothing without a demand. We must demand power.

Citizens, assemble!

We have become accustomed to those at the top making decisions without meaningful input from citizens – a legacy of our feudal past – but new forms of democracy are possible. One innovation we should be rushing to embrace is the citizens' assembly: diverse groups of around a hundred randomly selected people – accounting for gender, age, ethnicity and socioeconomic status – who meet over a defined time period to figure out answers to difficult questions. Think of it like jury service for the voice of our nation. Ireland arguably leads the way, with citizens' assemblies leading to major breakthroughs such as the legalisation of abortion and same-sex marriage, while an assembly on biodiversity loss in 2022 has prompted calls for the rights of nature to be enshrined in the national constitution.[29] The efficacy of mass deliberation is supported by work such as Stanford's 2019 'America in

One Room' initiative that showed how discussion among a large sample group, informed by expert analysis, can change attitudes in favour of greater consensus. Championing citizen's assemblies is a rejection of crass sloganeering in favour of enlightened, representative politics. Not all of them will work, but in our quest to disabuse our leaders of their hegemony over 'what the people want', we must demand citizens' assemblies play a greater role in our democracy. And what's more, by facilitating purposeful, consensus driven input, these assemblies will serve to strengthen the very meaning of our citizenship.

Speak English

When my grandad was sorting mail for the Post Office during the 1960s, alongside his Punjabi colleagues, their white manager berated them for not speaking English. My grandad proposed a compromise: they would continue to use Punjabi words but promised to laugh in English. As a confident global nation, hearing foreign languages should not surprise or offend us. But I'm ashamed to say that when I was a child, I would sometimes get embarrassed if I was out with BG – her English was less than perfect and I would find the disdain with which white shop assistants treated her uncomfortable. As I grew to develop a deeper understanding of the world, however, I saw things differently: Britain had been responsible for the horrors of Partition in 1947, setting in motion the series of events that led to her impoverishment and subsequent migration to the UK; as long as she was being understood, she had every right to use imperfect English. As does every newcomer. Especially those fleeing disaster. But since language is the framework of national consciousness and unity, new arrivals should also have access to and be encouraged to gain fluency. A report by Refugee Action states:

> The importance of language for people's effective integration in the UK has been demonstrated time and again. The evidence shows that those with low English language proficiency are less likely to be in employment, something that disproportionately impacts on women. And the effects of learning English are not just felt in the job market; the ability to speak English is also related to health outcomes, with those who speak English proficiently more likely to be in good health. This is certainly the experience of refugees in the UK.[30]

A real act of patriotism would be to provide the resources necessary to welcome new arrivals into the fold of our society. But despite government assertions that 'everyone living in England should be able to speak and understand English', funding for English to Speakers of Other Languages (ESOL) was cut by almost 60% from £212.3m in 2008 to £105m in 2018.[31] There is no justification for such cuts when better language skills would undoubtedly cover the cost through increased employment. We must demand that our framework for national unity be properly funded.

World-beating bank holidays

For all the talk of Britain being 'world-beating', we are bottom of the league when it comes to public holidays. England and Wales have the lowest number in Europe with eight. Scotland enjoys nine, whereas Northern Ireland gets ten days off work. Compare this to Germany (11) Portugal (13) and Finland (15). Not to mention people in the UK work some of the longest hours in Europe. In August 2021, the Trades Union Congress called on the government to create four new bank holidays. We must add our voice to the chorus. And we must do so in the name of national unity. Labour's 2019 manifesto proposed four UK-wide bank holidays to promote unity and celebrate the patron saints of our Home Nations. And in 2014, Conservative MP Bob Blackman championed an e-petition signed by more than 120,000 people calling for Diwali and Eid to be made bank holidays: 'Wouldn't it be a statement that we as a nation embrace these religions, and the people who hold them dear, and we are ready to recognise their place in our society?' Damn straight! It would also be a bold and confident way of acknowledging history. Modern Britain was largely built with the wealth extracted from undivided India, creating the economic conditions that led to so many who belong to these religious groups migrating to the UK. Not only would such public holidays create a tangible sense of national belonging for adherents but they would create space for all Brits to learn about their history and resulting diverse modern society. The stock answer to any call for new public holidays is that it costs the economy too much. But no one is talking about cancelling Easter or

Christmas to increase output. Society is not simply a machine that churns out profit, it is a framework for belonging. Let's be world-beating.

End montage. These are only a handful of the battlegrounds upon which we can fight for a more representative national culture. But they are essential fights because none of us, mixed or otherwise, can enjoy any sense of belonging and community without a truly representative and dynamic national culture. You may disagree with some of my assertions. You may think I've missed something obvious. Good. I'm just one voice. I encourage you to raise yours. It is when we come together, with goodwill, open ears and clear intentions for a more just world that we achieve greatness.

Patriotic citizens of the world

In 2016, then Prime Minister Theresa May told the Conservative party conference: 'If you believe you are a citizen of the world, you are a citizen of nowhere.' Despite the journey I've been on, I still believe this to be an entirely ridiculous, divisive statement. In an extremely literal sense, yes, citizenship is the bond between a citizen and a state. And since there's no global government, there are no (literal) global citizens. But to pretend we do not live in a global society is a backwards-looking delusion. Climate change, the threat of nuclear war, the pandemic, technological upheavals and refugee crises are all issues we face as a global community. No amount of travel bans or 'my country first' politics is going to solve any of these challenges, just as no country can cut itself off from the global economy and be entirely self-sufficient. International cooperation and global solutions define the modern world.

My mistake was to think that this meant national identity was an outdated hangover of a bygone era, an assessment that felt vindicated by the fact that racists and xenophobes had hijacked British and English national symbols in defence of an imagined past. I emerged as a cosmopolitan citizen of the world, spurred on by the borderless connective power of the internet, proudly rejecting nationalism and disowning my need for a national identity on the TEDx red circle. But I now see things more clearly. We live in geographic spaces. Territories governed by national institutions, inhabited by our fellow citizens. As comforting as it might be to exist in the cosy echo chambers of the online world, associating only with those who share our values, as residents of nation states we have to find ways to live meaningfully alongside our real-world neighbours. We might all own a smartphone, but we also have a postcode and a desire to belong. National identity is the means by which we foster that belonging. National identity is the means by which we thrive as a nation.

Equally, concepts of global citizenship are essential for protecting the future of the planet on which our nations exist. For too long we have been presented with a false dichotomy: are you a patriot or a globalist? This is not dissimilar from the questions that sparked my national identity crisis. Was I British or Indian? English or Punjabi? British Asian or Anglo-Indian? My solution was to reject national identity but real power comes from rejecting the premise of the question. It is entirely possible, indeed desirable, to be both. To be a patriotic citizen of the world.

We must recognise and champion national identity as a unifying mixed identity that accepts that, by virtue of history and the realities of the present day, many citizens have ties that cross borders. And we must countenance a borderless future. Patriotism is about a love of place. Be it your street, village, town, city, region, nation, continent or planet. It is about fostering belonging. National identity isn't something ancient and unchanging, handed down from on high for us to either accept or reject, it is simply a useful fiction in an ever-evolving story, of which we are all the authors.

And if you want to tell an entirely different story, I'm all ears. Whatever your position, nationhood will never be politically neutral and it cannot be ignored. My attempts to disrupt ideas of national identity have been a crucial step towards embracing my power as an active participant in society, striving for a better tomorrow. And the more active I've become, the more ways I've found to belong and to resist.

6

ADVENTURES IN MASCULINITY

The boxes on the page
ask our age and sexuality
we give them the power
to define our humanity

RAMANIQUE AHLUWALIA, 'OTHER'

'I WOULD FEEL so uncomfortable with our scene if I didn't know that you were gay.' She said it with such ease that it took me a moment to realise Katie was talking to me. I was around 16 years old. She was in the year above. My stomach felt strange, as if I were standing on a ledge, about to jump, or be pushed. We were in an English classroom that was serving as a green room, across the corridor was the drama studio where we were rehearsing the school play, *The Merchant of Venice*.

'Sorry— What?' I replied, suddenly feeling hot in my body. There were others around and this sudden shift of conversation into my sexuality felt deeply embarrassing.

'Our scene: I feel so much better about it knowing you're gay.'

'But … I'm not gay,' I replied.

Katie looked confused. Almost as if I'd told her the sky was not in fact blue but purple. Despite us having never had any conversation about my sexuality before, it seemed to be a certain fact in her mind. It also became apparent that others in the green room were under the same assumption. My stinging sweats passed and were replaced by a righteous bemusement. I interrupted the ongoing rehearsal across the corridor to check with the teacher who was leading the run-through. 'Do you think I'm gay?' The teacher now looked as confused as me. 'I'd assumed so,' she replied.

I set the record straight (no pun intended) and we returned to our rehearsal, now wondering where I stood with Katie. As a teen desperate for female attention, I had been enjoying the flirty banter we had been developing away from the scrutiny of the playground and year group divides. Did she no longer feel safe? Was my heterosexuality a threat?

I got in touch with Katie recently to ask her what she remembered of this episode and she shared something I hadn't been aware of at the time.

[11:13 AM, 7/22/2022] Katie: I mean from my side it wasn't an assumption, it was having been told [that you were gay] by older people at school. Which is actually worse because it was a widespread issue, which I know several men suffered from. You might remember people in my year – Chad, Jack, Rakkesh. All had rumours about their sexuality, which was so normalised then. And so disgusting to look back on. It isn't a coincidence that many of the men who suffered those rumours were usually the people involved in drama, debate, music. Just huge assumptions on what was 'straight' and 'masculine'. I know David definitely felt the need to be hyper masculine sometimes to balance it.

I hadn't been fully conscious of this culture of students policing male sexuality at my school, but thinking back it makes sense. Because as unsettled as I felt in that green room, I don't remember feeling all that surprised. It was known in the school that I had been attending ballet classes for several years at this point. I was into musical theatre. I didn't hang out with the rugby lads. I preferred the debating club over football at lunchtime. My friendship group was largely female. I was the guy many turned to for advice. To many, I was a kind of 'gay best friend'. I cross-dressed for a friend's fancy dress birthday party one time. My behaviour was not typically masculine and therefore it was decided: I was gay.

And little did I know, I was already internalising this binary: the idea that anything less than total, axe-wielding straightness equalled gay. It would take me almost 15 years for me to unpick this mental block. And my biggest inspiration would be my sister, Ramanique.

Ramanique Ahluwalia

We were teenagers, sitting on the shore of Lake Geneva, perched on boulders. The Swiss city of Montreux lay behind us and the snow-capped French Alps towered opposite.

Strolling down the promenade earlier we'd passed a statue of Freddie Mercury. Unveiled in 1996, one fist raised, the other gripping a microphone, the dramatic bronze by sculptor Irena Sedlecká stands as monument to the six albums Queen recorded in the city, including their final studio release, 'Made in Heaven'. 'He's Indian!' our dad would frequently remind us, in a manner not dissimilar to Sanjeev Bhaskar's iconic *Goodness Gracious Me* character. We were amazed to learn that our dad was telling the truth, that Freddie Mercury was indeed born Farrokh Bulsara, the son of Parsi parents. But we weren't there for the culture that day, we were there for the Nutella crepes and a taste of freedom.

In search of some time away from the adults, and with almost everything in Switzerland out of our budget, we had taken ourselves off to explore the lakeside and hang out on the rocks. As the clear water lapped around us, our talk turned to dating and Ramanique grew uncomfortable. Being an older brother, I delighted in this. I probed and eventually teased out, literally, what I had somehow intuited to be true: she was into girls.

Deep down, I wanted my sister to know that it was okay. That I supported her, loved her no matter what. That I was there for her. But as an ignorant teenage boy I only knew how to take the piss. My logic was that if we were joking about it, it wouldn't seem like such a big deal. It wouldn't have to be a 'coming out', it could be banter. 'Your Cheryl Cole obsession makes sense now.' I grinned. Ramanique laughed uncomfortably.

Looking back, I can see that my attempts at humour were

actually an expression of my own discomfort. Speaking to Ramanique while writing this, she tells me that I had actually made several jokes in front of the adults earlier in the trip, almost goading her to come out. I wanted to be supportive, but I didn't know how. We had a gay elder in the family but had only really learnt about this after their HIV diagnosis. All things LGBTQ+ were shrouded in a sense of taboo and mystery. I had also, I suspect as a way of coping with our parents' deteriorating marriage, appointed myself to a quasi-parent role when it came to my sister. I felt I needed to have answers. To be in control. To make it all okay. And so, instead of creating a safe space to let Ramanique open up, I teased her into coming out on my terms. 'What about kids?' I asked on our walk back to the house. I quite clearly didn't have all the answers.

Ramanique slowly came out to family and friends over the next few years and her journey to becoming the proud, fierce and inspiring queer artist she is today is her story to tell. But what I never envisaged was that my story would begin to run in parallel with hers, that my experiences of alienation as a white Punjabi, and her trials as a young woman discovering her pride, would bring us closer together. Our timelines began to crossover in the wake of the Punjabi wedding I attended in 2015.

I'd been telling her about the little brown girl who couldn't make sense of my bhangra moves, and the uncles who had implored me to reel off some Punjabi for their WhatsApp groups. 'This is probably your first experience of being othered isn't it?' Ramanique asked. It was such a simple question, and it landed with profound force. In asking that question I suddenly began to understand her experience. I suddenly realised how my one-off was her everyday. Humbled and a little shaken, I replied, 'I hadn't thought of it like that.'

It was as much a realisation for her as it was for me. As a young mixed woman who had experienced racist and gender-based abuse at school, being othered was a fact of life. As we spoke, she told me of her most recent experience: how she'd been out for drinks in London, and how when a guy had approached her, she had politely declined his advances by explaining that she was gay. 'But you're Indian?' he had replied, unable to reconcile her heritage with her sexuality. It was just another example of how she was frequently made to feel she was an oddity, an anomaly, something 'other'.

The idea that homosexuality doesn't exist in certain communities is a form of erasure that is thankfully being increasingly debunked by LGBTQ+ activists and groups. Visibility is crucial. If you can't see it, you can't be it. As such, the inability to reconcile culture and sexuality can be an internal struggle too. The writer and activist (and my good friend) Sharan Dhaliwal writes in her book *Burning My Roti: Breaking Barriers as a Queer Indian Woman* about how she was 'unable to identify [her] sexuality within [her] own culture' because she didn't have the language, the Hindi or the Punjabi, to express those experiences. She explains how this is largely due to the influence of the British in India and how English words, along with their attendant moral judgements, became more commonly used to describe sex and homosexuality. This was a fascinating insight that had me reaching for my sticky tabs. And it's made me eager to discover this vocabulary, to create the linguistic framework for belonging. Because if there's not a word for something in our language, how can it exist in our culture? It's a task many queer South Asians and their loved ones are already undertaking: 'I have a cousin who calls me v instead of veer [brother], a cousin-niece who calls me vassi [a compound of veer and massi: brother and aunty], queer and trans youth who call me massi [aunty],' prabhdeep singh kehal shares with me on Twitter. ('I do not capitalize my name in English-printed media and you may also use ਪ੍ਰਭਦੀਪ if you prefer.') It's a beautiful thing to see, especially for a culture that has a long history of gender nonconformity in the shape of hijra and khwaja sira communities. (The British criminalised these communities under Section 377 of the colonial penal code, which outlawed sexual activity that went 'against the order of nature'. The legacy of this hate is still felt, but India, Pakistan and Bangladesh all legally recognise a 'third gender'.)

I wish I'd had this level of insight and curiosity at the time, but I didn't. It was another missed opportunity. As a result of years of struggle, Ramanique was able to sympathise with my experience at the wedding and made me feel seen and understood. But while I suddenly had new insight into her journey, I was not yet ready to become a true ally. I was too wrapped up in my own nascent identity crisis. Plus, at the time, I genuinely thought I was doing everything right.

In 2015, I visited Ramanique in New York for her drama school graduation and we spent a night out at Marie's Crisis, a West Village piano bar with a long history of being a safe space for the gay community. I was more than comfortable with, and indeed a little flattered by, the attention I got while I was on the dance floor. One guy went as far as dramatically lifting up my jacket to better check out my butt. I'd been working out a lot that year and I appreciated his connoisseurship. I laughed, thanked him for the compliment but politely explained that, 'I'm straight, sorry!' Surely this made me a great person? I clearly wasn't homophobic, was this not allyship? Short answer, no. Much in the same way that racism can only be defeated by anti-racist politics – not doing racist stuff isn't enough, you have to be engaged in dismantling the structures of racism – the 'system of power and control that positions cis-straight white males as superior and normative' can only be overcome by queer liberation.[1] The truth was, in 2015, as comfortable as I was with gay attention, I was uncomfortable with queer politics. It would be another year before Ramanique's bravery, in the face of tragedy, would force me to confront this truth.

*

I had seen the news before Ramanique. It was 12 June 2016 and she was living in LA at the time. She was still asleep when, at just after 9am in the UK, the BBC reported at least 20 dead.[2] The shooting at Pulse, a gay nightclub in Orlando, Florida, would turn out to be the deadliest terrorist attack in America since 9/11. The nightmare began just after 2am local time and only came to an end following a three-hour hostage crisis. Forty-nine people had been killed, and over fifty were wounded. I saw the news. And then got on with my day. I didn't think to message my sister and see how she was feeling. I didn't reach out to let her know I loved her. It didn't occur to me that she would be waking up to news of the deadliest act of violence against the LGBTQ+ community in US history.

I feel deeply ashamed by my failure. But even more so when I look back at the WhatsApp messages I exchanged with Ramanique in the days that followed. The attack was a turning point for her. In a message in our 'Ahluwalia Cousins' group chat she shared how, 'In light of last night's events I realise how much bigger than myself this is.' Until then, she had been out, but not proud. That was about to change. Later that day, Ramanique would attend LA Pride, her first Pride event, despite the fact that a man en route to the festival in West Hollywood had been arrested that morning, his car full of assault rifles and explosive chemicals. The full force of who Ramanique Ahluwalia is was beginning to blossom. And again, I wasn't ready.

When Ramanique raged that the news in the US was ignoring the fact that the attack was on a gay club, focusing instead on the shooter's Muslim identity, I replied that, 'It's a cocktail of politics and people are focused on the ingredients that serve their narrative.' When she lamented that a close family member had failed to reach out to her, I replied, 'You can't expect everything all of a sudden. You've never had these conversations before. It's a long process.' And when she rightly pointed out that I suffered from 'a general lack of knowledge' on LGBTQ+ issues, I replied, 'I feel like you've had some incredibly powerful and life-affirming realisations and the immediate reaction is to want to transfer that enlightenment to all. Whereas actual wisdom and the ability to impart that wisdom will come from taking the time to fully process it for yourself.'

Ramanique hit back, 'Please do not do that. I think we should talk about this another time. I've been processing this for years. This is NOT an immediate reaction.'

It makes my skin crawl to read this all back. Revisiting my chat history and writing these last few paragraphs has taken me hours. I want to reach back through time and hug my little sister, the young woman who was halfway across the world. When I fell off my tricycle and smashed my face on a rock as a child, it was Ramanique who led me by the hand to safety, as tears and blood streamed down my face. She was now hurting, reaching out to me, and I was resisting. I was focused on my own discomfort. I didn't have the strength to support her. I was fragile.

The term 'white fragility', coined by author Robin DiAngelo, first appeared in 2011 in the *International Journal of Critical Pedagogy* but gained wider recognition after the release of her 2018 book of the same name. In that 2011 paper, DiAngelo lays out what the term means:

> White people in North America live in a social environment that protects and insulates them from race-based stress. This insulated environment of racial protection builds white expectations for racial comfort while at the same time lowering the ability to tolerate racial stress, leading to what I refer to as

White Fragility. White Fragility is a state in which
even a minimum amount of racial stress becomes
intolerable, triggering a range of defensive moves.
These moves include the outward display of emotions
such as anger, fear, and guilt, and behaviors such
as argumentation, silence, and leaving the stress-
inducing situation. These behaviors, in turn, function
to reinstate white racial equilibrium.[3]

Looking back at my messages with Ramanique, I can see that
this assessment was just as applicable to me in 2016. I was
suffering from a kind of straight fragility. The minimum
amount of gay stress I was feeling was making me extremely
defensive. I felt frustrated. I felt argumentative. I felt accused.
So I pushed back. And in doing so, I was functioning to
reinstate the heteronormative equilibrium.

I opened myself up to the idea that I wasn't getting it
right. That I needed to listen. As I doomscrolled, I spotted
a headline: 'Your Queer Loved Ones Just Lost 49 Family
Members. Be Patient With Them.' It was a HuffPost
piece by Joseph Erbentraut and one particular paragraph
jumped out:

In the days that have passed since the shooting,
I'm also reminded of how many people simply
don't understand or care to learn how to *begin* to
understand what it feels like to move through the
world after experiencing this layer of trauma on top of
the already overwhelming feelings of fear and grief.

This was the slap in the face I needed. Had I really understood? Had I really begun to learn? I thought because I had gay housemates and went to drag bingo one time I knew all I needed to know. This was a wake-up call. I revisited the article Ramanique had posted the day before in our cousins chat – 'To my heterosexual friends: this is why Orlando hurts' – I read it properly this time. I'd skimmed it before, thinking it didn't really apply to me. I saw now that it did.

Ramanique and I hadn't been in contact for about 24 hours. We were cooling off. But on 18 June at 11.45pm UK time, with characteristic grace and unfaltering faith, she reached out to say, 'Love you so much xx' I replied a few minutes later with the link to the HuffPost article, 'Love you too. xxx'

It was a small gesture. But it had a huge impact. 'Thank you so much for sending that. Thank you thank you thank you. Crying a little bit. It means so much. Gonna go get ice cream and lie in the sun and try to switch the brain off now xxx' I said goodnight and went to bed with love in my heart, we were thousands of miles apart, but I felt closer to my sister than ever before. And as I closed my eyes, I felt a fire begin to burn within me. I never again wanted my sister to feel like her big brother wasn't there for her. I was now in this fight.

*

The following year, on 8 July 2017, Ramanique was back in the UK and we attended Pride together for the first time. This is when I first started to understand that I had been under the spell of 'respectability politics'. The term originates from

1993, the year Ramanique was born, when Evelyn Brooks Higginbotham published *Righteous Discontent: The Women's Movement in the Black Baptist Church*. The final chapter of her book, titled 'The Politics of Respectability', explains how:

> While adherence to respectability enabled black women to counter racist images and structures, their discursive contestation was not directed solely at white Americans; the black Baptist women condemned what they perceived to be negative practices and attitudes among their own people. Their assimilationist leanings led to their insistence upon blacks' conformity to the dominant society's norms of manners and morals.

Higginbotham continues:

> Although the black church offered women an oppositional space in which to protest vigorously social injustice, this space remained, nonetheless, situated within the larger structural framework of America and its attendant social norms. Black church women, therefore, did not escape the influence of the dominant society. The women's movement in the black Baptist church reflected and reinforced the hegemonic values of white America.[4]

From this academic beginning, the derivative term 'respectability politics' has come to be understood, mostly negatively, as both the external pressure and the internal impulse felt by marginalised social groups to conform to the dominant culture of the society in which they exist, in order to be respected. It's the politics behind such sentiments as, 'I don't have a problem with it, I just wish it wasn't so in-your-face.' The underlying want is quiet assimilation, to become part of 'the norm'. But what if 'the norm' is the problem? What if The Norm Club only accepts male or female members? What if you can only get in if you have to declare whether you consider yourself Indian or British. What if – as in Boots Riley's brilliantly surreal 2018 satire *Sorry to Bother You* – you can only thrive if you bow down to corporate capitalism and adopt a 'white voice'?

The counter to respectability is liberation, freedom from the shackles of 'the norm', a transformation of society that affords justice to all. It is no coincidence that in the wake of the Stonewall riots in New York in June 1969 – triggered by police raids and spearheaded by Black people such as Stormé DeLarverie and Marsha P. Johnson – the groups that were founded declared themselves the Gay Liberation Front. These activists had no desire to be respectable. And this was the origin of Pride. An explicit protest against the hegemony of heterosexuality.

Partying on a Shoreditch rooftop on 8 July 2017, I didn't feel oppressed, or threatened, or out of place. As we hugged and danced, laughed and whooped, I felt solidarity. I felt free. What if this could be the norm?

It was during this time that non-binary gender identities were gaining more mainstream attention. In 2014, Facebook introduced an option for they/them pronouns and expanded its range of genders to over 50 terms that were decided in consultation with LGBTQ+ activists. In 2015, a free text option was added, allowing users to define themselves, for themselves. That same year, The American Dialect Society announced 'they' as their Word of the Year, defined as a 'gender-neutral singular pronoun for a known person, as a non-binary identifier'. And in 2017, the year I was at Pride in London, the singer Sam Smith announced that they were genderqueer, before later coming out in 2019 as non-binary and changing their pronouns to they/them. Mere days after Smith's announcement on Twitter, Merriam-Webster – the oldest dictionary in the US – officially added a non-binary definition for they, while also acknowledging that '*they* has been in consistent use as a singular pronoun since the late 1300s.'[5] Within the space of five years, non-binary people and language had become more visible in the UK and US than ever before.

It was in 2019 that I also articulated 'Both Not Half'. I didn't immediately make the connection, but by the time I'd written up my personal essay I had become aware that my resistance to being described as 'half' was an expression of non-binary thinking.

Binaries dictate that things must be one thing or another. Indian or British. Good or bad. Gay or straight. He or she. It's a shorthand we use to feel a sense of certainty in a complex and paradoxical world. And letting go of that certainty can feel scary, particularly when faced with difficult politics and unfamiliar ideas. Often our preferred response is to simplify and categorise or, when forced, use fractions so as not to upset the either/or framework. In doing so, in pursuit of comfort and reassurance, we sacrifice accuracy and blunt our curiosity. Binary thinking is in many ways a refusal to think for yourself, opting instead to put trust in assumptions or the values imposed on you to guide the way. But as I said in my TEDx talk, non-binary approaches force us to engage with detail and nuance.

I had come to this realisation because I was having to engage with detail and nuance in my own family. Ramanique was now in a relationship with someone who had recently come out as non-binary, changed their name and switched to they/them pronouns. I didn't know the full story of what that meant for them, but that was immaterial – I didn't need to know. Their discovery had freed them to live a more personally authentic life and, just as I now began to flinch every time I heard the word 'half' used to describe me, and how joyous it felt to hear 'both', I knew how incredibly affirming it would be for them to have their gender identity respected. It was a small change I could make in an effort to break free of the binary matrix. I of course made mistakes. I misgendered them several times, both in their presence and when they weren't around. But I learnt to apologise, correct myself and moved on. I learnt to embrace the fact that breaking free of the matrix required practice. I was so used to thinking in terms of he and she, but I knew from how easily 'both' had displaced 'half' in my mind that it was entirely possible to think in new ways. It was genuinely exciting. It was a way of creating a new norm.

Breaking the binary

I should perhaps take a moment to expand on non-binary gender identity. It is something I had to learn and while awareness is increasing all the time, it is not, at the time of writing, common knowledge. The first thing to note is that there is no one way to be non-binary; just like mixed, it refers to a multitude of experiences while also existing as a distinct identity. Non-binary people experience their sense of self beyond the dichotomy of man and woman and this can take many forms.

It is also very much a gender identity, not a sex. This is where it can get confusing, as sex and gender are so often conflated. But put simply, sex is defined more by biological traits, whereas gender is more socially constructed. I say 'more' because thinking of them as entirely distinct is a binary of its own that denies their interconnectedness. Sex is assigned at birth by looking at a baby's genitals. Gender is learnt and experienced as we grow up. And the way in which we learn and experience gender is largely dictated by the sex we were assigned at birth. (It's also important to remember that intersex people exist, an umbrella term for people with reproductive or sexual anatomy that doesn't 'fit' the male/female binary. This isn't always noticeable at birth but when it is, doctors sometimes perform surgeries to 'normalise' the child. There is currently no specific law in the UK prohibiting such surgeries despite them having been deemed a human rights violation by the UN.[6]) As Meg-John Barker and Alex Iantaffi describe in their book

Life Isn't Binary, 'gender can be defined as a complex biopsychosocial construct', a combined product of biological, psychological and social factors.

Cisgender people's experience is that their sex and gender is aligned as per societal norms. Trans people experience their sex assigned at birth and their gender identity as incongruous with societal norms. Non-binary people experience a similar disconnect and can identify with both genders simultaneously, neither, or move fluidly between one and the other. Despite being cisgender, I hugely relate to certain aspects of the non-binary experience; I sometimes feel more Punjabi, more British, both, or neither, depending on how I'm feeling and what I'm doing.

We must also acknowledge and celebrate the existence of non-binary sexuality – sexuality that goes beyond the straight/gay dichotomy. Bisexuality exists. You may think that this is obvious, given that the word 'bisexual' is not uncommon. Despite my school experiences drilling me in the gay/straight binary, the word bisexual was well known. But that didn't matter. When a rumour began to circulate that a straight classmate had had a same-sex experience at a sleepover, he was immediately labelled gay – not bisexual.

This tendency to erase bisexuality – as a reality or even as a possibility – was not unique to my school. When I first drafted the earlier part of this chapter, I described Freddie Mercury as gay. I had only just turned one when he died and got to know him through popular culture as a gay icon, a musical genius whose life was tragically cut short by AIDS. But while I would eventually unlearn the homophobic 'gay disease' narrative surrounding HIV, it was only when checking my facts that I discovered that, while he never publicly identified his sexuality, Freddie Mercury's 'attractions and behaviour were openly bi'.[7] The song 'Love of my Life' was about his one-time fiancé Mary Austin, to whom he would ultimately bequeath his home and music royalties.

In a pivotal scene in the 2018 biopic *Bohemian Rhapsody*, Rami Malek, as Freddie, nervously confesses, 'I think I'm bisexual.' Lucy Boynton, as Mary, retorts, 'No, Freddie. You're gay.' This is blatant bi-erasure. And while that may well have been a deliberate creative choice to highlight the reality of Freddie's romantic struggles, the film does little to establish and present this explicitly *as erasure*. Instead, watching it for the first time, it feels a lot like Mary is confirming a truth to a confused Freddie – that he is identifying as bisexual on his journey to coming out as gay. And it's a narrative that persists. A 2021 article on Smooth Radio's website begins, 'Freddie Mercury and Mary Austin were engaged before the Queen star came out as gay.'[8]

Thanks to bi-erasure, I grew up in the noughties understanding bisexuality to be a niche experience, a 'confused' minority among the more 'self-assured' gays and lesbians. It came as something as a surprise to me when during my research for this book I discovered that 'people who identify as bisexual comprise about half of lesbian, gay, and bisexual people in the United States' and that 'many Americans, especially young Americans, identify as something other than heterosexual, gay, or lesbian.'[9] In the UK, figures from 2020 show that among people aged 16 to 24, 2.7% identify as gay or lesbian, while 5.3% – almost double – identify as bisexual.[10] Bisexuality is far from niche.

None of this is to say that some people don't come out as bi before later identifying as gay or lesbian, or vice versa. But the idea that bisexuality is inherently a phase, some kind of stepping stone before you reach a more 'certain' or 'confident' stance, is a harmful trope that upholds the sexuality binary.

Looking back on the attitudes that pervaded during my youth, something else also jumps out: same-sex behaviour was encouraged in women without their straightness ever being questioned (so long as they remained romantically interested in men), whereas guys would be instantly denigrated for even expressing curiosity. School bus banter openly glorified threesomes, but only between a man and two women; the alternative, I was told, was the evil and corrupt sounding 'devil's threesome', to be avoided at all costs.

Programmer and writer Vaneet Mehta explores this double standard in his book, *Bisexual Men Exist*, and explains it is an expression of phallocentrism – the societal centring of the penis, stemming from patriarchal norms that privilege cis men. Through this lens, sex is only considered legitimate or socially relevant when there's a dick involved. As such, women can sleep with women all they like and retain their straight identity. For men on the other hand, even *attempting* to perform oral sex on *yourself* can be considered gay. I found this insight deeply illuminating and so I reached out to Vaneet.

The story of Vaneet's book is not too dissimilar to mine. Frustrated by a lack of visibility and understanding, he created the hashtag #BisexualMenExist. 'The main reason was to help those who were like me, who felt so alone and trapped and who struggled to accept their identity.' It all spiralled from there. For obvious reasons, I related. But I also felt a more specific connection. I felt that we were both fighting the same thing: the binary. He felt similarly and we arranged to meet up for a drink.

We spoke for over two hours and discovered all manner of commonalities, not least because of our shared Punjabi heritage. I shared how assertions that I 'don't look mixed' had inspired #BothNotHalf and how, in that sense, I felt a deep kinship with his experiences of bi-erasure and the need to change the narrative. But the most significant revelation for me came when I mentioned how I had come to realise that non-binary identities require active effort rather than passive acceptance – using they/them pronouns for example, is an action. You cannot simply ignore it: it is something you either choose to respect or reject. Similarly, I wondered whether some bisexuals may struggle to find true support in their families or communities, since such support requires people to actively embrace an idea that goes against a societal norm: the non-binary notion that attraction to more than one gender is possible and valid.

'So there's an interesting idea around essentialism – the idea that we have some immutable and innate essence,' Vaneet lent in. 'You have the whole "born this way" mentality and a lot of gay people have used this to successfully challenge homophobia and fight for equality. When the accusation "you're making a choice" is levelled, you can reply, "No, I was born this way." But if it's possible to have a gay or straight essence, it follows that a bisexual essence is also possible, an essence that allows for a degree of choice. This is where bisexuality causes a disruption.'

I hadn't considered this before, but I started to realise the implications. I was familiar with the Kinsey scale and the idea that sexuality was a spectrum, but I hadn't really considered how, in a binary world, a monosexist world – a world in which it is presumed that everyone is, or should be, attracted to one gender – fluidity is felt as choice and thus a threat, both to those advocating for same-sex rights and wider society. Bisexuality challenges us to break free from the fetters of monosexism and embrace, as Lois Shearing puts it in their book *Bi The Way*, 'the possibilities of sexual fluidity and self-determination'.

To be clear, a lot of people do feel they were born a certain way. Their sense of their sexuality feels innate and immutable and I fully support a global ban on conversion therapy. This does not, however, invalidate the fact that some people do experience a sense of choice and acknowledging this is crucial in our collective quest for belonging. As writer Brandon Ambrosino shared in a 2016 article for BBC Future, 'I am gay – but I wasn't born this way':

> I don't think I was born straight. I was born the way all of us are born: as a human being with a seemingly infinite capacity to announce myself, to re-announce myself, to try on new identities like spring raincoats, to play with limiting categories, to challenge them and

topple them, to cultivate my tastes and preferences, and, most importantly, to love and to receive love.[11]

Sometimes, individuals use the 'born this way' narrative as a moral get-out clause so that they can feel like allies without letting go of their prejudices. I once heard an elder say about Ramanique, 'I love and accept her no matter what but, you know, it's not something you wish for in your family.' A similar trope exists for bisexual people, 'Well, at least there's a chance you'll end up in a normal relationship.' The prejudice may even be disguised as concern for 'how hard life is for LGBTQ+ people'. These attitudes are rooted in heteronormativity, a rigid sexuality hierarchy that privileges straightness, underpinned by binary thinking. The existence of bisexuality proves the hierarchy to be a false construct and draws our attention to the human capacity for change. But the status quo hates to have its true nature revealed. Where binaries are attacked, backlash usually follows. And nowhere is this being felt more keenly, at this moment in time, than in the trans community.

Trans liberation now

In July 2021, I received a call from my agent with news that a Bollywood production was interested in casting me in an upcoming Akshay Kumar film. I'd spent a bit of time in Mumbai in 2014 and while it had been a fun adventure, hunting down and surprising casting directors with my Punjabi, nothing came of it. It seemed now, seven years later, things were about to change. This was a chance to star opposite the 6th highest-paid actor in the world.[12] The email to my agent read: 'As mentioned in the call, we are happy with his showreel so at this stage we need to book his screen test as soon as possible, preferably this week.' I didn't even have to audition! I couldn't believe my luck. And then I read the character breakdown.

'He was raised in the UK and India. His mother, who is a magician, dies in a car crash. He blames himself and others for her death.' Interesting, I thought. 'Through the use of prosthetics, he transforms himself into his mother and goes on a killing spree … a police inspector tries to find the "old lady" killer … the cat and mouse chase begins.' Yikes.

Prompted by the increasing hostility in the press towards trans people, I was learning about transphobia and the many ways in which trans people are oppressed. Through listening to trans people speak and reading work by queer writers, I'd come to learn that one of the many media tropes that feeds this oppression is the archetype of the cross-dressing killer; an archetype that teaches us that trans people are depraved, deceitful and violent, and therefore deserving of contempt, mistrust and brutality. This felt familiar – *Psycho*, *Silence of the Lambs* – but it was only when I sat down to watch the Netflix documentary *Disclosure: Trans Lives on Screen* that I realised I had been inducted into this trope as a child.

I was a massive Jim Carrey fan. I couldn't get enough of his over-the-top comic genius and my love of dance was inspired in no small part due to the set pieces in *The Mask*. So, when my dad let me and my sister rent a VHS copy of

Ace Ventura: Pet Detective from Oadby library, I was giddy with excitement. I howled with laughter as Ace, disguised as a delivery man, threw a box labelled 'glass' around; I shrieked with horrified delight as Ace discovered he had kissed a trans woman – 'Einhorn is a man!' – and proceeded to vomit, use a toilet plunger on his face and burn his clothes; I grinned with prepubescent glee as Ace stripped Einhorn down to her underwear and turned her around to reveal a bulge tucked between her legs, prompting every police officer in the scene to spit, vomit and scrape their tongues. The transphobia could not have been more in your face and obvious. The film also presents Einhorn as a mental hospital escapee, connecting transness with psychological instability. Critics at the time did comment on its 'brutal and unpleasant stew of homophobia and misogyny', but it raked in $107m at the box office and became a nineties kids classic nonetheless. A spin-off animated series ran for 41 episodes and was shown in the UK on CBBC.

It was with this burgeoning understanding of the role the media has played in reducing trans people to jokes and threats that I decided to back out of the Akshay Kumar film.

I share all this because I think it's important to acknowledge that it's okay to be confused, so long as that confusion prompts learning and growth. When 'the transgender issue' became a headline event in the culture wars, I realised I wasn't entirely sure what I thought. The phrase 'trans women are women' had become a rallying cry for trans activists and allies but I couldn't quite make sense of it myself. Surely women were women, and trans women were trans women? Why the need, as I saw it at the time, to equate one with the other?

I also felt an instinctive kinship with the trans community; I knew what it felt like to have one's body and sense of self deemed incongruent by society. It all felt very confusing. But then I considered the lens of Both Not Half, and it began to make sense.

Both Not Half is an articulation of how I know myself and experience life as a Punjabi, as someone of Indian descent. It is a rejection of the accusation that I am a lesser Indian or a diminished Punjabi. With this in mind, I began to see what 'trans women are women' meant. It was not equating the two, it wasn't an erasure of womanhood or an attack on cis women. It was simply saying that trans women are a type of woman and are equally valid in that experience. And equally valid does not mean the same or typical. Again, reflecting on my own experience, I understand that while most South Asian people are brown skinned, some (like me) are not. Our experiences in a racialised world will of course be different, but there is no hierarchy of South Asian experience. Equally, while most women are cis, some are trans. Their experiences of life in a gendered world will undoubtedly differ, but there should be no hierarchy of womanhood either. Just as Both Not Half invites us to expand our understanding of what it means to be mixed, 'trans women are women' and 'trans men are men' invites us to expand our understanding of gender. If you rephrase it as 'trans people are people', it all becomes rather obvious. As ever, the only thing under attack is the binary.

'But trans people are perpetuating the binary! We shouldn't be encouraging them to play up to gender stereotypes.' This is a common argument beloved by those invested in maintaining the status quo; they attempt to present themselves as radically opposed to gender stereotypes, while at the same time denying the immense diversity of trans experience. What this argument typically fails to acknowledge, as highlighted in Stonewall's 2018 'LGBT in Britain: Trans Report', is that access to trans healthcare and gender recognition can be 'traumatic and demeaning, many can't or aren't able to engage with it, and those who do go through it say they have to fit outdated stereotypes of what it is to be trans, and what it is to be a woman or a man to secure recognition.' 'I've always known.' 'I feel like a man stuck in a woman's body.' 'I used to wear my mum's makeup.' 'I always used to play football with the boys.' 'I never used to play football with the boys.' While these experiences may be true for some, many trans people regurgitate stereotypes in an attempt to get the support they need. To be clear, there is also nothing wrong with identifying as a man or woman in such a way that may be considered stereotypical. Those experiences are entirely valid. After all, if a cis person can lean into convention, why not a trans person? But the constructs of man and woman become a constraint if you consider them a rigid 'either/or' and refuse to acknowledge the vast array of experiences beyond the binary. Because non-binary trans people exist, like my old housemate Alex.

*

It was through conversations with Alex that I learnt of the unique struggles of being a non-binary trans person.

Alex was assigned female at birth but felt uncomfortable being socialised as a girl. 'I also knew I didn't want to fully "switch" and be a boy,' they told me. Instead, they imagined their wardrobe as an eclectic mix of both male and female clothes. When they first shared this aspiration with their sister, she affectionately teased, 'Well, you'll need a lot of money!'

As Alex became more sure of their trans non-binary identity, they became less certain of how to exist in the world. They couldn't imagine how living authentically would make their life any easier. Plus, they were a committed feminist and had a strong circle of likeminded female friends – they worried that they would be ostracised for aligning themselves with anything 'male' and that it would be read as a betrayal.

Alex was also feeling guilt. They felt they 'should've known earlier'. From what little trans representation there was in the media during their childhood, it was clear that kids who asserted their trans identity before puberty were taken more seriously than teens, who were often dismissed as confused or seeking attention. That said, these examples were all of trans binary people: people who had a clear sense that they were either boys or girls. Non-binary trans experience was all but invisible. Realising that their identity was unable to conform to any sort of societal expectation, Alex decided to hide who they were and sought belonging within 'acceptable boxes', briefly identifying as a lesbian. They forced themselves to wear makeup and adopt a more feminine gender presentation so as to 'get a better result in the world'.

This was a survival instinct. Just as I had grown up watching *Ace Ventura*, absorbing trans tropes, so had Alex.

Trans people were presented as tragic figures, the victims of murders and rapes, or deceitful dissemblers who were not to be trusted. 'You learn to expect violence. Institutions that once felt safe, as an upper-middle-class white person – like the police or hospitals – take on a threatening character. You notice staff making disparaging remarks. You start to wonder whether you'll be treated properly, whether they might do you deliberate harm. It becomes a huge source of anxiety.' And this anxiety was not unfounded. When Alex did begin the process of seeking medical transition, their therapist threatened to have them hospitalised for pursuing their non-binary identity. 'In the end, I just decided to pretend to be a trans binary guy, just tell them the story they want to hear, don't threaten the system or the construct of gender. I couldn't risk authenticity.'

Alex also explained that their experience wasn't unique. 'Regardless of gender identity – man, woman, whatever – not all trans people want or get "full" surgery. This could be due to health reasons, financial constraints or just personal preference.' It's also worth keeping in mind that the notion of 'full surgery' relies on a binary understanding of gender, diminishing all other treatments as 'incomplete'.

The more Alex and I spoke, the more we began to find parallels in our experiences. When Alex first moved into our house, I had asked what their pronouns were and they had responded, 'he/they'. At the time, I had made the assumption that Alex was assigned male at birth and so double checked that he/they was correct. 'Yeah, whichever is easiest for you'. I later discovered that their actual preference is 'they', but they offer 'he' in new or uncertain situations as a way of avoiding problems with people hostile to non-binary pronouns. Similarly, until my mid 20s, I would never correct pronunciations of my name and always introduced myself to new people as 'Jassa' with a hard first 'a', as you might assume it sounds given how it is written in English. The actual pronunciation, 'juh-sa', required too much explanation and provoked too many questions. Alex smiled. 'It's a constant negotiation between how much of our identity we hide versus how much friction we are prepared to tolerate.'

This friction has resulted in us both developing set scripts that we run when meeting new people, refined over time to anticipate invasive questions and pacify people's discomfort. It can be exhausting, demeaning even – for a time, I used to explain my whiteness by including a joke that 'my dad didn't put much effort in that night' – but it's less tiring than constantly having to come up with new ways to explain your existence.

This is also why I describe myself as 'white presenting', rather than 'white passing'. I'm well aware that I do 'pass' as white and benefit from white privilege, but 'passing' centres someone else's perception. And I rarely allow that perception to persist if: 1) I have control over the situation; and, 2) It's relevant to the conversation.

This, I shared with Alex, was how I had come to understand the issue of disclosure – the act of revealing one's trans identity. When I meet people and they clock my name, many find it impossible not to enquire what my background is, what my mix is, which parent is which, what shade of skin they have – far more information than would otherwise be considered polite or necessary for a first encounter. Alex laughs. 'I can totally imagine someone asking, "But where are you really from?" with the same energy that they might ask, "But have you had the surgery?"' Sometimes it even becomes a game of 'guess the ethnicity'. During a shift waiting tables, Ramanique was once the subject of a bet. Without her knowledge, a group of men had been trying to guess her ethnicity and she was pressured into settling their debate when she brought the bill.

Just as no one is entitled to someone's ethnic background, no one is entitled to someone's medical history. As people get to know each other, these things may naturally come up. And it should go without saying that communication and consent are essential to any sexual encounter or relationship. But no one is owed disclosure. Cis people don't have to preface dates with a description of their gender identity or genitals, and neither do trans people. Many trans people, Alex included, do disclose – 'I stick to dating apps so I can do so safely. It just allows people to self-select out if they have an issue' – but cis people need to get their head around the fact that trans people are entitled to privacy. And while having a preference for certain genitals is a valid experience – as trans advocate Brynn Tannehill argues, genital preference 'can theoretically be applied neutrally across cisgender and transgender people' and is not, therefore, inherently transphobic – it is transphobic to rule out dating trans people or ending a date based on *assumed* genitals. [13] After all, the initial spark that may prompt a date rarely has anything to do with penises, vaginas or reproduction. And to expect trans people to lay all this information out before a drink has even been ordered is absurd. No cis man would think it reasonable to have to disclose their penis size and sperm count before arriving at a bar. Similarly, no mixed person should ever be expected to share their genetic makeup to validate their name or skin tone (and they definitely shouldn't have to do so to settle a bet). Fundamentally, any encounters with lived experiences that challenge societal norms should be treated with respect and self-reflection, not hostility and accusation.

And if you do feel an impulse to be hostile, reflect on where that is coming from. Is it fear? Is it perhaps shame? Is the fight for equality maybe forcing you to reflect on who you are? Discomfort is very often an invitation to learn something about yourself. What might you uncover? My own discovery came as a surprise.

Straight, mostly

In 2013, I was in Romania, filming *Dragonheart 3: The Sorcerer's Curse*. I'd been revelling in the B movie thrills, conjuring smoke, ducking from explosions, and talking to a tennis ball that would later be voiced by Ben Kingsley. One evening, during a night shoot at Castel Film Studios, I was waiting in my trailer when I received a text. It was from a girl. And it was quite flirty. This wasn't altogether out of the blue; we had some history and we were both single. But I could sense excitement in her, something daring and adventurous. It was hot. Moments earlier I'd been feeling a bit sleepy, but not now. No, now I was wide awake. Not even my scratchy druid's robes could distract me. We pinged innuendo back and forth – I tried not to catch sight of my bowl-cut hair in the mirror, not the sexiest of looks – and then she asked me a question that forced me to my feet. 'Have you ever thought about a threesome?' My heart started to pound. '*Damn*,' I thought. '*Is this going where I think it's going?*' I probed a little. I was now pacing my trailer, watching the 'is typing' animation, analysing every pause and praying that no one knocked on my door to call me to set. Yes! Oh damn, yes! She was definitely hinting at a proposition. I replied cautiously: I didn't want to spook her. But maybe I'd been too careful? She was really taking her time with her reply. What could it mean? My stomach was doing flips. Perhaps I'd misjudged? Had I come across too eager? I had just turned 23 and though I would never have admitted it, I was very much in my sexual infancy. I stared at my screen until my eyes started to blur. And then, *bzzz*. Her message popped up. I blinked. 'What if it was with a guy?'

What followed was one of the most bizarre sensations I've ever felt. I was simultaneously disgusted, disappointed and overwhelmingly turned on. My mind flashed back to my school bus journeys and the older boys' warnings about 'devil's threesomes'; their laughing faces seemed to bear down on me, suffocating me with humiliation. My chest felt tight. But the rest of my body could not have cared less. My heart was racing, pounding forcefully in my ears. My phone began to slip in my sweaty palms. And … Well, it was pretty obvious. The moment seared itself into my memory and before I had any time to process what was going on there was a knock at my door and I was being roped up and dangled over the parapet of a castle wall. Nothing ever came of the conversation that night and my brain began the process of suppressing my confusion. *I'd definitely still opt for two women if I had the choice anyway, so no need to stress about it*, I told myself. *It was late, I was lonely, forget about it.* But the experience was far too intense to forget. I tried ignoring it instead.

But other thoughts started to creep in. I began to reflect on my experience earlier that year of playing Vincent Featherwell in the second series of *Ripper Street*, a gay telegraph boy involved in prostitution and blackmail. It was an incredible role and I loved the character – a charismatic young leader unafraid to stick his finger up at society. In a press interview, I was asked, given that the story weaves in 'the modern theme of gay rights', did I research what it meant to be a gay Victorian? I was sadly too early in my journey with queer politics to refute the idea that the fight for gay rights is a modern phenomenon, but I did reply honestly:

The short answer is no. I'm a huge believer in the script and Toby Finlay penned an incredible episode, one of the best I've ever read. My research took the form of investing in the script and trusting [the director Kieron Hawkes'] vision entirely. What I focused my energies on was bringing Vincent to life as a human being. The episode does very cleverly intertwine modern themes but it's ultimately about a timeless idea – treating people equally. What really enthralled me about the project as a whole was that these ideas and our heroes are essentially in opposition; Reid [Matthew Macfadyen] is charged with upholding the law, but the law discriminates.

I felt this truly and deeply. Growing up hearing stories of racism and injustice, I relished the chance to throw myself into a role that shined a spotlight on how legality does not equal morality. It felt like a calling. But I had overlooked the specificity of this being a gay story. I was ignorant to gay history, as my later experiences with my sister would attest. And I was unaware of the discourse around the (in)appropriateness of straight actors playing gay. I was also very early in my career and, to be honest, the chance to play a guest lead in a primetime BBC One series was all I was really focused on. But I did have other thoughts in the lead-up to the shoot. Thoughts I didn't share in interviews. I was genuinely curious about what it would feel like to kiss my male co-star. We would have a film crew surrounding us, and professionalism would be paramount, but what would it feel like to be in bed together? Would I feel anything? Would I learn something about myself?

The shoot came and went without any revelation and I figured my curiosity was misplaced. Though looking back, I'm not sure I was being entirely honest with myself. My one intimate scene in *Ripper Street* had felt as devoid of genuine spark and emotion as any of my straight scenes in *Some Girls*: it didn't really mean anything. It was just a day at the office. But I did feel a sense of relief. Perhaps that was why I felt so panicked that night in Romania: it poked at something I had already tried to forget about. The niggle wasn't going away.

On my first ever trip to LA, in 2014, I found myself wondering if I would be open to a same-sex experience if one presented itself while I was there, far from home. The idea had occurred to me as I arrived at a Golden Globes party in West Hollywood. Knowing no one in the city, I'd turned up alone and was capitalising on my fish-out-of-water status to make new friends. With zero sexual intent, I got chatting to a guy in his 40s who offered to take me under his wing. He proceeded to introduce me to a group of attractive women in their late 20s and early 30s and I forgot all about my curiosity. As the awards telecast came to a close and the drinking began in earnest, we all crammed ourselves into a photobooth to memorialise our unexpected fellowship. Tight dresses and long legs were everywhere, my 23-year-old mind was going wild. The flash went off, blinding us all slightly. And then, as the women began to pile out, one of them shouted back with glee, 'Let's leave these two faggots to it!'

Before I had really registered the comment, I was alone with the guy and he was leaning in to kiss me, my back pinned against the wall of the booth. I stopped him before it went any further – and apologised. I felt guilty. I was worried that I had upset him. I tried to put him at ease and laugh it off. But I was feeling a bit queasy. Firstly, because the moment felt engineered on his part. And secondly, there had been such intense disgust in the woman's voice. I felt ashamed. I left the party not long after and decided to be extra clear about my heterosexuality for the rest of the trip.

Any curiosity I'd arrived with was now set aside. I didn't want a repeat experience. The disgust of women was too high a price to pay. The binary sucked me back in.

It was only after articulating Both Not Half and beginning to unpick my relationship with binary thinking that I began to revisit these memories. Only after I became aware of the central role of shame as an oppressive societal force did I become aware of my own deeply held personal shame. I noticed how, despite wanting to, I assiduously avoided clicking on the gay category on porn websites. I clocked my reluctance to admit to significant others that a MMF threesome did in fact hold some fascination for me, even when they themselves were being open about their own curiosities. I noticed that I had suppressed any interest in masturbation toys – the only one I'd ever owned was given to me as a joke birthday present and I felt deeply embarrassed when I was pressured into admitting I'd tried it out. I reflected on all of this and I began to see that I was shackled: trapped in a narrow definition of straightness that I had learnt from childhood. I was afraid to let go and step outside of the socially acceptable cell I'd built for myself. I was inspired to break free. I began to consciously plan my escape.

I clicked on the 'gay' category. A lot of the content did nothing for me. But some piqued my curiosity. A few, to my surprise, I found I was really into. It was fun to explore. After all, a lot of the straight porn I'd watched featured dicks so it wasn't exactly uncharted territory. And gay ninjas didn't kick down my door and swoop through my windows to revoke my sense of straightness. In fact, I grew more confident.

I felt my shame begin to shrink. I was being more honest with myself. True to myself. I was rejecting the fictions taught to me by society and opening up to the full scope of my capacity for experience. It was exciting. I felt my horizons expanding.

*

'Straight People Don't Exist, Research Says.' There were lots of headlines like this but I knew better than to take them at face value. I picked through the articles and eventually found the research in question, conducted by Dr Ritch Savin-Williams, the director of developmental psychology and the director of the Sex and Gender Lab at Cornell University. He's now retired but remains passionately involved in his field. And much to my surprise and joy, when I reached out via email, he replied within a few hours:

> I watched your TEDx talk and I'm <u>very impressed</u> with your clarity, humor, voice, and ideas! Indeed, maybe I should retitle my book "Both Not Ninety/ Ten." Most importantly for me is your perspective and values—which I totally identify with. We are so much in need of more "boths" and fewer "halfs" (I hope that makes sense).

It made total sense. Dr Savin-Williams' book, based on a study using pupil dilation as a measure of arousal, gave scientific support for an emerging sexual identity among young men: 'mostly straight' – people who are comfortable with their heterosexuality, do not identify as bisexual, 'yet remain aware of their potential to experience far more'. The 'Ninety/Ten' in his email is a reference to his attempt in his opening chapter to define this identity as 90% straight, 10% gay. Towards the end of his book, however, bothness enters the picture:

> Research shows that, like straight guys, mostly straight young men's genitals are aroused and pupils are dilated for naked female images. However, unlike straight guys, mostly straight young men have nontrivial increases in arousal responses to naked male images. They are, to use conventional terms, both heterosexual and slightly homosexual.[14]

I read the book with the fervour of someone discovering a long-guarded truth. Page after page became streaked with my highlighter. Could this be me? I've never really found myself attracted to men in person, but I have had fantasies, I have watched gay porn, and my experience in my trailer in Romania was as intense as it was unexpected. And these were exactly the kind of experiences being described in the case studies.

When I speak to Dr Savin-Williams, one of the first things he's keen to stress is that the romantic and the sexual do not always act in sync. 'I've interviewed young men and women who have been very romantically attracted to one sex but then very sexually aroused by the other.' Hearing him say this brings another suppressed memory to the fore.

I was listening to an episode of *The Guilty Feminist*

and the panel discussion had turned to the idea of being heteroromantic but sexually bicurious – romantically interested exclusively in the opposite sex, but sexually open to other experiences. While I had a sense of 'could this be me?' at the time, the conversation was led by women, not men, so I didn't instinctively apply it to my own experiences. After all, sexual fluidity among women is seen as far less threatening than sexual fluidity among men. Dr Savin-Williams agrees.

'You know, a lot of the researchers [in my field] are straight men, who have their own fantasies, and there's a history of thinking that all women are born bisexual, which is not true.' Dr Savin-Williams himself identifies as 'totally gay'. 'But because of that I think it is more acceptable for women to be mostly straight. And the literature would say at this point, about twice as many women as men identify as mostly straight. My argument is they're actually equal. I see no reason for there to be a difference. And in our physiological research, far more men [than those who identify as mostly straight] are actually mostly straight. Their eyes don't deceive.'

I know for a fact that my eyes wouldn't deceive. And it occurs to me, am I mostly straight? And why the need to use a label? With this question in mind, I sat down with my sister's partner, artist and queer activist Dominique Holmes.

'I really hate the term label,' they tell me, 'but, if there's a label, it means I don't have to have that in-depth, complicated conversation. I prefer to call it identity. Identity is something human, personal, emotional, the embodiment of who someone is.' Label is what you do to specimens in glass cabinets. It assumes clean boundaries, clarity and categories.

Labels are designed for other people to read. Identities, on the other hand, are linguistic expressions of lived experience. They are a shorthand for sharing complexity and, most importantly, ourselves. I explain to Dom that, much in the same way that referring to myself as 'both not half' made me feel more at ease in a racialised world, discovering 'mostly straight' feels like a more authentic way of understanding myself in a heteronormative world shaped by suffocating ideals of manhood.

'I know within the queer community some people get annoyed by the number of different identities out there now. But you know, if you find something that connects with you and resonates inside, that says who you are, to the level that you want to share, without the need to disclose anything personal if you don't want to. Without feeling compelled to go into detail about where you're from, what genitals you were born with, any of that – it is powerful. And the more words the better. Because the more you can really say "this is who I am" without having to delve into detail, it's better for everyone. It's better for us to have an understanding of our similarities and differences without invading people's personal experiences.' This sense of privacy is why Ramanique loves identifying as queer. It's specific enough to give her a sense of community, yet also private. It's also a political choice, claiming queerness is a rejection of heteronormativity. Perhaps that's why I'm feeling excited about embracing mostly straight. Not only does it feel more true to who I am, it's an identity that disrupts the binary.

Dr Savin-Williams writes that identifying as mostly

straight 'might well change the world – moving it closer to embracing same-sex sexuality in its many forms and degrees of expression.'[15]

I have no desire to present myself as a 'straight saviour'. But I do want to know myself. I want to share myself with others. And I want to change the world. It was this longing that gave birth to #BothNotHalf. It is that same longing that gives me the confidence to embrace mostly straight, or, as I've come to prefer: heteroflexible. Both are an articulation of who I am and a rallying cry for a new and more inclusive future.

But I'm also not relinquishing 'straight'. If straight women have the capacity for fluidity, then so do men. My exposure and deep sense of connection to queer politics, history and community has freed me from the fetters of fragile masculinity and introduced me to a more liberated straightness.

'I loved when you spoke Punjabi. It was great, you know, because of your skin colour, it was like an interruption,' says Dr Savin-Williams of my TEDx talk. 'It's about disrupting the categorical approach to our lives. I love that. I'm about destroying the categories. I consider mostly straight to be a temporary holding.' Likewise, I don't consider #BothNotHalf to resonate forever. It's an identity of sorts, but more crucially it is a tool. A tool for breaking down the binaries that strip our world of complexity, a tool with which to build a society that embraces and celebrates multiplicity, grounded in nuance and specificity.

In that sense, Both Not Half is a queering of identity. Embracing this, and allowing myself to be guided by it, has helped me to become a better LGBTQ+ ally. It has helped me to better understand trans, bi and non-binary experiences. And, most unexpectedly, in the writing of this chapter, I have discovered a new and more authentic way of expressing who I am. 'That's what us queers have been screaming at the straights for years!' Ramanique tells me, after reading an early draft of this chapter. Sorry it's taken me so long to catch up.

I hope that in sharing my journey so far, I may inspire you to better explore your own relationship with masculinity, sexuality, your attractions. Let your mind wander, click on that link, see that show, share that fantasy with your partner, wear that outfit, go on that date, try that app, buy that toy. See what happens when you let go of the binary. Free yourself. Know yourself. Identify as you see fit. And find the courage to stand in solidarity. Queer liberation is a fight to free us all.

7

OCCUPY THE BACK SEATS

The classless society would also be the tolerant society, in which individual differences were actively encouraged as well as passively tolerated, in which full meaning was at last given to the dignity of man.

MICHAEL YOUNG, *THE RISE OF THE MERITOCRACY*

I HAD MADE up my mind. I wasn't going to move. I can't quite remember how old I was, but my sister recalls that she'd just started at the school, so I must have been around thirteen. I was thrilled to be taking on the role of cool, older brother. The only problem was, I wasn't very cool. And my decision to lead a school bus revolt was downright embarrassing.

The bus had been my first experience of secondary school when I myself had matriculated two years earlier. Raised on tales of Harry Potter and Alex Rider, there was something thrilling and adventurous about boarding a double decker, parentless, and travelling into Leicester's city centre. It was a transition towards teenhood. But where to sit? I didn't really know anyone yet.

I opted for the top deck, the cool deck. Most of my vehicular outings to date had been in cars or coaches, all of which were boring single-storey affairs. But I was now in Year 6, primary school was behind me, I called the shots. Up the stairs I went.

Shit. I had emerged into a sea of unfamiliar and decidedly cool-looking faces and I suddenly remembered that I was a bespectacled soon-to-be-11-year-old weighed down by an oversized and overfilled backpack. The panic was rising and the bus had started to move. Heading back downstairs seemed the best way out but bus-physics had robbed me of my ability to control my body. Perhaps sensing my first-day dilemma, a couple of older lads beckoned me over and took me under their wing. Damn, this was cool.

Tree branches swept by the steamed-up windows as I sat laughing along to in-jokes I didn't understand. I was then initiated into a game that was won by being the first to shout out the temperature reading displayed at the top of the Leicester Mercury building. (I won!) But the frivolity wasn't to last. My novelty as a new kid soon wore off and it became apparent that I had to learn my place. Cool kids towards the back of the top deck, nerds and loners towards the front, younger kids stayed down below with the music geeks (they needed the space for their instruments) and the elevated back seats that faced each other was the premium lounge, belonging to the sixth formers and prefects.

Yes, prefects. This was a private school, complete with Houses and end of year exams. My parents had been warned by my primary school headteacher that the local state secondary my dad had attended would do me a 'disservice'. In her opinion, I would be stretched at private school, and so avoid boredom and trouble. It would be a major financial challenge, but my mum – brought up by her socially mobile father to respect the social and cultural advantages bestowed by private education – felt it was worth the effort. My dad, on the other hand, and as the main breadwinner, needed a bit more convincing. After all, he'd done well for himself through the state system. But when he revisited his old classrooms on an open day and saw that the periodic tables in the science labs hadn't changed since his youth, it was decided: they'd scrape the cash together and send me to Leicester Grammar.

I have been very reluctant to discuss the fact that I attended Leicester Grammar School when speaking about my past publicly. Not because I wish to hide the fact that I attended a private school – though I could probably be more forthcoming about this fact – but because I had such a bad time there. It's remarkable, for example, that I ever became an actor given how belittled and bullied I was by one of my drama teachers, a situation that escalated into a full-blown formal complaint, resulting in my first strong memories of anxiety and depression. Put simply, I've never wanted to give them credit. That said, I cannot deny that the quality of education was good and, most importantly, I was schooled in the intricacies of how to be middle class. A big part of the secret was respecting traditions and knowing one's place within the established order. It was all very well, admirable even, to have ambitions, but you must wait your turn and genuflect as you climbed the ladder.

And so it was on the bus: there was an established order. A tradition. Once you made it to sixth form and could wear 'business attire' instead of uniform, you were welcomed onto the back seats. You became part of the club. For the first two years of my secondary school life, I had thrown myself into propping up this system. It offered a sense of belonging and connection to something bigger. So what if I was a lowly Year 6? I was destined for besuited Upper Sixth greatness. I simply had to do my time.

But around 2003, something in me changed. Perhaps it was having read *Harry Potter and the Order of the Phoenix* that summer. Harry was only a couple of years older than me and he had led a student resistance against draconian rules. Or maybe it was seeing *Dead Poets Society* for the first time, sitting in Robin Williams' classroom and watching him rail against conformity. Or maybe I was simply longing to mimic my dad's disdain for all things pretentious. Whatever the cause, I began to intuit that the established order was not my friend.

And so it was, one afternoon, I found myself sitting at the back of the bus, occupying the central seat, before the end of school and without a haughty sixth former in sight. This was a stroke of luck. The school operated several buses dedicated to different routes serving various students. But during school hours, they doubled up as transport for afternoon games and PE sessions. Being located in the city centre, there were no rugby pitches (always rugby) within walking distance. As such, we would have to gather in the playground after lunch, pile onto the buses, head off to wherever we needed to be, and head back in time for the end of school. Once back, we'd file out and head off home. Unless of course the bus that had been used that day was the bus dedicated to your route home. In that case, you simply stayed where you were and waited for everyone else. That was rarely the case for me. But today, I'd beaten the odds. And we were back a bit earlier than usual. I had time to build up my courage and rally some support. I enlisted a friend who lived near me and we decided to stay put.

The bus started to fill up and the first sixth former made his way towards us with an intimidating air of entitlement. He seemed to expect that his presence alone would cause us to take flight. But we held firm. I planted my legs across the wheel arches, blocking the way and informed him that the ancien régime was being overthrown. He could join us if he wanted, on equal terms, but we would not be moved. An officious prefect came to his aid and reminded us of our inferiority. We informed her that prefect privileges pertained to discipline, not seating arrangements, and refusing to move was not against any rule. Feeling the rush of defiance, we invited uniformed friends to join us in the sanctum. The suits felt their grip on the situation weakening and became increasingly agitated. As the driver called out that everyone needed to sit so we could move off, they bitterly conceded defeat. There were rumblings about loss of 'tradition'. My sister was mortified. I was elated.

When I sat down to write this chapter, I thought I'd be writing about mixed class identity, examining terms like 'class-passing' and investigating the emergence of Multicultural London English, the dialect born of mixed working-class identities that I employed to play Rocky in *Some Girls*. These are interesting conversations to have, but they are not what I have truly learnt. The real lesson has in fact been an essential and timely reminder of what I discovered on the bus that day: social hierarchies can be challenged and dismantled.

The claws of apathy

GCSEs came and went, and I did very well. My mum was elated, my dad considered his expectations met. And we decided it was time for a change. I ditched Leicester Grammar and its fees and enrolled at my local comprehensive for my A-levels. I was now following in the footsteps of my dad, uncle and aunties.

I was remarkably unapprehensive about this transition. If anything, I was excited. To be shunning the staid atmosphere of Leicester Grammar and striking out on my own was thrilling. And Beauchamp College was a revelation. Whereas my dad's secondary school had seemed stale and dated, Beauchamp had undergone a transformation. No strict dress codes. Grants to support extracurricular activities. Sports facilities on site. A subsidised gym. A new library. And a truly diverse student body. The classes were a bit bigger and rowdier, but armed with my private school toolkit, I flourished. And my favourite subject turned out to be 'Government and Politics'. Two years of learning about legislatures, standing committees and political parties meant

I began university primed for the 2010 general election. And I got thoroughly swept up by Cleggmania.

This was the year of the first televised leaders' debates. And it was the first general election I was eligible to vote in. I was stoked. In my halls, debate viewing parties proved as popular as any club night. Drinks were knocked back, opinions were thrown around and democratic zeal spilled from every corridor. This was our chance to change the world! The Liberal Democrats had emerged from the 2008 financial crisis and the 2009 parliamentary expenses scandal relatively unscathed and were positioning themselves as a champion of 'change' with the two-party system in its sights.[1] But the biggest appeal to me as a newly enrolled university student was Nick Clegg's pledge to abolish tuition fees.

I listened hard, and then I proselytised. I made it my mission to convince everyone around me that Clegg was our saviour and that Cleggmania was the one true doctrine. When the day of the election finally came, I chirpily updated my Facebook status to read 'Jassa Ahluwalia is going to agree with Nick after a spot of breakfast', 'I agree with Nick' having become an election catchphrase. I even shared that I was 'well jealous of Jamie Marcus who actually got to vote for the Cleggster himself!' Jamie was an old school friend, studying in Clegg's constituency at Sheffield Hallam. I was so Cleggmaniacal that I was even celebrating when the coalition government was announced five days later: 'Clegg is Deputy PM and four other Lib Dems in Cabinet … yeah baby!' Cringe.

By the end of the year, my lord and saviour had reneged on

his promise and supported the Conservatives to triple tuition fees to £9,000, an obscene increase that sparked furious protests, building occupations and violent confrontations with police. I'd like to say I was in the thick of it, railing against the injustice and hypocrisy of it all, but I wasn't. I'd been put off by the acts of vandalism, the thought of getting arrested scared me and I felt humiliated by the betrayal. The only cuts being made were to public spending. And that's when reality punched me square in the face: Leicester-Shire Arts in Education was having its funding pulled.

The history, success and legacy of Leicester-Shire Arts in Education cannot be overstated. It began as the 'County School of Music' in 1948, founded by Eric Pinkett OBE on the principle that 'children everywhere should be given the chance to play instruments.' Funding was scarce in post-war Britain but 'despite the initial difficulties, the service had by the early fifties grown in size, and had gained an international reputation with its European tours'.[2] By the mid-1970s, dance and drama classes were made available. I began attending Knighton Fields Centre, the service's home on Herrick Road, in the mid-1990s. Twice a week, I learnt the rigours of ballet from ex-Royal Ballet principal Graham Fletcher. The service also operated in my primary school, where I learnt to play the tabla, under the tutelage of Bhai Gurmit Singh Virdee, a Leicester local who also happened to be a world-renowned master. Darbar Festival, now a regular fixture at the Barbican Centre, was established in his memory, following his death in 2005.

Kate Stevenson, now a policy lead at the Ministry of

Justice, was seven years old when she began to learn the violin through Arts in Education. In 2011, as the cuts were coming into force, she penned an overview of its achievements for the education journal *FORUM*:

> Leicester-Shire Arts in Education grew considerably from its limited beginnings, and now caters for over 10,000 students. Around 6,000 students in 200 schools receive instrumental tuition, and various performance groups meet to rehearse on week nights and Saturday mornings. These range from ballet to bhangra; from a symphony orchestra to a steel pan ensemble – all reflecting Leicester's diverse population. The groups are involved in around 80 public performances a year, including the annual Christmas concerts held at Leicester's De Montfort Hall.[3]

These concerts were where I discovered performance could be a profession. My BBC documentary *Am I English?* features a brief clip of me dancing the role of Mercutio in Prokofiev's *Romeo and Juliet* at De Montfort Hall. The sword I'm wielding was a real rehearsal foil borrowed from the Birmingham Royal Ballet, the choreography was Sir Kenneth MacMillan's original and the music was performed live, by the Leicester-Shire Schools Symphony Orchestra. We had costumes, sets and lighting design. It was as close to a Royal Opera House performance as any child or parent could dream of. And we knew that because Graham would organise coach trips to Covent Garden for us to experience the real deal. We had no concept of ballet being 'elite'. Classes cost next to nothing and financial support was available for those who needed it. It was only when *Billy Elliot* came out in 2000 that I gained any sort of understanding that ballet might be viewed by some as feminine; Graham was training the largest number of young male dancers in the country outside of full-time dance schools. We brawled and illicitly traded Pokémon cards and BB guns in the dressing room, before dashing to the studio to pas de bourrée across the floor.

When I think of my mixed upbringing and the fluidity it exposed me to, I do not limit myself to my ethnic identities. The corridors of Herrick Road, echoing with the sounds of ballet, kathak and jazz, taught me that high and low art was a false classist binary. It also taught me that the arts had value because they were the means through which belonging can be expressed: performing together, watching together, sharing in joy and sorrow as part of a collective effort to better understand ourselves and imagine a better future. This is the power of the arts. And perhaps that's why the political elite frequently belittle performance as a waste of time. They feel threatened by it.

Against a backdrop of covid-fuelled arts cuts, a government poster published in 2020 showed a Black ballet dancer tying her pointe shoes, emblazoned with the caption: Fatima's next job could be in cyber (she just doesn't know it yet). Meanwhile, the arts remain highly valued by the wealthy and the privileged. London's private schools boast more theatres than the West End, which probably explains why 67% of British Oscar winners and 42% of British BAFTA winners come from independent schools, despite the fact that only 5.9% of British kids attend such schools.[4] The message is clear: the arts are the plaything of the wealthy and the privileged, not a legitimate career prospect for anyone else. You might be able to make it as a working-class artist, but most likely only if you kowtow to the demands of the middle-class gatekeepers. Make it traumatic and gritty and you might get the green light; try to make it as a ballerina and you'll be told to retrain in cyber.

Leicester-Shire Arts in Education now seems like a utopia. But it was once real and it changed lives. By providing high-quality, subsidised classes, it was actively dismantling the class barriers that dictate who gets to engage in what forms of culture. It was giving kids who would have perhaps never stepped inside the Royal Opera House the chance to feel like that was somewhere they had a right to be. We didn't need to know the shibboleths of high society: we knew the choreography and we belonged there. And all this was scrapped in the name of austerity.

I didn't have the strength to cope. It was a body blow. The fall of such a historic, overwhelmingly successful institution made me acutely aware of my absolute powerlessness. I had always imagined that, despite inevitable setbacks and disagreements, we were collectively working towards an ever brighter and more prosperous future, for all. I now saw how naive I had been. The state gave zero fucks about accessibility in the arts. *Welcome to adulthood*, I told myself. Apathy and disillusionment sunk their claws into me. I focused on self-preservation and getting ahead as an individual.

By 2012 my efforts had started to pay off. I had dropped out of uni, presented *Art Attack* for Disney, shot the first series of *Some Girls* for BBC Three and guest starred in an episode of *Casualty*. I'd also come close to playing a younger version of one of the lead cast in Edgar Wright's *The World's End*. And so, armed with my burgeoning CV, I reached out to my dream talent agency: Independent Talent.

I had done my work experience week at Independent's Oxford Street offices back in 2006, when the agency was still known as ICM. How did 15-year-old me get through the door? Nepotism. The founder of the agency, Duncan Heath, is my late grandmother's cousin. I'd met him once at her funeral in 2000 but my only memory was that he had the latest Nokia with Snake II on it. Seven years later, my mum reached out to him and he agreed to let me run office errands for a week during the summer. This was my first taste of show business. The whiteboard in the office had 'BOND 21' scrawled across the top, the in-house name for the yet to be released *Casino Royale* – 15-year-old me felt like he'd infiltrated MI6 itself.

During my week at Independent, I had a meeting with Duncan Heath in which he imparted that in order to get ahead I would 'need to be prepared to walk over my grandmother's grave'. I wasn't entirely sure if he remembered that my grandmother was his departed cousin, and that she'd been cremated, but I lapped it up like the hungry puppy I was. He did also counsel that unemployment in acting was about 95% and I should have a Plan B, preferably in IT, but the message *I* took away was: 'I must forsake all shame and morals. To succeed, I must commit myself fully, spare no prisoners.' I was also gutted to learn that nepotism wasn't going to get me on to Independent's books. Well, at least not immediately. I'd have to earn my place.

When I arrived back at Independent's refurbished offices six years later in 2012, I walked into reception like a prince entering his kingdom. I'd done the impossible. I was in the 5%. Aged 22, I found myself a client of 'Europe's leading talent agency'. Over the next 12 months I shot the second series of *Some Girls*, I slayed Goliath in the US miniseries epic *The Bible*, spent a month filming in Malta on BBC One feature *The Whale*, and went head to head with Matthew Macfadyen in *Ripper Street*. I felt unstoppable. I stopped calling myself an 'aspiring' actor. I was now an actor. And to sanctify my newfound sense of professional status, I decided to join my trade union.

'Thank you for your application to join Equity. I am delighted to inform you that your application has been approved.' The email hit my inbox on 1 November 2013. What a rush. I had no idea what a trade union really did, but what I did know was that to be an Equity member meant that you were a bona fide professional.

There is power in a union

'You should stand for the Race Equality Committee.' It was now 2018, one week before Christmas, and Bec Boey and I had just bumped into each other outside the BBC Radio Theatre at New Broadcasting House. We were there for 'An

Audience with Nicole Taylor' – the BAFTA-winning writer behind BBC One's *Three Girls* – our reward for having successfully submitted scripts to the BBC Writersroom (as mentioned in chapter 3). I was still as yet unaware of what a union actually did, I was also not yet fully conscious of the fact that inequalities in society are fundamentally about economics. Racism was invented as a means of justifying class hierarchy, but I'd only ever been taught to fight against racism, not the economic system underpinning it. So I was intrigued by Bec's proposition.

We'd met doing a play together in 2014 and I'd felt an immediate kinship with Bec. An actor and writer of mixed British, East and South East Asian heritage, she was one of the first to make me feel truly seen and understood in a rehearsal room. I was telling her all about my script and my Anglo-Indian protagonist. I hadn't yet articulated Both Not Half – that would come after the holidays – but I shared how frustrated I was that our industry had such a narrow interpretation of what it meant to be 'mixed race'. 'That's why you should stand for election.' She grinned, piquing my curiosity. 'Would I even be eligible?' I asked.

Saying it out loud was one of those moments when I realised how much I had internalised the narrative that I was 'not the right kind of mixed'. 'Of course! I'm on the committee myself,' she reassured me. 'We need more people prepared to fight.' As she was speaking, the cogs in my head started to whir: my problem was that no one in the industry took my brown heritage seriously, but if I was an elected member of a committee dedicated to ethnically minoritised actors and creative workers, they'd have to pay attention, surely? Plus, it would be a welcome return to activism. Campaigning to change the industry to help mixed heritage performers felt like a battle I could win.

I was sitting on a bus, a regular hierarchy-free TfL bus, travelling home from a long day of side hustling for rent money. I was on the phone to Nicholas Pinnock, star of 50 Cent's ABC drama *For Life*, telling him about my plans to stand for election. He had doubts. Big doubts. In his experience, Equity was an ineffective bureaucratic dinosaur that implored people to pay their subs without offering any real benefits. 'What if I can change that?' I appealed. 'From the inside. Everyone keeps telling me we'll be able to change things once we "make it", but I don't want to wait.' Another friend had shared his own frustrations with me about the asymmetrical power structures in our business and even though he'd recently starred in a massive Hollywood blockbuster, he still didn't believe he had enough influence to do anything. Nicholas sympathised. 'I want you to succeed, but I just want you to go in with your eyes open. Equity just doesn't have the power of a union like SAG in the US.' My Hollywood-blockbuster buddy had said much the same thing. The American actors' union the Screen Actors' Guild was formidable. Its number one principle being that a 'member must always work under a union contract around the globe'. Due to anti-union UK law, Equity had no such clout.

Maybe being back on a double decker reminded me of my school bus revolt, or maybe reality was hitting me that I wasn't about to get plucked out of obscurity to star in the next

Marvel hit, but I felt a resolve forming. At the start of 2019, my first #BothNotHalf skit had gone viral and the sentiment behind the hashtag was resonating with people. What if I harnessed that as part of an election campaign?

Getting elected, getting sued

Jassa's flat. Day. Jassa addresses the camera. His Thaiya-ji (paternal uncle) – played by Jassa wearing a turban with a glass of salted lassi in hand – sits in a corner and chimes in. We cut back and forth. Jassa speaks in English, Thaiya-ji in Punjabi. Everything is subtitled.

Me:	Hi, my name is Jassa Ah-
Thaiya-ji:	Jasseh!
Me:	Sat sri akal, thaiya-ji.
Thaiya-ji:	What are you doing?
Me:	I'm recording my election statement.
Thaiya-ji:	You've become a politician? Do you know that dog-man Boris?
Me:	Er … no …
Thaiya-ji:	If you meet him, throw a lassi over him for me – salted. [slurps a gulp] Ahhh …
Me:	I'm actually standing for the Equity Minority Ethnic Committee.
Thaiya-ji:	Why? You look white, you should be happy.
Jassa:	That statement needs examining.

Thaiya-ji: Give me your statement then.

Jassa: [reading off his phone] Owing to my
             mixed British-Indian heritage, I am
             passionate about championing minority
             ethnic representation. [snores can be
             heard, thaiya-ji has been bored to sleep]
             Not just in terms of faces, but also
             stories …

Thaiya-ji: [jolting awake] That's a good point,
             there's a need for stories.

Jassa: Being white presenting has also given
             me insight into the universality and
             complexity of minority experience.

Thaiya-ji: [affirming] Mmm …

Jassa: I'm particularly keen to change attitudes
             towards mixed heritage performers.

Thaiya-ji: Meaning?

Jassa: [to thaiya-ji] "Mixed race" is often used
             with very little consideration to the
             diversity of mixed experience, or it's like,
             overlooked entirely in favour of binary
             "us and them" narratives.

Thaiya-ji: You know what, I've never thought
             about it like that …

Jassa: [back to camera] 'Both Not Half' is the
             distillation of my struggles with my
             sense of self, it appears to be resonating
             and I'd love to continue this work to
             effect meaningful change.

> Thaiya-ji: Vah! Where do I vote?
> Jassa: Oh, you have to be a minority ethnic
>   Equity member to vote.
> Thaiya-ji: Then why are you wasting my time,
>   you idiot!

Thaiya-ji throws his glass of lassi over Jassa. In shock, dripping in lassi, Jassa stares at the camera as the subtitles read: VOTE! – (for me please) – equity.org.uk/elections.

Writing this script, I was conscious to favour 'mixed heritage', or 'mixed', over 'mixed race'. In my TEDx talk I say, 'I feel that the term "mixed race" is itself, problematic. A linguistic hangover of scientific racism, complete with fears of "race mixing". I prefer to think of myself as mixed heritage, and of one human race.' In the same way I've since changed my opinions on nationalism, I'd like to offer a corrective here. I don't think 'mixed race' is problematic. It is an identity that many people feel an affinity to. I do not personally wish to give the fiction of race any positive credence, but I also have no issue with other people describing themselves that way. But my preference, and my choice when describing myself, is mixed heritage. Heritage has universal resonance and I'm far more interested in how my experience is similar to others. One of my favourite things about doing events is the chats that come after, speaking to people of all backgrounds who hadn't ever considered themselves mixed. I hear 'I know it's not the same, but …' so regularly and I absolutely love it. I assure them it is the same. #BothNotHalf was born of mixed heritage experience, but the sense of grappling with one's multiplicity is a universal experience. It is always an immense privilege to share in that intimate moment when someone suddenly sees themselves, and in turn the world, differently and more joyfully.

I shot the script on my phone with the help of my sister and posted it just after 6pm on 30 June 2019. When I was recognised outside a bar in Hoxton by an actor I'd never met, I realised it had found its audience. On 12 July, the polls closed and my election to the committee was confirmed.

I still didn't really know what a union did. I attended an induction day but it was more about internal bureaucratic structures than industrial action. The first committee meeting I attended was exciting for its officialdom – I was new to agendas, quorums and motions – but how would I actually make a difference? I was convinced the committee needed to be more active on Twitter, to rally the wider membership and make them feel like they had a voice. So when an actor went on *Question Time* and accused mixed heritage university lecturer Rachel Boyle of racism for calling him a 'white privileged male', we drafted a thread in our WhatsApp group, voted on it and hit 'tweet'. All hell broke loose.

We had shared that 'as far as we were concerned' Laurence Fox was 'a disgrace'. This got a lot of support from the people we were trying to engage with and upset others who felt Equity shouldn't be making such statements. That we were a committee of volunteer activists sharing our opinion seemed to pass people by – or was wilfully ignored. Right-wing commentators cast us as both dangerous power brokers who had influence over the entire 'acting community', and as 'rogue' operators to be dismissed.[5] It was an amusing contradiction. What was less amusing was that Equity's senior staff, fearing legal blowback, had hastily decided to delete our thread, lock us out of our committee's Twitter account and publicly censure us. Amidst outcry from members and keen to find a way forward, we got to work with the union's leadership team to put together an official joint statement. It was a difficult process, but we were quite proud of the result:

> Equity deeply regrets that the events of 17 January 2020 created a division between the union and our Minority Ethnic Members Committee [since renamed the Race Equality Committee] at a time when the unity of our actions is crucial.
>
> The MEM Committee is right to address racism in our industry, especially instances where its existence is being questioned and discussions closed down; it is their mandate. However, in order to protect the union and the overall membership, Equity has procedures and protocols to help us deal with the possible consequences of any actions we take.
> The MEM Committee accepts that Equity's deletion of their posts and temporary suspension of their Twitter account was ordered by the General Secretary to protect the union. This created a damaging perception that the union had arbitrarily silenced our MEM Committee, and Equity has come

to acknowledge and understand that actions like these
can perpetuate ingrained racism.

This statement was dated 5 February 2020, almost four
months before the killing of George Floyd and the heightened
awareness of structural racism that followed in the wake of
global Black Lives Matter protests. The acknowledgement
of 'ingrained racism' was hard won.

And then, the very next morning, a scary-sounding letter
from an expensive solicitor arrived at Equity HQ. Our
statement was mothballed and never saw the light of day.
Equity would go on to issue Fox a public apology and pay
his legal fees of around £10,000 plus VAT. Our committee
was incensed. We'd only been told about the settlement the
night before the press release went out. We only had one way
in which to register our protest: we resigned en masse. Others
tore up their membership cards and left the union altogether.
It was a shameful chapter in our history. It seemed Nicholas
Pinnock had been right. There was no winning here.

But some ember in me refused to be extinguished. Our
resignation had made headlines. We might be out in the cold
but perhaps we could still exert influence? Was this perhaps
the moment of despair from which radical hope emerges?
After all, it was now abundantly clear that Equity's way of
doing business – quietly, behind closed doors and with little
media attention – wasn't going to fly with the next generation
of activists. Maybe this was our moment.

I led on organising an open letter in *The Stage* and
gathered over a hundred signatures from prominent actors

and theatremakers. Our demand: new Equity leadership. Was this a bit opportunistic? Perhaps. A leadership election was already scheduled for that summer. But in making such a statement, and against the backdrop of Black Lives Matter, we ensured that anti-racism would become a defining issue for any future general secretary.

I ended up endorsing Paul Fleming, a union organiser responsible for central London theatres. I hadn't met Paul before but actors I respected were backing him. When he emerged as our new general secretary, he issued a 'radical statement of intent' in which he acknowledged that '[a] lot of things have gone wrong' and spoke directly to 'Black, Asian, and Ethnically Diverse artists who have left, or never joined [the union]' committing to 'build a union you can trust'. He also issued an apology:

> Our most recent Race Equality Committee had one of their most productive periods ever, with tireless work to improve opportunities for UK based Black artists and artists of colour, pressing for real strategies to increase work and opportunities for British East/Southeast Asian artists and driving a new approach to monitoring. When their union has not supported any members or activists in the way they've needed, whether wittingly or unwittingly, I am sorry.

Not everyone was convinced that this was the dawn of a new era, but the statement couldn't be easily dismissed as lip service. He'd actually said 'I am sorry' and had concluded by saying, 'Allyship cannot just be asserted, Equity and I will fight to earn that status.' In response to my congratulations at the time of his election, Paul had replied:

> I'm so sorry you've felt so frustrated in this first stab at union involvement, and I hope we'll have you on the fight as we go ahead. Your social media voice on the issues and perceptions around #bothnothalf are an absolute challenge to the efficacy of our structures to give a voice to the full range of under-represented voices - and we need that!

Cautiously confident that our union was now committed to an actively anti-racist agenda and with the knowledge that my voice was valued, I stood and was re-elected to the Race Equality Committee. But my approach had changed. During the run-up to the election I'd shared my frustrations with Paul: why was it that no one seemed to know what Equity actually did? His answer set me on a new course that would result in some of the most meaningful activism I've ever been involved with.

'We've not been very good at communicating what a trade union is. And because the UK has the worst anti-union laws in Europe, we have, historically, resorted to promoting ourselves as a sort of club that offers perks. Yes, we offer benefits like public liability insurance and discounts on theatre tickets – and these are valuable – but these are not the primary function of a trade union. A union is its members – workers – coming together to fight for better pay, terms and conditions. We are not a pressure group: we are a union. We have unique status in law which allows us to negotiate contracts and agreements and take legal action on behalf of members. This industrial work is where we derive our power. This is not to say that we are not political. The idea that the industrial and the political can be separated is a false dichotomy. Unions exist to build worker power, exert that power, and so shape a more equal society. But we can only do that if we organise effectively. And it is the job of union staff – and my role as general secretary – to empower members to do just that.'

I had come to Equity thinking of it as some sort of service provider. Despite my role on the Race Equality Committee, I had seen it as separate from me. The headquarters in Covent Garden and the staff that worked there: they were the union. I was just a member. I paid them my monthly direct debit and expected to get something in return. I mouthed off about problems and expected the staff to deliver results. The lack of return on my investment had left me feeling disillusioned. Now, I began to see things differently. This was not a capitalist, transactional relationship. I *was* the union. My fellow members were the union. We didn't have control over the industry, control would always lie with the bosses. But as a collective, we had power. Industrial power. We needed to organise. And in February 2021, we did just that.

Getting organised

When I volunteered to join Equity's self-tape working party as a representative of the Race Equality Committee,

I was cautious about what was to come. Could we actually do anything?

We had been formed to tackle the spike in complaints about self-tapes – audition tapes, filmed by actors themselves, usually at home, without input from a director or casting director. I was first asked to shoot one in 2012 when I was away filming *The Bible* in Morocco. It was a welcome way of getting my hat in the ring. This is how self-tapes emerged – as a solution. But in the years that followed, they started to become a problem. They began to replace first-round auditions entirely and, freed from the constraints of time slots and studio space, unrealistic deadlines and excessive scripts crept in, becoming a major source of stress and anxiety for actors.

The pandemic poured petrol on this fire. With nobody able to meet in person, self-taping became the go-to and complaints soon followed. Equity's subsequent survey of members was, at the time, the most responded to questionnaire in the union's history and revealed that a significant number of actors had been asked to produce a self-tape in less than five hours, while some reported having to prepare nearly 50 pages at a few days' notice. These extremes were shocking, but not altogether unexpected. Actor and comedian Jonny Weldon produced a sketch in April 2021 in which he receives a phone call from his agent before dashing downstairs to tell his girlfriend to cancel her evening plans. 'I've got to do eight scenes, four costume changes and six accents by 9 o'clock tomorrow morning.' His panic and anxiety struck a chord with almost every actor on Twitter. 'The accuracy tho!' replied Jade Anouka.[6] 'Depressingly accurate!' lamented Ben Lamb.[7] Four-time Olivier-nominated performer Emma Williams responded with a video of her own showing her attempting a tape while holding her infant daughter, highlighting the impact on those with caring responsibilities.[8]

Initial talks revealed that casting directors faced time pressure from producers and agents disclosed that they were frequently having to start work before office hours, processing tapes for morning deadlines. We all agreed that change was needed and so our working party sprang into action. This is where I saw what a committee of committed trade unionists was really capable of in the face of an established hierarchy. Brilliant ideas on issues that had never occurred to me were suggested. Ideas that sounded great were properly interrogated and flaws ironed out. Some people wanted to make certain concessions to get us over the line, others wanted to dig in and make them dealbreakers. I experienced every side of it and changed my mind on various issues. When we went into negotiations with the Casting Directors' Guild and Personal Managers' Association, we acted collectively and as one, knowing that we spoke as representatives of almost 50,000 members.

We amazed ourselves with what we achieved: a four-day minimum turnaround, a maximum of two scenes and six pages of script, plus protection for bank holidays. These were the kind of utopian ideals I'd shared with Nicholas Pinnock back in 2017. That these were now published in black and white was huge. Critics rightly pointed out that these were guidelines; they were not yet contractual or enforceable. But this misunderstands the win. What we had achieved was a shift from the individual to the collective. In 2017, I had had to find the courage to reject a last-minute audition on the basis of my own personal values. Now, actors could point to the industry standard as agreed by their union with leading agents and casting directors.

And the shift wasn't just happening in the UK. We were leading the way for performers globally. In September 2023, I was elected as an Equity delegate to the International Federation of Actors conference in Istanbul, a global network of performers' unions. I was a panellist for a discussion on self-tapes and it was thrilling to hear SAG-AFTRA's executive vice president, Ben Whitehair, share that Equity's guidelines had 'sent waves through America' and had informed their strike demands.[9]

We had laid the groundwork for a change of culture. It was a move towards a more dignified and respectful way of doing business. It started a meaningful conversation that showed that change was possible, giving me hope that positive change for mixed heritage actors could also be realised.

I really knew what a union was now. My confidence in the power of the collective was growing. So, when I was unceremoniously booted off a job in August 2021, I knew I could fight back. Not as an individual, but as a union member. The decision to fire me had been out of my control, but I wasn't powerless. The contract I was on wasn't an Equity agreement, but that didn't matter. I now knew I could turn to my union for legal assistance for anything work related. The producer stonewalled my agent – 'Our Dignity at Work Policies are only for our staff and not for artists. Everything agreed for Jassa can be found in his signed contract.' But I knew they'd change their tune once Equity staff threatened legal action on my behalf. I walked away with a four-figure settlement and my head held high. My agent, James Penford, refused to take any commission. There is power in a union.

This was the moment I realised that despite my middle-class upbringing, I was a worker. That is not to say I suddenly began to identify as working class. Rather, I now understood my position within the economic system we live in. I was entirely dependent on waged labour for my survival. 'There exists a widening gulf in experience between those whose survival depends on work and social security, and those whose prosperity is guaranteed by assets and inheritance,' writes Eve Livingston. 'While the latter are insulated from economic hardship and emergency by their wealth, the former – the vast majority of us – need unions in order to have any hope of comparable protection, regardless of what our specific experience of work looks like day-to-day.'[10] Though I may one day have some inheritance, I had no property to fall back on or investments I could live off. Artistically, I was an actor collaborating with producers to realise a creative vision. But industrially, I now clearly understood that I was a precarious and frequently low-paid worker, employed by bosses on lacklustre terms and conditions. I was becoming class conscious.

*

Awakened, empowered and determined to use the insight I had gained in order to deliver on my 2019 election statement, I volunteered to represent the Race Equality Committee at Equity's 2022 conference – the annual gathering of representatives from across the membership that sets our policies for the year ahead. I was there to present a motion calling on our Council to 'commit to work with Spotlight [the UK's leading casting database] and the Casting Directors' Guild to review the Spotlight 'appearance' category, enabling a more genuine, sophisticated targeting of relevant performers that is inclusive of mixed identities by default.'

On 22nd May 2022, I took to the stage at the Leeds Marriott Hotel, introduced myself as a first-time speaker, and began:

> I have spent my life being told I do not look like I
> have South Asian heritage. And yet I do. My dad
> is a brown man, born in India. I grew up speaking
> Punjabi, eating dhal and roti, and my summer
> holidays were spent playing gully cricket in the streets
> of Punjab. This is the fundamental problem with
> 'appearance' when it comes to casting. It privileges
> producers and casting directors' preconceptions over a
> performer's reality.
>
> The mixed-ethnic population is the fastest growing
> demographic in the UK. It is estimated that by the
> end of the century, Britain will be 30 per cent mixed
> race. By 2150, that figure is projected to rise to

nearly 75 per cent. People of mixed heritage are the future, but our industry does not yet have the tools to meaningfully reflect this reality on our stages and screens.

At present, Spotlight databases performers based on 'appearance', with all mixed heritage performers lumped together under 'mixed race', a label that has become shorthand for Black and white mixed heritages, to the exclusion of other minority mixes. This lack of nuance and specificity is unhelpful to performers and to casting directors alike.

Mixed heritage performers also often find themselves excluded from ethnically specific casting on the basis that they appear either 'too X' or 'not X enough' – this feedback is frequently from gatekeepers unversed in the nuances of ethnic heritages. The appearance category on Spotlight also lacks consistency of specificity; Pakistani and Indian sit alongside the all-encompassing Black-African. This flaw in the UK's primary casting database is deeply unhelpful at a time when the industry is striving for better and more accurate representation on stage and screen.

While the REC acknowledges that appearance is undoubtedly a central part of any casting process, a better system and greater awareness of the diversity of mixed heritage performers is needed. We believe

casting should be as inclusive as possible, where
possible, and accurate and specific where necessary.
This motion is the first step towards creating that
better system.

The motion was passed overwhelmingly, meaning Equity
was now formally committed to seeing this through. A couple
of months later, Equity's indomitable equalities officer, Ian
Manborde, facilitated a meeting with Spotlight and I was
able to make suggestions directly to the people who could
make the changes happen. My main ask was for all search
filters to include mixed heritage performers by default. For
example, I wanted to be able to list myself as mixed but also
appear in results alongside my South Asian peers. If casting
directors chose to look at my headshot and decide I don't
look right, fine. But I wanted to prompt conversation. It was
no longer acceptable that mixed performers were bunched
together as a homogeneous other and excluded by default.

I also pitched the rather bold idea that Spotlight should
amalgamate every known list of ethnicity, geographic region
and religion to create a searchable mega list. The system
should be dynamic enough to allow for multiplicity, I argued;
whatever heritages a performer may list, none should take
precedence over another.

I was told we'd have an update in August. And we did!
Well, August 2023. But our year of persisting paid off. The
system Spotlight came back with was more than I could've
hoped for. And they'd even gone and created the mega list.

The new system allows performers to select from a

range of 'broader backgrounds': Black/Black African/Black Caribbean; East and South East Asian; Indigenous/Native; Latin American; Middle Eastern/North African; Mixed; Pacific Islander; South Asian; White. You can select as many as you want. You then have the option to add up to ten specific 'ethnicity or heritage options'. Mine currently lists: British, English, Indian, Punjabi and Sikh. I can choose whether I want this information to be publicly visible, and the hope in future is that individual heritages can be hidden from public view – a request we took onboard from listening to the union's Gypsy, Roma and Traveller (GRT) Network, as well as Jewish members.

This new system is not a silver bullet for the problems of representation on stage and screen; it is still ultimately people with biases in positions of power who decide who gets to work. But this is a radical new tool that empowers performers and casting directors to shift the dial. The more accurately we can represent ourselves and the more accurately we see ourselves on stage and screen, the more accurately we begin to understand ourselves as a society. But make no mistake, as proud as I am of this achievement, it is just one front in a larger battle.

The right to strike

Both Not Half challenges racial hierarchy by refusing to accept the binary thinking required for it to function. There is no us and them, only humanity. But racism did not create inequality, racism was invented in order to justify social hierarchy. As Kenan Malik explains in *Not So Black and White*, 'Nineteenth-century thinkers looked upon the working class as a racial group, physically and anthropologically distinct from the rest of society'.[11] He goes on to say:

> It is not racial differences that have led to unequal treatment but the persistence of social inequalities in societies with a commitment to equality that has led many to view such inequalities as ineradicable, and hence natural, and to place people into different racial categories.[12]

You will recall that this was the attitude at play in colonial India, where 'common British soldiers ... belonged, like Indians, effectively to another race.'[13]

In order to create a world in which mixed people feel they truly belong we need to fight racism and rid ourselves of the fractional, hierarchical thinking it spews forth. But racism cannot be defeated without overcoming economic inequality. Racism is an expression of class inequality. Or, as Stuart Hall, the Jamaican-born, UK-based political theorist famously said, 'race is the modality in which class is lived.'[14] True equality – and thus belonging for all mixed people – will only be won through raising class consciousness and wielding collective power by acting in solidarity. Social equality is a prerequisite for lasting mixed belonging. That is why unions are so important. They offer us the most powerful means of fighting back. And though they are loath to admit it, those with power and wealth know this to be true. Culture wars and identity politics are the perfect distractions to their economic dominance. They fear trade unionism and instead try to fob us off with the myth of 'meritocracy'.

I grew up under the spell of this myth. On all sides, my family had pulled themselves up and climbed the ladder. From a village in Punjab, my grandad had become a respected teacher in Leicester. Through attending night classes, my grandpa had become an architect and shaped the skyline of Birmingham. I was middle class. A product of meritocracy. And my parents had raised me with what Annette Lareau calls 'an emerging sense of entitlement'.[15] It was my responsibility to follow in their footsteps and climb higher.

But there was a contradiction at play. My dad's ascent from a Punjabi village to a British suburb was a tale replete with stories of working twice as hard for half as much, stories familiar to anyone with immigrant heritage. Clearly, society wasn't a level, meritocratic playing field. But it was an attractive myth and it had become received wisdom. 'I want Britain to be the world's great meritocracy,' proclaimed Theresa May in September 2016, 'a country where everyone has a fair chance to go as far as their talent and their hard work will allow.'[16] Sounds reasonable? Sure. Apart from the fact that the guy who coined the term 'meritocracy' did so as a scathing critique.

In 1958, sociologist Michael Young published *The Rise of the Meritocracy* at a time when grammar schools were propelling people of modest means to university and into the kind of jobs usually reserved exclusively for the privately educated elite. This shift was considered progress. But Young saw in this the formation of a new and insidious class system. 'Merit' would lend legitimacy to 'the eminent', while those at the bottom would become stigmatised as 'dunces' or layabouts who just needed to try harder. This was not, his satire warned, what a more equal society looked like. But that didn't seem to matter, 'meritocracy' entered our political lexicon as a utopian vision, extolled by ministers across the political spectrum.

One leader did, however, break with this tradition. In 2019, Jeremy Corbyn announced he would be scrapping social mobility as a Labour goal in favour of opportunity for all. 'The idea that only a few talented or lucky people deserve to escape the disadvantage they were born into, leaving in place a social hierarchy in which millions are consigned to the scrap heap, results in the talents of millions of children being squandered.'[17] *Spiked*, an online magazine not exactly known for its left-wing politics, agreed. 'Corbyn is correct to call this orthodoxy into question … more graduates does not, in and of itself, create more highly paid professional careers – it just increases the competition for those that do exist.'[18]

Meritocracy is social hierarchy disguised as equal opportunities. It is a lie that we cling to so as to avoid the difficult task of addressing the fundamental problems with the way in which our society is structured. Unions exist to educate workers and change that structure. 'We need to sell our labour at a rate that allows us to live a decent life, while [bosses] want to extract it at as low a price as possible, for as big a gain as possible.'[19] No individual worker can effectively take on a boss, but a union of workers, or an individual with the support of their union, can. That is why the wealthy and the powerful fear them and continue to try and crush them. And they were winning, until 2022, when the tide began to change.

In the lead-up to that summer, the Trades Union Congress – a federation of the majority of trade unions in England and Wales, with around 5 million members – released the following statement under the banner We Demand Better:

> Working people have had enough. Everything's going up but our wages. Ministers partied while people died. They did nothing while P&O lays off hundreds of workers on the spot. And they dithered and delayed whilst living standards plummeted. It's time for a new deal for working people. We need help with energy bills and a real pay rise for every worker. Let's take matters into our own hands – and get out on the streets.[20]

I heeded the call. And I wasn't alone. As a TUC affiliate, Equity joined the protest on 18 June en masse. We flew our national banner and were cheered on by West End front of house staff as we passed their theatres on our way to Parliament Square. And I wore a Both Not Half T-shirt.

'#BothNotHalf in solidarity with #WeDemandBetter! The future is mixed and we must #DemandBetter for the generations yet to come,' I tweeted. 'An honour to march alongside my @EquityUK comrades today.'

Until this moment, I hadn't had the confidence to

embrace the language of trade unionism. During the self-tape working party negotiations I had referred to my Equity 'colleagues', adopting the language of business so as to appear more respectable. But just as I had come to reject 'half' in favour of 'both', I now began to embrace 'comrade' as a vocal commitment to trade unionism as a force for change. And change was coming.

Just three days later, following a breakdown in negotiations with rail companies over pay and working conditions, members of the National Union of Rail, Maritime and Transport Workers (the RMT) walked out on strike. Transport Secretary Grant Shapps dismissed the union's calls for him to come to the negotiating table as 'a stunt', while Prime Minister Boris Johnson opined that their demands were 'stuff that maybe the union barons are more attached to perhaps than their workers.'[21] Neither seemed to have paid attention to the fact that thousands of workers had been venting their rage in Parliament Square just 72 hours prior.

Sudden surges in labour movements are not without precedent. These 'leaps', as identified by Eric Hobsbawm, are best understood as 'accumulations of inflammable material which only ignite periodically, as it were under compression'.[22] Compression in this case took the form of the pandemic and lockdowns, which made it abundantly clear whose work actually mattered to the functioning of society and who was insulated through the benefit of home offices and gardens. A Trust for London report from September 2021 found that 45% of supermarket workers and 31% of care workers are paid less than the benchmark for decent living standards.[23] Against this backdrop, the Enough is Enough campaign was launched on 8 August 2022, with the stated aim of 'winning back dignity for working class people'. With a Labour Party focused on courting business leaders, it fell to unions and community organisations 'to push back against the misery forced on millions by rising bills, low wages, food poverty, shoddy housing – and a society run only for a wealthy elite.'[24] As Britain hit 40 degrees celsius for the first time in recorded history, 'hot strike summer' became the talk of the nation. Winter followed and as Big Ben announced the arrival of 2023, support for striking workers showed no signs of abating. In fact, a Sky News poll showed 'Rising public support for unions despite widespread strikes'.[25]

The phrasing of that headline is revealing. It presumes that the public and those striking are different people. And while the report mentioned that strikes had spread from transport and communication sectors to the NHS, it made no mention of solidarity. It's a presumption that Peter Brookes tried to exploit in his cartoon for *The Times* on the day of the first Demand Better march. He depicted a train driver sitting with his feet up on a cobwebbed train saying 'Up the workers!' while various workers stranded on the platform bellow back in angry unison, 'We are the workers!'

'My cartoon Saturday [in] @TheTimes asks "what about all the other workers?" #RailStrikes' he tweeted. I gave him an answer: '"All the other workers" were marching in solidarity with the #RailStrikes through the streets of

London today. I was there. We were chanting our support in Parliament Square. Everyone from firefighters to nurses to musicians and actors.'

Rishi Sunak, having become PM by default following Liz Truss' disastrous 45 days in office, tried a similar tack in the lead-up to Christmas 2022: 'What I'm not going to do is ask ordinary families up and down the country to pay an extra £1000 a year to meet the pay demands of the union bosses.' Back when I believed I was a middle-class luvvie, back when I considered my union as a separate entity from myself and back when I believed in meritocracy, I might have been swayed by this argument. But not anymore. Now, I saw right through the lazy rhetoric and I tweeted my response in a fit of rage: ''Union bosses' have far stronger mandates than this gutter government. They represent their members, workers from ordinary families, who were balloted and voted overwhelmingly for strikes. Our participation-prize PM can only dream of such legitimacy.'

I had grown up without any real understanding of trade unions as a means of political engagement. In fact, the narrative I'd consumed was that unions were collections of outdated militants with a tendency towards violence. I now understood that this demonisation was no coincidence. Just as Macaulay's *History of England* was used to wrest the national narrative away from the Chartists, modern governments and the media work tirelessly to keep popular working-class movements at bay. To understand how we change the future, we must first understand how we got here.

*

Right at the advent of the labour movement, at the start of the 19th century, the Conservative government passed laws to outlaw all strike action. These Combination Acts – which 'sentenced to three months in jail or to two months' hard labour any workingman who combined with another to gain an increase in wages or a decrease in hours' – were only repealed in 1824 in response to activism led by Francis Place and MP Joseph Hume.[26] Thanks to their efforts, the trade union movement was able to grow, leading to the Trades Union Congress being established in 1868 and the Trade Union Act in 1871, which gave a legal framework for strikes and organising for the first time.

The following century saw the formation of the Labour Party as the parliamentary wing of the labour movement, with its crowning post-war achievements being the welfare state and NHS. With a more equitable society coming into being, women working as sewing machinists at Ford Dagenham went on strike in 1968 to protest unequal pay, sparking the formation of the National Joint Action Campaign Committee for Women's Equal Rights. Their combined efforts led directly to the Equal Pay Act of 1970. But progress wasn't to last. The 1970s saw high inflation and economic stagnation bring trade unions and the Labour government into conflict. During the winter of 1978–79, dubbed the Winter of Discontent, strikes were rampant and Prime Minister James Callaghan's mandate lay in tatters. Following the loss of a vote of no confidence by one vote, Labour was ousted and Margaret Thatcher moved into

No.10, setting the stage for the most draconian anti-union laws since the Combination Acts.

The media was complicit in manufacturing consent for these crackdowns. On 18 June 1984, striking miners at Orgreave coking plant were met by thousands of police, 'including forty-two mounted officers holding staves twice as long as truncheons'. Echoing the events of Peterloo, workers were 'met with mounted charges' after which other 'units then ran into the field, attacking miners at random with baton blows'.[27] These attacks were unprovoked, and miners sustained significant injuries. But when the BBC broadcast footage of the confrontation, it was edited out of sequence to depict the miners as the instigators.[28] *The Times* reported that police had only acted after being 'overwhelmed by the pickets' while the *Sun* gleefully celebrated the 'amazing cavalry charge'.[29]

Public opinion was, predictably, heavily impacted. In August 1984, sixty-two percent of respondents to an NOP poll believed that picketing miners were responsible for the violence during the dispute. A few weeks after the events at Orgreave, twenty-seven percent said that their opinion of the police had actually improved.[30]

The three Employment Acts passed during the 1980s, together with the 1984 Trade Union Act and two further laws during the 1990s, gutted union power in the UK. The picketing of a place of work other than one's own –

secondary picketing, used to exert pressure and foster worker solidarity – was outlawed. Political strikes were made illegal, stripping working-class people of their voice in the realm of public affairs. Secret ballots and notice periods became a requirement for strike action. Closed-shops – the practice of employers agreeing to only hire union workers – were made illegal. And the election of union executives and industrial action ballots required postal voting, curtailing turnout and union engagement.

I personally felt the impact of this restriction in 2022 when I successfully stood for election to Equity's Council, our executive committee. I had to implore voters to fill out their paper ballots and post them in time. Such has been the success of Thatcher's legacy that many I spoke to didn't realise that this was a legal restriction and instead complained that Equity needed to modernise its voting practices. It's easy to see why this is the case when both Labour and the Conservatives elect their party leaders using online platforms.

The New Labour government did little to reverse this vandalism. In fact, during his 1997 election campaign, Tony Blair used the pages of *The Times* to proudly assert that 'The changes that we do propose would [still] leave British law the most restrictive on trade unions in the Western world.' And these restrictions were ratcheted up again by the coalition government in 2016, with strike action requiring a 50% turnout of relevant union members. With this history in mind, it becomes blindingly obvious that the wave of strikes seen in 2022 and 2023 were far more legitimate than Rishi

Sunak's premiership. Before standing unopposed, Sunak lost his party's leadership contest – voted for online – and didn't face a general election. Every union on the other hand cleared monumental legal hurdles before they got anywhere near their picket lines.

This onslaught of anti-union legislation saw union membership fall from a peak of over 12 million in 1979 to under 6 million by 2012, the lowest level since the 1940s.[31] And the impact was devastating. As union membership halved, the share of income going to the top 1% more than doubled.[32] The Institute for Public Policy Research reported in 2018 that 'inequality has risen to levels not seen for nearly a century' and noted that 'countries that have higher rates of collective bargaining have lower levels of inequality; and within firms where there is a trade union present, pay inequality is less.'[33] The Nordic countries, frequently held up as paragons of economic opportunity and equality, have the highest union density in the world and 80–90% of employees are covered by collective bargaining agreements.[34] The IPPR called for radical action to reverse the decline in collective bargaining and union membership in the UK in order to reduce inequality and boost wages. The Conservative government listened and we all lived happily ever after …

No. By the start of 2023, with the government claiming that pay rises were unaffordable, corporate profits in the UK hit an all-time high.[35] Shell's profits doubled to almost $40bn off the back of Russia's invasion of Ukraine.[36] And we were back on the streets, protesting yet another anti-union law. In response to mobilisation to challenge this extreme inequality, and with support for strikes showing no signs of waning, the Conservatives tabled the Strikes (Minimum Service Levels) Bill. This bill was labelled 'not fit for purpose' by an independent review and the government's own analysis warned it could lead to more strikes. The Joint Committee on Human Rights also found the bill likely to be incompatible with human rights law.[37] And yet, its proponents doggedly claimed they were bringing the UK into line with other European countries, prompting the European Trades Union Congress to issue a vehement retort: 'The UK already has among the most draconian restrictions on the right to strike in Europe, and the UK government's plans would push it even further away from normal, democratic practice across Europe.'[38]

This draconian history is why I came so late to class politics and trade unionism as a force for change. Many of my generation have grown up with little knowledge of what unions are, what they once were in the UK and what their role in a healthy democracy and economy is. Indeed, the silencing of working-class politics through anti-union legislation and the establishment of neoliberalism – that is free-market capitalism, deregulation, and limited government spending – as the economic norm, has seen class distorted into an issue of culture. As Kenan Malik observes:

> When the working class had a significant presence
> in politics, it was easy to see how issues of housing
> or wages related to economic and social policy. The
> more the working class was marginalized, the less class

was employed as a lens through which to understand social problems. As class declined as an explanatory tool, culture increasingly became, as we have seen, the medium through which social issues were refracted.[39]

I was my own obvious example. I didn't get involved with Equity out of a sense of class solidarity, I articulated Both Not Half and stood for election to the Race Equality Committee – the only way I knew how to have a political voice was to leverage my identity.

I'd perhaps be being too harsh on myself to say that my lack of class consciousness made me part of the problem. But I definitely wasn't yet part of the solution. By failing to ground my anti-racism in class politics, I was helping leave the door open for a wealthy and powerful few to weaponise the 'working class' in order to undermine the solidarity needed to fight inequality and social hierarchy. The 'UK Race Class Narrative Report', published by the Centre for Labour and Social Studies in May 2022, explains this as a 'divide-and-rule strategy', which aims:

> To racialise the working class as a white cultural minority, presenting them as the victims of immigration and advances in racial and gender equality. Rhetorically, such framing obscures from view the essential questions of inequality, power, wealth and oppression. Indeed, rather than reject class, certain Conservative politicians proclaim to be "the champions of the white working-class".

> Meanwhile, progressives are portrayed as class
> traitors – "the woke mob" – obsessively focused on
> race and ignoring the "real" working-class.

Populist politicians and shock jocks frequently invoke the
'white working class' while migrants and people of the global
majority are implied to be classless. It's a divisive, racialised
framing of class that 'has been so successful that some figures
in the political centre, and even on the left subscribe to it.' As
Robbie Shilliam explains in *Race and the Undeserving Poor*,
'the "white working class" is not a natural or neutral category
of political economy … Rather, this constituency must be
apprehended as an elite artefact of political domination.'[40] In
other words, the wealthy and powerful invoke the deserving
'white working class' as a tool to maintain their position,
and the overall class hierarchy, by drawing attention away
from the economic and social structures that perpetuate
poverty and inequality, and instead direct anger towards the
'undeserving poor', who more often than not are people of
the Global Majority.

If progressives fail to anchor issues of race and diversity in
the politics of class, we won't ever change the system. When
Liz Truss became Tory leader, the *Telegraph* trumpeted how
she had formed the 'most diverse Cabinet in history with no
white males in top jobs', with no mention of the fact that the
proportion of her senior ministers who had attended private
school was the highest for over 25 years.[41] Douglas Murray,
writing in the *Spectator*, criticised this headline, not for its
lack of class consciousness, but because 'it isn't remotely

new … after Theresa May, thank God a woman is back in charge, eh?' Bemoaning 'the diversity cult', his article goes on to predict that the Tories 'will keep pointing out that Labour has never been led by anyone other than a white man. And yet despite all this, Labour MPs will still accuse the government of institutional racism'.[42]

This criticism of Labour leadership is warranted and the party must be unflinching when it comes to examining why. But the case of white men leading Labour doesn't render its accusations against the government null and void. As Eve Livingston put it in 2017, 'a vote for an old white man can feel more progressive than one for a woman or minority wedded to a political status quo which has inequality at its core.'[43] At the general election that year, 73% of Black and Minority Ethnic votes went to Labour (led by old white man Jeremy Corbyn), just 19% voted for the Conservatives, while 'homeowners continue[d] to vote disproportionately Conservative, while renters tend to support Labour'.[44]

To be crystal clear: representation matters. Rishi Sunak becoming Britain's first PM of South Asian heritage (and a Punjabi!) was a big moment and seeing him light divas outside his Downing Street residence for Diwali in 2020 had an impact on me. I can't begin to imagine what that has done for brown kids who aspire to lead our nation. But discovering in 2023 that Sunak paid a lower rate of tax on his investment earnings in the previous year than I did on my income from work had an even greater impact.[45] Representation without class consciousness is window dressing.

*

We have been convinced by our overlords that there is no alternative to the status quo. The rich and powerful consciously design laws to keep the system rigged in their favour, while simultaneously telling us that nothing can be done and that our own visions for a more equal world are fantasies. This is a deliberate strategy to foster apathy. Their dominance doesn't need our consent, it simply requires us to stay silent. We don't need to win over the hearts and minds of these people, they know exactly what they are doing and why they are doing it. We win by making noise and mobilising our disaffected allies. Class consciousness and solidarity are our strongest weapon and armour. And our armies are our unions and community organisations. Join them. Shape them. Fight for their right to exist, to strike, to bargain collectively and to shape society. And fight especially hard when we disagree with them. As my Equity Council comrade Sam Swann recently put it to me: 'Unions are a site of struggle, not a person to cancel.'

Unions are also places of community and education. I articulated #BothNotHalf at a time when I felt lost and was questioning my sense of belonging, a journey that led me to my union. It was in union meetings that I learnt that I, as a mixed person, had a right to speak on matters of race, but also a duty to listen. At the end of my very first Race Equality Committee meeting, fellow committee member Nana St Bartholomew-Brown gave me a big hug, reassured me I belonged there and showed me photos of her mixed heritage grandchildren. It was an overwhelming moment. And it marked the start of a new and profound chapter of my political education, a journey that revealed with blinding clarity that the fight for mixed belonging is in fact the fight for social equality.

I now frequently find myself speaking to anyone who will listen about the essential need for unionisation within our society. I encourage people who have never been to a protest to come along and experience the palpable power of collective action. I'm also very conscious that I don't want to be overbearing and turn people off. Whenever I'm in conversation I make a habit of leaving some dead air to allow people to change the subject. But they rarely do. I've been amazed. People lean in. More recently, they've been starting the conversations, knowing that I might have some answers. They ask questions. They come alive. Because they're being presented with a way to fight back.

If that's you, come join the resistance.

8

ONE NOT BOTH

We shall not cease from exploration
And the end of all our exploring
Will be to arrive where we started
And know the place for the first time.
T.S. ELIOT, 'LITTLE GIDDING'

'I HELP RUN a nearby trattoria called La Pizzica Restaurant at which you must let me feed you! I am the older one after all! Sikh filial piety and all that!' His email had come through at close to midnight. I got back to him the following morning, sympathising with his sense of duty, 'I know the feeling too well. My younger sister often crashes with me and my compulsion to feed her is bizarre.' It was June 2018. We set a date for the following month.

This was to be my first meeting with Gurbachan 'Gorby' Jandu, a PhD researcher from the department of politics at Birkbeck College. He had reached out via my agent with an interview request, explaining that he was seeking out 'a newer generation of diverse Sikhs who are making real headway in fields hitherto less common for the community … it's a nice thing to see a Punjabi Brit doing such work'. The email had come out of the blue and had taken me aback. I replied, eagerly, 'I can't tell you how much joy it brings me, looking the way I do, to be recognised as a British Punjabi outside of my family.' 2018 was the year I wrote my Anglo-Indian TV pilot, the script that laid bare my inner turmoil and mental health struggles, and Gorby's email felt like a lifeline. A warm hug of acceptance. I hoped our conversation might give me some answers.

A couple of weeks later, I set off down Fulham Road to meet Gorby. He reminded me of my dad. He didn't look like him, and he was younger, but his cropped hair, stubble and hirsute forearms felt familiar. We started with a glass of prosecco, before moving on to a montepulciano. While Gorby's interest lay in quizzing me on my sense of national identity, I was much more concerned with the ease with which he referred to me as a Sikh. Reflecting on our conversation five years later, in 2023, Gorby recalls his surprise at my discomfort.

'I remember telling you I'm not an outwardly looking Sikh either; I used to wear a turban but I don't anymore. But I've never had to confront whether I was a Sikh. I approached you as a subject for my research but I really came to see you as a context for my own mixed heritage daughter, because I suddenly realised that race could be a problem for her. I'd never thought about it that way. I gave her an Indic but not a traditionally Sikh name, and instead of Kaur she has a Welsh middle name, because her mum's family are all from Wales. I wanted her to feel comfortable with all aspects of her heritage. But I had never considered that she might grow up to not feel Sikh.'

For Gorby, I was obviously Sikh. I spoke Punjabi. My name was steeped in Sikh history. There wasn't any doubt. But for me, asserting myself as Sikh felt like a big step. I felt far more comfortable calling myself Punjabi. That was an identity grounded in culture and custom, whereas Sikh felt explicitly religious. I wasn't religious. I knew how to conduct myself in a gurdwara but, other than some very basic principles of equality, I knew very little about the specific teachings of the gurus. I claimed Sikh *heritage*, but I was concerned that were I to call myself 'a Sikh' I would be opening myself up to interrogation. Were I a brown man, like Gorby, I doubt it would raise any eyebrows, but a white guy with short hair? That required explanation. I'd come to this dinner hoping to find some answers, but I left with yet another question: am I Sikh?

By the time we came to do the formal interview in January 2019, just two weeks after I'd coined #BothNotHalf, I was struggling for an answer. We met up in West London again. Thinking it a fitting event, I had invited Gorby as my guest to the launch of *Turbans and Tales: Portraits of Contemporary Sikh Identity* at the National Army Museum, the event that would prompt me to journal and eventually write the essay that became my TEDx talk.

We arrived an hour early and found a table in the mezzanine café. While the events team were setting up, Gorby clicked on his dictaphone and I found myself doubling down on my answer from six months prior: I didn't feel I could call myself 'a Sikh', but I was confident in my Sikh heritage. I was 'culturally Sikh'. I had grown up in a Sikh household and was familiar and comfortable with Sikh spaces and practices, but I had no religious practice of my own. The kara I wore – a steel bangle, an article of faith that had belonged to my late grandfather – was a symbol of that cultural connection. That was the answer I gave. But whereas articulating #BothNotHalf had brought with it an immediate and profound sense of relief and ease, calling myself 'culturally Sikh' left me feeling dissatisfied. Before I could dwell on it, the event was underway. I filled a paper plate high with complimentary samosas and began to examine the portraits that were now on display: men and women, mostly brown but a couple of white and Black faces also, and all of them wearing turbans. Not one of them looked like me, which seemed to confirm my suspicion that I was not 'a Sikh'.

But maybe I was? Maybe I wanted to be? A seed had been planted in my mind just before Christmas. A germ of a thought that I had yet to properly examine. Why hadn't I mentioned this to Gorby? Why had I felt the need to give him such a concrete answer? What was I afraid of?

Growing up Sikh

I have a distinct memory of coming home from primary school, standing in the hallway, taking off my coat and asking BG, 'Is God real?' She replied with emphatic certainty, 'Of course.' I didn't ask any follow-ups. The perturbed look on her face and the shock in her voice had thrown me. At school,

I'd sensed there was some debate on the matter. But for BG, it was as if I'd questioned the existence of gravity. I felt almost stupid for asking. But my doubt lingered.

I grew up in a Sikh household, but not a religious family. Portraits of Guru Nanak and Guru Gobind Singh hung on the wall, their long beards and haloed turbans radiating saintliness. But on the opposite side of the living room was a photo of my grandad, clean shaven with a short crop of hair; he had adopted the look as a concession to the politics of 1960s Britain. By the time I was born, his hair was as long as BG's once more and his pagh was back – a mark of his confidence and success – but he would still get his beard trimmed at the barbers. I have no memory of prayers being recited at home and the only mention of the divine tended to be BG exclaiming '*Hai Rabba!*' whenever she heard bad news or her arthritis was playing up. But we were weekend regulars at the gurdwara.

Ramgarhia Gurdwara on Meynell Road was housed in an old red-brick industrial building. The only indication that it was a place of worship was the bright saffron Nishan Sahib, the triangular Sikh flag, fluttering in the wind, and a sign in Punjabi that I couldn't read. We would arrive in the bustling entrance hall, full of people that looked like Grandad and BG. And it would be loud. The high ceiling and the hard floor amplified every conversation into a cacophonous din. Through the mass of voices, someone might call out to BG, an old friend from her factory days maybe, or to Grandad, an ex-colleague from the Post Office perhaps. I never knew who they were but they always seemed delighted to see me.

After we'd taken off our shoes and stowed them in a pigeonhole, I would check that my head was covered. My rumaal of choice was one of my English grandmother's old silk handkerchiefs. I loved it and I loved wearing it. The paisley design felt right at home among the women's patterned shawls – the motif having originally travelled to Britain, and the looms of Paisley, from colonial India in the form of imported Kashmiri textiles. I would tie it on my head in exactly the same way as when I dressed up as a pirate. BG would then hand me a couple of coins and we'd weave through the sea of shoes to the diwan hall.

As we passed through the fire doors that reminded me of school, chaos would give way to calm. The commotion of the entrance hall gave way to the melodic drone of the harmonium, and my feet would welcome the warmth of the carpet underfoot. Men sat on the floor to the left, women to the right, on large white cotton sheets, with a clear stretch of carpet running down the centre. This walkway led to the palki, an ornate canopy, under which the Guru Granth Sahib was housed on a platform, supported by cushions draped with colourful fabrics. Here, an elderly man with a regal blue turban would be sat, fanning the holy book with a chaur, a fly whisk, as a sign of reverence.

I have no memory of not knowing what to do. I would walk down the central aisle to the palki, place my coins on the edge of the golak, the collection box, and watch with glee as they slid out of view and made a satisfying *ching* as they landed. I'd then matha tek: bow down before the Guru Granth Sahib and touch my forehead to the soft rug.

We'd then stand with our palms pressed together, before Grandad would take his place on the men's side, while I'd follow BG to the women's. All the while, kirtan crackled over the ageing PA system.

I had no understanding of kirtan as devotional singing, nor that the words the musicians sang were verses from the Guru Granth Sahib, sung in particular raags so as to evoke particular emotional states. But as soon as I heard the tabla, I was transported. The sound of the dayan, the smaller drum, rang in my mind with blissful clarity, while the modulating bayan, the bass, resounded thrillingly in my gut. As I grew older and braver, I would venture away from BG and creep to the very front of the men's side where the performers sat on an elevated platform. I would sit, transfixed by the tabla players' hands, dancing over the skins with impossible speed. And I would dream of one day learning the secret for myself.

My heart would sink when the kirtan ended. As I clung to the last few notes of the tabla a man with a flowing beard and a regal blue or saffron turban would approach the lectern on the other side of the palki and begin talking in Punjabi. I knew that I understood Punjabi, that I spoke it, but the exegesis and formal announcements were wasted on me. The sounds were all familiar but I could glean no meaning. I would grow bored, start to fidget and distract myself by examining the various turbans and chunnis on display. I would find myself pleasantly and a little melancholically confused by how everyone looked so familiar, like family, but with the knowledge that they were absolute strangers.

Eventually the talking would come to an end and the kirtan would start again, but only briefly, much to my disappointment. I'd then take my cue from those around me to stand and fold my hands for a prayer I didn't know, before sitting for a reading from the Guru Granth Sahib that I didn't understand. But my patience was about to be rewarded. The sweet fragrance of karah parshad would now begin to waft through the hall. Equal parts wholemeal flour, sugar and butter, karah parshad was the most delicious thing in the world. Volunteers would circulate, dishing out small handfuls of the warm thick paste and I would eagerly await my turn with palms outstretched. If I was lucky, and grinned hard, I'd get an extra-large portion, along with an approving smile. I'd fold my hands in thanks, feel the warmth of the parshad press against my fingers, and then tuck in.

It would now be lunchtime and with my appetite whetted, I'd look to BG for the signal to make our way to the langar hall, the free community kitchen on the other side of the building where we'd fill our steel trays with dhal, vegetable curries, rotis and rice pudding prepared by volunteers. It was the same food we had at home but for some reason it was always more delicious here. 'Langar always tastes better,' BG would tell me – a fact, not an opinion. I'd go back and ask for seconds, in Punjabi, and would be rewarded with more than I could eat. But I did, or BG came to my rescue. We'd then say our goodbyes, find our shoes, and head to the car. It was the most perfect way to spend a Sunday. I felt at home, but I understood none of it.

What I did know, however, was what we weren't. We

weren't Christian, but we did Christmas presents, hunted for Easter eggs and my dad read me and my sister Bible stories. My mum had grown up in a largely secular family, but my dad had attended St Joseph's Convent School in Bathinda, Punjab. He was fond of the parables and was keen to ensure we were familiar with them.

We weren't Hindu. I had Hindu friends at school but their names sounded different. They worshipped multiple gods with multiple arms. But we all celebrated Diwali. By observing my grandparents' behaviours, I came to understand Hindus as a kind of distant relative. Muslims, on the other hand, seemed to be regarded as strangers, enemies even, and I found this perplexing. Whenever BG recalled fleeing her burning house during Partition, she spoke with great respect for the Muslim family that had sheltered her. Without them, she and her family would have likely perished in the violence. Equally, my grandad spoke proudly of how his family had protected a Muslim child in their village by claiming she was their Sikh daughter. But he treated my aunty, who had married a Muslim, like a pariah. As he grew more elderly, his prejudice waned, but I was well into my teens before I ever met my uncle.

Growing up, this was my experience of religion. A Sunday outing, tabla, karah parshad, langar, Christmas presents, Easter eggs, Diwali fireworks and family trauma. Rituals, festivals and conflicts. Everything was external. At a distance from me. And it all seemed somewhat optional. I was never pressured into anything, and I was far too young for marrying a Muslim to be a concern.

Into the wild

In May 2016, I felt invincible. I'd started the year on set with Cillian Murphy shooting *Peaky Blinders*. *Skin A Cat*, a play by Isley Lynn, had taken Vault Festival by storm and I'd just finished the tour of *Wipers*. I was feeling deeply satisfied, exhausted and I needed a holiday. I soon discovered that my measly budget wasn't going to get me to a sunny beach, and as I daydreamed about all the places I longed to visit, it occurred to me that I had never explored my own backyard. I had never been to the Lake District. Inspired by a scene from *Wipers*, I began to imagine cooking up some dhal in a mess tin and repurposed my holiday funds for camping equipment. Wandering off into the wilds had always appealed as a child; I was now 25 years old and could do it.

My 65-litre backpack, a gift from BG, found at Age Concern for £5, was abominably overpacked and the hip belt left me with bruises the size of fists. But when I stood atop Scafell Pike, having climbed up the steepest route after two nights alone under the stars, I literally googled 'how tall is Everest'. I felt on top of the world. And deeply moved. Walking solo among the tarns, beneath cloudless skies and listening to the *Lord of the Rings* soundtrack, I found myself tearing up. The sheer beauty of the natural world was overwhelming. It was coaxing something out of me. On my third and final night, with my tent pitched high on Illgill Head, overlooking Wast Water, I felt profound clarity, serenity and inspiration. This was the very spirit of adventure.

And then a few months later, in August, I was in hospital recovering from the emergency surgery to remove my ruptured appendix. I was unable to raise my arm for a glass of water, let alone walk. I had never felt so weak in all my life. I'd previously looked at my body in the mirror as a way to gauge my progress at the gym, but after 10 days at The Royal London Hospital I just wanted it to work.

While convalescing on my mum's sofa, I clicked 'book'. I couldn't fathom being well enough to take the flight, but I had been assured that by January, I would be sufficiently recovered. New Zealand and its unparalleled beauty would be my reward for surviving and the salve my bruised soul sorely needed. Sat on the plane on New Year's Day 2017, at the request of my sister, I started a journal: *I've put my ear plugs in to write. The same strange pink candy looking buds I used in hospital. A small but stark reminder of how lucky I am to be going on this adventure.*

This was going to be the trip of a lifetime. A physical challenge, but a much-needed escape and a return to the bliss I'd experienced in the Lakes. But the South Island had other plans for me. I had travelled to the other side of the world in search of peace but I was about to discover a deep disquiet lurking within me.

*

Another wave slammed into me and the icy salt water burnt the cracked skin of my armpits, now lacerated by the coarse seams of my buoyancy jacket. My fingers were frozen around my paddle and I was pulling furiously at the frothing sea, but our kayak could do nothing to fight the headwind. Seb was sitting behind me in the driving seat, urging me to dig deep. But I was spent. I was exhausted before the storm even hit. I felt weak. And I was angry. Seb's plans had been too ambitious and now he was trying to turn the unfolding nightmare into a teachable moment. We were only caught in this weather because we'd had to turn back to get the camera he'd forgotten at our lunch stop. Our friends Zak and Henry had pulled ahead under blue skies and were almost at the mainland. The best we could do was hold our position and pray we didn't capsize.

But I couldn't maintain my rage. His relentless positivity cut through the gusts and kept me going. We held our position, and he rallied me to drive hard in the lulls. We inched towards the coast and when we finally approached the shore I fell into the shallows on my hands and knees. I was now so cold, the sea water felt like it was boiling. And I did my best to hold back tears. I hadn't been able to take in anything over the last three days. *I'm struggling*, I wrote in my journal. *I'm finding it hard to relax into Seb and Zak's easy going outlook. I'm not comfortable not being in control. It's horrible because I don't feel entirely present. It's like I'm witnessing everything at a distance. Saw dolphins, but felt like I didn't really see them.* This was not the peace I had come looking for. And it continued to elude as we wound our way south along the west coast.

I feel a dull and lonely ache inside of me, I wrote on 14 January. *It feels like waiting to sit an exam and all the joy in the world is tinged with a sense of dread and unhappiness.*

It makes me feel like a helpless child. I'd called my mum to let it all out and felt like I'd failed as an adult. And following my grandpa's stroke on Christmas Eve, I felt newly aware of her own mortality. *Imagining a time when I can't call to hear her voice, and know I'm loved and it's all okay, terrifies me.*

The majesty of my surroundings seemed only to amplify my despair. I'd hit rock bottom. The day before, I'd misjudged a distance while driving our hire car and dropped our front right wheel into a steep ditch. The wheels spun uselessly and though it wasn't long until a passing lumberjack crew came to our aid with a winch, I felt utterly stranded. Why wasn't anything working? Why did I feel so damn miserable?

At the time, and despite the candour of my journal, I didn't recognise the signs that my mental health was in a bad place. I didn't know I needed help. I didn't know that I was desperately searching for a way to understand myself, to find a sense of peace and belonging. But looking back at the video diaries Henry was shooting on the trip, it's abundantly clear that I was grasping for answers. After a particularly gruelling and wet trek in Nelson Lakes, he'd asked me what the appeal of the wilderness was:

'When you're on a hike it stills your mind ... By connecting with those basic needs ... It relaxes your mind and allows thoughts to flow more freely, I feel. It relaxes your grip on the thoughts at the back of your mind. It allows you to reconnect with yourself, your inner life. I feel like a lot of the world is filled with distractions that are stopping you from accessing your inner life ...'

I was certain that I was fine and that I simply needed to reconnect with the 'real me'. I suspect this is also why I offered Gorby such a concrete answer about my Sikh identity in early 2019. Having articulated #BothNotHalf, I became convinced I had the answer I needed. It was easier to commit to 'culturally Sikh' than consider the alternative: I still wasn't entirely sure of who I was.

And so, back in 2017, in the hope of finding some personal stillness, we agreed I would have three days in Wanaka to hike alone. Traversing Jack Hall's Saddle at a height of 1,275 metres, I didn't find any answers, but the view was breathtaking and the problem seemed to form more clearly in my mind. *I'm finding I'm in pursuit of solitude and intimacy,* I journalled, without any consideration for the contradiction, *I'm discovering a deep fear of life beyond parents. A new shift into adulthood. A woman on the way up told me a friend of theirs had died on the route we were walking. She said it with such lightness and humour but I felt it so keenly. The horror of such a fall. A life affirming walk becoming their death. I seem to have forgotten how to ignore death.*

I returned to Seb, Zak and Henry feeling lighter and our final few days together were full of laughter, high jinks and the certain knowledge that lifelong friendships had been forged. I returned to the UK with wonderful memories, stunning photographs and a newfound curiosity about my own being. And it was this curiosity that prompted me to ask Seb what he'd been talking about when he'd been taking himself off to 'do some headspace' each day. 'It's a meditation app,' he replied.

Into the mind

I'd always been a bit wary of meditation. And yoga. Basically, anything Eastern that was popular with hippies and Instagram. The most challenging rehearsal day I had when doing *Skin A Cat* was a scene in which my character, Gerry, a middle-class white man in his 50s, tells Alana about his spiritual connection to India. I played all the men in the play and had no issue embodying teenage angst and workshopping ways to stage anal sex, but simply sitting in front of my co-star and saying the line 'this cave I go to in Ajanta, inside is this enormous carving of Amitabh' felt almost impossible. And I struggled to articulate why. Sharan Dhaliwal encountered a similar problem while writing her book *Burning My Roti* and found an answer through speaking to Kallie Schut, a British-born yoga teacher of Indian heritage: 'This practice about healing, recovery, spiritual enlightenment, working through the cycles of life and death, has been taken away from people of South Asian heritage and been sold as a commodity, as a packaged box with a pretty bow and some essential oils in it.'

Looking back at that rehearsal day, I see now that the problem wasn't Gerry: the problem was me. I was yet to confront my own relationship with Eastern spiritual traditions.

When I sat down to try Headspace for the first time, I was not actively exploring my spiritual heritage. I was simply trying to shake off jet lag and control my emotions. The app's lack of religious trappings and language avoided my Gerry-reflex going off, while the fact that it was co-founded by a former Buddhist monk assuaged any doubts I had about the legitimacy of the endeavour. Had I stopped to think about it, I might have recognised that the absence of cultural context was another kind of box and bow. I was being sold a commodity but the minimalist packaging had caught my millennial eye. And I liked what I was sampling.

This was the first time in my adult life that I'd consciously sat down to sit in silence and do nothing. In doing so, childhood memories of attending Sikh meditation groups with Grandad and BG rose to the surface. I worried that boredom would get the better of me, but Andy Puddicombe's guidance kept me focused on my breath and I soon began to experience something quite familiar. This was the kind of calm I found while out walking, usually on day three of a multi-day hike. But here I was, connecting to it, after just a few minutes of breathing. This was a revelation. The salve I needed to cope with the stresses of life. It wasn't long before I'd tapped in my card details, paid for an annual subscription and was obsessing over my run streak.

Cut to a year and a half later: my 28th birthday party, where my friend Andrei reflected that everything I was saying about my wild camping adventures, meditation and the pursuit of peace sounded a lot like a school of thought he'd recently taken an interest in: Stoicism.

*

[21:51, 07/01/2019] Jassa Ahluwalia: Been doing more stoicism reading today. It's like stumbling on Yoda or something. I've been really working with it alongside Sikh philosophy these last couple of months and I feel so damn content.

I sent this message to Andrei a couple of hours after posting my Quorn dhal skit on Instagram. It's quite bizarre looking back through my messages, I hadn't realised how closely linked these events were. But it's no coincidence, I suppose, that my #BothNotHalf journey began around the same time as my first foray into philosophy. I wasn't just looking to resolve my sense of mixed identity, I was looking for answers about how to live.

The connection Andrei had made between my outdoors adventures and meditative states was the Stoic idea of 'cultivating a relationship with poverty'.[1] In a letter to Lucilius Junior, procurator of Sicily, philosopher and statesman Seneca wrote, 'Set aside now and then a number of days during which you will be content with the plainest of food, and very little of it, and with rough, coarse clothing, and will ask yourself, "Is this what one used to dread?"'[2]

My camping trips were far cries from poverty, but I saw what Andrei recognised: I was courting simplicity and discomfort in order to test and better know myself. I ate oats and lentils, my clothes were purely functional (and changed far less frequently than in regular life), my transport was my own two feet, and I had to find ways to cope with my eczema without the comforts of a warm shower, a soft towel and an industrial sized tub of moisturiser. This was, in a way, my attempt to live 'in accordance with nature'.

This is the fundamental principle of Stoicism. As Robin

Campbell explains in the introduction to his translation of
Seneca's letters, 'the Stoics saw the world as a single great
community' governed 'by a supreme providence' known by
various names including 'nature, the spirit or purpose of the
universe, destiny, even (by way of concession to traditional
religion) "the gods"'. The purpose of life was to 'live in
conformity with the divine will' and joyously accept all that
fate bestowed.[3]

The idea that I could live a life of profound peace, free of
reluctance, was deeply attractive. And I was amazed by how
accessible and relevant these ancient texts were. I had always
assumed that the likes of Zeno, Seneca, Cicero, Epictetus and
Virgil were readable only through, and for the purpose of,
scholarship. *It's like I've discovered it's for me and to be used,
not academic material for study*, I wrote in my journal. And it
wasn't just the mononymous Greeks and Romans who had
caught my attention.

Just before Christmas, I'd stumbled upon a video on
Twitter emblazoned with the caption 'Guru Nanak's
Greatest Message'. I'd tapped on the video with a fair amount
of scepticism. The video showed a Sikh man, Satpal Singh,
dressed very traditionally, wearing a blue dumalla turban
that marked him out as an Amritdhari Sikh, with a flowing
beard, sat in front of a microphone in what appeared to be a
gurdwara hall. I was expecting a sermon on the superiority of
the Sikh way of life, the need to grow one's hair and wake up
early. What he actually said came as a shock. 'Guru Nanak
Dev Ji did not believe in God,' he began.

Guru Nanak Dev Ji knew God, and there's a very
big difference ... we talk about: dedicate your life
to God ... well what is God? Maybe with a white
beard, sitting in the clouds? Is this the God that Guru
Nanak Dev Ji's talking about? The whole of [Sikh]
wisdom has been summarised most beautifully and so
intelligently into one single digit: '1'. 'Ik' means that
everything in the whole entire creation is one thing,
that looks like many different things. You go out into
nature and you look at a mountain and you look at
lakes, but the thought that comes in our mind is wow,
Waheguru, this nature that you've made is beautiful.
Because for us, Waheguru is far away ... When do
we ever say, 'I can see you in the river, I can see you
in the birds, I can see you in the sky, I can see you
in everyone, I can see you in me.' The wave doesn't
understand that it is the ocean, the human doesn't
understand that it is God. 'Sabh Gobind Hai, Sabh
Gobind Hai, Gobind Bin Nahi Koi ... Everything
is God. Everything is God. There is nothing except
God.' The God that we're praying to is right here.
What do we do with this wisdom? How does it
change our life?

The video cut off after two minutes and twenty seconds,
the maximum upload time on Twitter, and I sat in stunned
silence. I remembered asking BG about the existence of God
and her answer suddenly seemed to make more sense. I'd
been asking about the dude in the sky, she'd been talking

about the essence of reality. And the mention of mountains and lakes resonated with unexpected force. During my first wandering in the Lake District, I found myself welling up at the sheer magnificence of the tarns, glistening in the midday sun, framed by lush green marshes and dramatic outcrops. Was this … God? I had never thought to thank an Almighty for what I was witnessing, I was looking out on prehistoric geological processes, explained by the natural sciences, not intelligent design. But the experience of it? The experience of beauty, that sense of myself and the world suddenly melding into each other, that bliss, was this what Guru Nanak was talking about?

What had really struck me about the video, before really listening to what was being said, was that it was in English. Sikh ideas have largely been confined to Punjabi despite the fact that the Guru Granth Sahib is written in multiple dialects and languages. This is often overlooked by virtue of the fact that the text is presented in a single script – Gurmukhi – which is now most commonly associated with Punjabi. To hear Sikh discourse in English was incredibly refreshing and encouraged me to lean in. But I remained cautious. After all, I still maintained that I was not a religious person.

I was explaining all of this to actor and filmmaker (and photographer of my author headshot) Cristian Solimeno over a pint. 'I'm getting really fascinated by Sikh philosophy,' I shared with him. 'It doesn't seem all that religious, it kind of reminds me of the Stoics. I've always been taught that Sikhism was a religion that believed in one God but the more I'm digging into it, Guru Nanak was talking about the idea that there's no real separation between anything, that everything is One. Non-duality.' This is a very inaccurate recollection. I have no WhatsApp messages, journal entries or voice notes to go on, but I said something like it. Whatever my exact words were, the prevailing feeling was one of recognition: non-duality spoke to my conflicted sense of identity. If there was only One, then my whole 'am I English or Punjabi, British or Indian' debate dissolved into irrelevance. In my TEDx talk I say that #BothNotHalf came to me in a moment of spontaneous realisation, prompted by seeing the word 'half' in the comments. That's true. But if I had to pinpoint when the seed for that realisation was planted, this conversation would be my best guess.

I returned to Satpal Singh. He had founded a YouTube channel in 2013 called Nanak Naam and I soon discovered a whole series of lectures, in English, on the meaning of Japji Sahib, the opening composition of the Guru Granth Sahib. I had first encountered Japji Sahib during a brief stint attending the Punjabi school at Meynell Road Gurdwara. I had been made to memorise the opening verse, known as the Mool Mantar, and I had never forgotten it. But I had also never been taught what it meant. They were just sounds. I had no idea that this 'root mantra' contained the very essence of Sikh thought, that the rest of Japji Sahib was an explanation of these ideas, nor did I have any clue that these 40 verses contained the entirety of Sikh philosophy, acting as a thesis for the 5,824 verses that followed. I began to crave long Tube journeys for the opportunity to listen and make notes on my phone. This was still very much an intellectual exercise for me. But there was something else too, a sense of connection. I was beginning to forge my own relationship with my Sikh heritage.

The first stanza after the Mool Mantar, pauri one, the 'first step', begins by saying that ritual practice is a futile endeavour.

> By bathing a hundred thousand times purity is not attained,
> Through silence in meditative poses, quietness of the mind is not achieved,
> The hunger of the desirous is not alleviated by
> seizing all that the world offers, nor does hunger and abstention.

Wow. This seemed entirely at odds with my experience of Sikh practice, bathing in and drinking the holy waters at sites of pilgrimage, meditation, reading all the texts, fasting. My whole understanding of Sikhi was being turned upside down. Who was *this* Guru Nanak? The final line of the pauri reads: *hukam razai chalna nanak likhiya naal.* 'Says Nanak, walk on the path of hukam, the command that is written and resides within you.' As soon as Satpal began explaining the concept of hukam, I was struck by a flash of recognition. 'It doesn't say accept hukam,' Satpal said. 'It doesn't say obey hukam, it says *walk* on the *path* of hukam.' This was what the Stoics taught! 'For Fate the willing leads, the unwilling drags along,' writes Seneca, quoting Cicero. Neither the Stoics nor the Sikh gurus deny human agency, but they both understood that the universe is unfolding without regard for human emotion and much of life is outside of our control. Satpal likens this to swimming in a river. You can swim wherever you desire. You can fight the flow and head upstream, or even plead with the river to take a different course, but your efforts will ultimately tire and disappoint you. You risk drowning. Become one with the flow of the river though and the water will carry you. Your strokes will feel effortless as you wind your way through life.

The metaphor made perfect sense. I loved it. What a brilliant concept. I noted it on my phone with satisfaction. But I had skimmed over a line in the middle of the verse: *Even if your thousand clever ideas become a hundred thousand theories, not a single one will help.* Later that year, in the summer of 2019, I would be confronted with this lesson in the form of a very real river.

Vishnu Schist

When Kevin Shen first asked if I was interested in joining his Grand Canyon expedition holiday, I had zero sense of how lucky I was. The permits for independently rafting the Colorado River are like gold dust and only available by lottery. Some people go a lifetime waiting for their shot. So precious are the permits that the application process allows you to name a successor, at the point of submission – if you or they can't use it, you have to forfeit it. Kevin had inherited his from a friend whose wife was having a baby.

Kevin knew I had outdoors experience and shooting *The*

Rezort had been an intense adventure, so he figured I'd be well suited to 18 days off grid, with six strangers, under challenging circumstances. I resolved to treat this opportunity with the same reverence as I would an acting role. It would be a huge step up from my three-night hikes in the English countryside, but I couldn't wait to discover what I would learn.

With a few exceptions, the rapids of the Colorado River get more violent the deeper the river cuts into the canyon. As a guide for rafters, each rapid is assigned a rating on a scale of 1 to 10, with 1 being flat water, while 10s are rare monsters requiring expert oarsmanship. We wouldn't have to worry about the 10s for several days yet, with the real behemoth – Lava Falls – acting as our expedition finale. Plus, I was just along for the ride. We had four experienced oarswomen who would be doing the real work, my job was simply to spot obstacles, throw my weight and hold on. But it became clear on day 1 that I had underestimated what lay ahead. What I thought was our first rapid turned out to be an unmarked riffle. The waves felt huge. A fear I hadn't experienced since childhood began to gnaw at my stomach. My logical brain told me I'd get used to the rapids day by day. But what about tomorrow? Acting like a sphinx guarding the entrance to the canyon's depths was the rapid known as House Rock, an 8.

As our first major encounter, we pulled in upriver and scouted the rapid from land. The heat of the day was beginning to hit and cicadas serenaded us. I couldn't read the water yet, but I was told there was a clear and easy line to the right of the big standing waves. Cool. But there was a new seriousness to our oarswomen and I felt a little tense as I clipped up my life vest.

I was in Elizabeth's raft, our trip leader, and I was comforted by her authority. The only drawbacks were: 1) We'd be the first to go; and, 2) Her raft carried a cooler in its front, meaning I would be riding on top, at the level of the inflated side tubes, rather than nestled in the bow.

The rapid was out of sight and the river had become glassy, smooth and silent – the tell-tale signs that we were on the approach, Elizabeth informed me. I could hear my heart pounding in my helmet. Then, as we rounded the bend, a roar unlike anything I'd ever heard was unleashed. A primal, eternal sound. It slammed into my gut – terrifying and electrifying. I could feel my adrenaline brewing and as white froth slipped into view, I gripped the perimeter line.

A massive wave looms over me, the jaws of a beast, frothing violently yet motionless, anchored to the riverbed. I cower before the gaping maw. I'm looking down. Fuck. We're falling in. Riding up. I don't know what's going on but my gut tells me this is wrong. This isn't the line. This is the hole. The one place we're not meant to be. I hear shouting but I don't hear what. My face is close to the torrent now, my face wet with its wrath, we're tilting up sideways, fast approaching 90 degrees. The raft is slow, sluggish, water rushes over the bow with impossible force. I know what's coming. And there's nothing I can do.

Our raft, fully laden with all our equipment and food, was

flipped like a rubber duck. As I began to fall into the torrent, I kicked away from the cooler to ensure I was clear of the steel frame as it came crashing down. I was underwater now. Clear green water. Bubbles swirling. No sense of up or down. Something struck my helmet, an oar maybe. The cold was intense. I'd barely managed to take a breath before the plunge. When would I pop up? Oh fuck. This was real. This wasn't a theme park ride. I was at the bottom of the Grand Canyon, our only communication was via satellite, the only way out was the river, or rescue helicopter. The realisation hit that there was no guarantee I was going to survive. I had never known fear like this.

And then I popped up, my life vest tight and secure. I could barely breathe but I remembered Kourtnie mentioning that your windpipe closes up when the back of your throat is hit by cold water. That key bit of information kept me calm long enough to remember I needed to try and breathe in the trough of the waves to avoid sucking in water. I was still in the rapid. The raft appeared on my right and I grabbed the perimeter line once again. Elizabeth was on the other side. She looked shaken and shocked, like a parent in danger, but she gave clear orders and we swam the raft into an eddy. The river gets warmer the deeper it goes but here, only a few miles down from Glen Canyon dam, more than eight minutes in the water risks hypothermia.

Guru Nanak was right. *Even if your thousand clever ideas become a hundred thousand theories, not a single one will help.* I had read this stuff, theorised, but I wasn't yet living it. One of the first things I'd done when we'd reflipped the raft was retrieve my ammo can, a small watertight steel box used to store personal items. It had been suspended upside down in the water for a fair while and I was worried my journal had gone the way of the bread. Thankfully, the rubber gasket had held firm and the water damage was minimal. Only my copy of Epictetus' *Discourses and Selected Writings* had warped slightly. I fanned the pages in the sun and read the first couple of pages. One line jumped out: *I must die. But must I die bawling?*

So, this was the lesson I was here to learn. To confront death. It feels quite overblown writing this now, but at the time, cut off from the world and surrounded by 1.7 billion-year-old rock named Vishnu Schist, this kind of thinking felt entirely apt. The gauntlet had been thrown down. Would I pass the trial?

To discover the calm beyond the drop, the present
ever changing moment, the clarity of mind in the
flip to know my inability to breathe was a natural
reaction … it is deeply rewarding to know I can push
beyond that fear and find not victory, but peace. I
feel I have met Fear on this trip, not the casual jump-
and-see of a bungee or a skydive, I've seen its face in
the holes of these rapids, gaping, frothing jaws formed
by rock and time. Been thinking of Mool Mantar:
nirbhau [without fear]. And the Stoics. Fear is like
expectation, both are fabrications of the mind.

Fear had taken on a physical form in my mind. A face

formed of coal, existing in darkness, illuminated by the red glow of his burning eyes. Every time I closed my eyes he was there, taunting me, mocking me. But over the next week I underwent a transformation. I began to court Fear. As the rapids grew more technical, I welcomed him in. I sought him out. Because in his presence I melted into the moment.

And then it was Day 14: Lava Falls, the 11-metre drop where the Colorado River explodes. We scouted the carnage of water and rock with calm efficiency and as we pushed off to begin our run, Fear returned to stare at me from the shore. But he couldn't touch me. I saw that now. He could only watch. And I smiled. I smiled so hard. I pulled my life vest tight, buckled my helmet, gripped the perimeter line. I was ready to die. Truly prepared. An enormous standing wave shrieked into vision on my left. Our line was good. We dropped in.

*

As I recounted my tale of the Grand Canyon, two months later in September 2019, Parmjit Singh looked at me with that glint in his eye I'd come to love. We'd known each other for just over a year now and our friendship was somewhat unexpected. He was a historian and writer who had helped found the UK Punjab Heritage Association and its publishing wing Kashi House, an intellectual force who leafed through disintegrating parchment in much the same way I scrolled on Twitter. We'd met at the opening night of *Empire of the Sikhs* at SOAS in 2018, an exhibition he'd been instrumental in organising. Parmjit is about as typical a looking Sikh as they come but he truly didn't care that I looked white, had short hair and was sipping a glass of complimentary wine. Instead, he recognised that I was on a path of learning, the literal meaning of 'Sikh'. He'd taken me under his wing that evening and, in the depths of my pre-#BothNotHalf turmoil, I felt like I'd found a home.

I'd been nervous to share how Sikh ideas had inspired me on the river, it still all felt very new. But that glint had settled me. Parmjit took a beat before he replied, looked knowingly at Sukhdeep Jodha, the linguistics genius of the Kashi House team, and proclaimed, '*Sher da dil.*' I didn't know what he really meant, I understood the Punjabi – 'heart of a lion' – and I felt it as an affirmation. But I didn't get the significance. Parmjit would go on to explain that this was a concept he'd encountered through his work with Nihangs, a fearsome (and now somewhat fringe) Sikh warrior order, some of whom imbibe cannabis as part of their meditation practice. As he saw it, *my* 'sukha parshad' had been Lava Falls.

Nihangs were so outside the mainstream of what I understood a Sikh to be that I would never have made this kind of connection. But in doing so, Parmjit opened me up to a whole new way of thinking: there was more than one way to be a Sikh. Parmjit himself was proof. Yes, he had a big turban and a beard to match but his Sikhi wasn't grounded in regular attendance at a gurdwara, it lay in unearthing and disseminating the diverse history of Guru Nanak's legacy. When the pandemic hit in 2020, this mission went online in the form of the UKPHA Virtual Book Club and one talk in particular made a lasting impression.

When I logged on to watch Amardeep Singh give his presentation on the Nanakpanthis of The Indus in June 2020, I had no idea what to expect. I'd never heard the term Nanakpanthi before. Thankfully, he began with an explanation:

> In short, it's basically 'the followers of Guru Nanak's philosophy' ... Guru Nanak, who is attributed with founding the Sikh faith, actually founded nothing. He was just on a quest to attach the people to the Oneness of mankind and he had a philosophy to share with the world. The people who followed him – in many cultures, practices, in different geographical regions – in the past were known as Nanakpanthis.

Guru Nanak was born in 1469 and for over 200 years the vast diversity of people who venerated his philosophy of Oneness coexisted and were referred to in Persian sources as Nanakpanthis. Then, in 1699, for reasons of spiritual sovereignty in the context of persecution at the hands of the Mughal Emperor Aurangzeb, Guru Gobind Singh, the tenth guru, instituted the Khalsa – a collective identity for the Sikh community and the name of a specific group of Sikhs, initiated as warriors. This initiation into the Five Ks and its attendant code of discipline is where the image of the modern Sikh began.

A hundred years later, and with the Guru Granth Sahib having been installed by Guru Gobind Singh as the eleventh and eternal guru, the term 'Khalsa' was adopted by the Sikh leader Maharaja Ranjit Singh for his Punjab-based empire – Sarkar Khalsa – and the numbers of initiated Khalsa Sikhs swelled. Nevertheless, diversity and syncretism remained alive and well in this 'Sikh Empire'. Indeed, its estimated population of 12 million was made up of 70% Muslims, 24% Hindus and just 6-7% Sikhs – though as we're starting to discover, these strict categories are not particularly useful for understanding the prevalence of Guru Nanak's teachings.[4][5]

Following the demise of Maharaja Ranjit Singh, the British swept in to annex Punjab in 1849, bringing with them Christian missionaries, prompting resistance in the form of Hindu, Muslim and Sikh reform movements, each of which found themselves in conflict with each other and competing for political influence. Amidst this proselytising, it became expedient to define what a Sikh was and the Khalsa definition proved simple and attractive. Fluidity began to erode and communities began to calcify. The British also encouraged Sikhs to think of themselves as 'a totally distinct and separate nation', feting them as a 'martial race' in reward for their loyalty during the 1857 uprising.[6] During the census of 1891, it was still possible to record oneself as a Nanakpanthi, but by the early 20th century, the clarity offered by Khalsa initiation had won out as the standard for Sikh identity. Partition in 1947 cleaved Punjab in two and concentrated Sikhs as a religious majority on the Indian side of the border, further consolidating the Khalsa tradition. In Indian Punjab today, Sikhs total 16 million, while in all of Pakistan they are estimated at fewer than 20,000.[7]

Discovering this history of the formation of Sikh identity blew my mind. I felt an immediate resonance. My personal conflict, I realised, was to do with the Khalsa form. I did not feel inclined towards the strictures of full initiation, but I now saw that that did not preclude me from being a Sikh. There was a diverse history I could connect with. And I wasn't just harking back to some bygone era, the Nanakpanthi tradition lives on. In his travels through Pakistan, Amardeep Singh has encountered Muslims engaging in group discussions on the Guru Granth Sahib, people with Hindu names confidently asserting their Sikh identity, as well as a gurdwara in Lahore where he witnessed a Khalsa Sikh sat before the Guru Granth Sahib, while two Sindhi Hindus and a Muslim performed kirtan. This was the very essence of Guru Nanak's message.

ਕੋਈ ਬੋਲੈ ਰਾਮ ਰਾਮ ਕੋਈ ਖੁਦਾਇ ॥
ਕੋਈ ਸੇਵੈ ਗੁਸਈਆ ਕੋਈ ਅਲਾਹਿ ॥

koee bolai raam raam koee khudhaae
koee saevai guseeaa koee alaahi

Some say Raam Raam, and some Khuda
Some serve the divine as Gosain, others as Allah
GURU GRANTH SAHIB, ANG 885

Less than a month after attending Amardeep Singh's online talk, and in response to a vocal minority pushing for the inclusion of Sikhs as an ethnic group on the 2021 UK census, I tweeted: 'Sikh is not an ethnicity.' I attached four photos of Sikhs: a Black man, a white woman, a Black woman and me. I concluded my short thread by sharing that, 'I believe diversity of Sikh representation is sorely needed … Sikhs are not a monolithic group. Our history is defined by diversity, our future should be too.'

The summit of the Gods

On Friday 2 October 2020, I woke up and read some panicked WhatsApp messages on the family group chat. BG had been in hospital and it appeared things may have taken a turn for the worse. But I stayed calm. I tried BG's mobile. No answer. I was still in bed, cold grey light creeping through the blinds. The sound of rain. I got up, sat in my armchair, closed my eyes and recited 'Waheguru'.

This was a new practice for me. Naam simran, the meditative recitation and remembrance of the divine, is an integral tenet of Sikhi, designed to foster continuous awareness of hukam. My first encounter with it had been on the day of my grandad's funeral in August 2017. As his body lay at home, with close family and friends gathered, we waited for the funeral directors to return and seal the coffin. Unannounced, a distant relative confidently began to chant, 'Satnam, Waheguru.'

'Satnam' roughly translates as 'truth and existence are the name and essence of the Oneness' and 'Waheguru' is both an expression of awe (Wow! Divine wisdom!) as well as a compound of 'wa' (dark), 'he' (light), and 'guru' (teacher), meaning 'the carrier from dark to light, ignorance to wisdom'.

I opened my eyes, feeling more at ease now with what was unfolding. I picked up my phone.

My dad didn't sugar-coat it. He told me straight. 'BG died this morning.' *I felt the shock*, I wrote in my journal, *but once I stopped resisting, I felt at ease.*

> Maybe I've just not processed it. But even watching our interview recordings last night, when I realised I wouldn't be able to sleep until I'd checked the backups, seeing BG smiling, chatting and full of life, it only brought joy. Is this hukam? Contentedness? A small part of me longed to feel grief but the rest of me marvelled at this special day. This once in a lifetime day, the day BG died, and I tried my hardest to drink it all up. I marvelled at how her love seemed entirely undiminished. I smiled at the thought of her merging back into the vast unknown. She was always so at ease with death, it felt hard not to be at peace.

I had not that long ago felt bereft of belonging. Three years earlier, I had been sat on my bed crying out of a smothering sense of loneliness and despair. And yet now, what I'd always feared would be a cataclysmic moment of loss, felt like celebration.

*

On the second anniversary of BG's passing, I was in Nepal with my mum and sister to trek the Annapurna Circuit. And the country's capital, Kathmandu is not short of historic shrines. You cannot move for pagodas and stupas, with some, like Pashupatinath, dating back to the 5th century CE. And the boundaries between Hinduism and Buddhism are far from distinct. Nepalese Buddhists frequent the Shaivite inner sanctum of Pashupatinath, while carvings of Hindu deities can be found at the famed Buddhist stupa, Swayambhunath, known colloquially as the monkey temple. Tantra – the 6th-century philosophy of Indian origin that 'challenged distinctions between opposites by teaching that everything is sacred, including the traditionally profane and impure' – is visible everywhere.[8] Guru Nanak pioneered an approach, but Oneness has permeated the philosophical traditions of South Asia for millenia. It is the essence of the Hindu symbol and sound 'Om', has parallels in the Muslim (specifically Sufi) concept of Tawhid, and the curled nose beneath the 'Eyes of Buddha' is a direct reference to the number 'one' in Devanagari numerals, almost identical to the Gurmukhi numeral that opens the Guru Granth Sahib.

Aware of this immense spiritual history and with a suspicion that Guru Nanak must have spent time in Nepal during his travels, I wondered if there were any historic Sikh sites hidden away. My googling threw up something tantalising: 'It is not on the tourist map. No coaches park below the small forested hill by the river … The temple is left to bird song and the occasional visitor who either knows it is there or by chance comes upon the small weathered sign which says, Guru Nanak Math.'[9]

I felt like I'd found a treasure map. Hagiographies record Guru Nanak embarking on five *udasis*, extended periods of travel, to engage in spiritual and philosophical discourse. The third of these, in the early 1500s, brought him through Kathmandu and the Math marks where he is meant to have stayed and sat in meditation in what was then an expanse of jungle.[10] And it was within walking distance of our hotel. In BG's memory, we went in search.

I had the route on my phone but the GPS on my offline map was lagging. We took a couple of wrong turns, taking us past 'BG Bakery House' – we stopped for a photo – before we eventually came to the river and crossed a treacherous road, finding ourselves in front of an unmarked gate. This was meant to be the spot. But a hoarding suggested this was a college and there was no trace of the shrine. Uncertain, we walked around the block to see if the entrance was hidden elsewhere. Nothing. And none of the locals I spoke to seemed to have heard of the place. I was worried I'd perhaps got it wrong, that I should've double checked the actual coordinates rather than relying on Google Maps. But the faded red gates we'd passed did look similar to those I'd seen in a photo online. Maybe the signage had changed? It was worth a look.

We wandered back and climbed up the tree-lined path, stepping through another gate at the top of the hill to find a ceremony underway – for Fulpati, the 7th day of Dashain – in what appeared to be a mandir hall. I couldn't see anything that suggested a Sikh presence. My mum and sister hung back while I explored the wooded surrounds, but my only discovery was a pungent toilet block. I felt like I was leading us on a wild goose chase. My hope was starting to fade and we began retracing our steps, passing a small side door to what I'd thought was the hall we'd already passed. But then I looked up and saw a sign. A literal sign. My Devanagari was rusty but 'नानक' jumped out: Nanak.

An ecstatic rush of discovery washed over me and I called out to my mum and sister. We took off our shoes, feeling the hot concrete underfoot, and entered the courtyard within. At the centre, on a plinth, sat a small bronze statue of Guru Nanak, wrapped in a saffron yellow shawl, shaded by a parasol. This was a totally new encounter for me. The Guru Granth Sahib is highly critical of idolatry: 'One stone is lovingly decorated, while another stone is walked upon. If one is a god, then the other must also be a god.'[11] And Japji Sahib makes clear that: 'That which is worthy of worship cannot be created nor made.' But, in my opinion, this critique is not absolute. 'The ways to love the One are countless,' says Nanak. Through developing a deeper understanding of the Hindu tradition, I'd come to understand murtis, devotional images, much like I saw the mountains. They are a concession to the mind, a means of focusing, a way in. The concrete plinth was no less part of the Oneness than the bronze, but the serene image of the meditating sage certainly helped prompt my awareness of it.

In a cloister to one side sat an old man, sporting a beard and long hair tied in a topknot, a look I now registered was uncommon in Nepal. He glanced up from where he was sitting on the floor while a young man with a fresh tilak and an Om necklace attended him. They didn't seem used to visitors, at least not Western tourists, but nor did they seem surprised by us. I asked if this was indeed the place we'd been looking for and the old man, whose name I learnt was Naiyam Muni, confirmed that it was and asked if I was a 'sardar', a Sikh. I replied in broken Hindi and showed him my kara. He then motioned to an enclosed mezzanine, carved of wood, on the opposite side of the courtyard. '*Yeh gurdwara hai.*' 'This is the gurdwara.'

Govind, the young man, led us across and took a rumaal for himself from a plastic bag hung from a nail on the wall. As we all covered our heads, he opened up a trapdoor to reveal the intimate gurdwara within. The sense of discovery, of magic, of such a unique experience was overwhelming; BG was at the front of all our minds. I held back the tears, climbed up into the gloom and bowed before the Guru Granth Sahib.

We sat in silent meditation and the quiet was majestic. Traffic raged at the base of the hill but here, all we could hear was birdsong and insects buzzing between flowerpots. Naiyam Muni joined us and distributed mishri, rock sugar, as parshad. And as I let the sweetness dissolve on my tongue, I began to feel an urge building in me. I searched for some confidence – was it appropriate? – and then I asked, 'Can I read a verse?' 'Of course,' came the reply.

Naiyam Muni helped me move aside the embroidered pink and orange fabrics and fresh flowers that protected and adorned the Guru Granth Sahib. I turned the heavy pages to the opening composition, Japji Sahib, and I began to read. I only went as far as the end of the first verse, it took me less than a minute, and the experience of it is impossible to convey. But when I finished and spoke the salutation '*Waheguru Ji Ka Khalsa, Waheguru Ji Ki Fateh*', Naiyam Muni joined in, as is the custom, and any doubts I'd had about my legitimacy dissolved. As soon as we'd left, my mum burst into tears.

*

On 26 February 2023, I found myself back on a plane to Kathmandu. I was off to join One Family's Annapurna Base Camp expedition in aid of Maiti Nepal, a phenomenal charity, led by the indomitable Anuradha Koirala, dedicated to fighting the trafficking of women and girls.

In the weeks prior to my departure, my sister and I had been working with Soho Theatre, developing a pitch for a play based on our shared and differing mixed heritage experiences. It was a creative five days but deeply challenging. A major rift in our thinking had revealed itself and neither of us really knew how to bridge it. I had a desire to be seen and welcomed by Ramanique, an equal in our mixed experiences, but she was resistant. I was white, she was brown, I was straight, she was queer. It became a hurdle we couldn't clear and our writing stalled. We decided we needed time to process independently.

As I was drifting in and out of sleep on my flight, a monologue began to form in my head. Half-conscious and bleary eyed, I pulled out my iPad and began to write. I didn't think, I just let it out and didn't dare reread anything. Once I was done, I drifted off again. By the time I'd arrived at the hotel, I'd forgotten all about it.

The previous year, unseasonal monsoon rain and landslides had devastated the tourism industry in the Annapurna Conservation Area, ending our family adventure before it had even really begun. Walking back the way we'd come and witnessing the destruction was heartbreaking, so I was immensely grateful for the opportunity to be returning. And the weather report was good.

After several days of hiking, the final push to base camp started at 4am, crunching through snow and ice with shooting stars streaking over the faintly visible peaks, I felt entirely where I was meant to be. Connected to myself and all. I understood now what Guru Nanak meant when, discussing the ineffable experience of the divine, he wrote, 'On paper, with a pen, no writer can express this.' I recalled the image of Natraja, Shiva as the cosmic dancer. Joseph Campbell describes the icon as 'the visage of the Unmoved Mover, beyond, yet present within, the world's bliss and pain … non-dual, Being-Consciousness-Bliss (*sat-chit-ānanda*)'. Satpal Singh draws on the same image to explain the Sikh concept of 'Karta Purakh', the being that does all, explaining that in the same way that the dance and the dancer cannot be separated, the Oneness is both formless and manifest. I felt myself dancing. As the sun rose and the summit of Annapurna blazed, I kneeled in awe. I was there but there was no me.

Back in Kathmandu, I returned to Guru Nanak Math with One Family's Saad Awan and Waleed Khan. Naiyam Muni recognised me instantly, confused at first, then a smile filled his eyes. He recounted my previous visit to Saad, whose Hindi was far better than mine, and implored us to stay for tea. He welcomed us all into the gurdwara and Saad tried to explain that though he and Waleed were Muslim, they had grown up around and had a great affection for Sikhs. But he only got as far as saying, '*Hum musalman hai, liken ...*' before Naiyam Muni gently chimed in with, '*Hum sab ik hai.*' 'We are all one.'

On the journey back to the UK, I reflected on all I had experienced over the past fifteen days. I struggled to fathom it. Something in me felt different. Something fundamental. What I'd experienced on the mountain felt like a surrender. I had offered myself up and relaxed into my being. If I never acted again, so be it. If this book turns out to be a flop, fine. That bliss I'd experienced asked nothing of me. It was simply present, within me and everywhere, always.

Don't worry, I didn't fool myself that I had achieved enlightenment. As I packed my bags and worried about my baggage allowance, I definitely noticed my awareness becoming veiled. But, *this is the journey I am now on*, I wrote in my journal, *remaining connected, knowing that joy resides within, that 'playful carefreeness'. The canyon was a major moment of self death for me, but this time it feels more nuanced.*

Sat on the plane, I remembered the monologue I'd written. I decided to revisit it. And I realised I'd come to the end of a chapter in my journey.

I need you to want me by your side. I need to feel welcome. I need to feel your love. I'm just a scared little kid who got left at Grandad and BG's and wet the bed and cried and cried until you were there to cry with me. You only used to cry when I started crying. BG used to try to get me to stop because she knew I'd set you off. But when you were crying I felt less alone. I didn't want you to cry but it made us closer in that moment. We were together.

But you always knew how to … be. You never got homesick the way I did. In India, that Christmas. I couldn't bear it. Christmas was home and I wasn't there but you were there and you felt like home and you made it home. You made the crackers, wrote the jokes, you didn't cry.

I'm scared. I'm scared to step out by myself. Because I don't know who me is. I'm the white Punjabi. I'm Mr Walia's grandson. I'm Rocky from Some Girls. I'm that guy whose video you saw. I crave being known so I don't have to introduce myself. I thought it was because it made me feel seen. To not have to explain who I am. All the same questions. All the same answers. But I'm just scared. Because who am I? If I'm not the white Punjabi. The Both Not Half guy. I'm scared I might just be who I am. Just another confused, scared kid calling out for his mum.

I've asked too much of you. I see that now. You've fought so hard for you and I've felt defeated. Because despite the doubt I've had it easy. My crisis came in my 20s and I made it a book deal in my 30s. I get DMs about how I've changed people's lives and I feel like a fraud so I try and find more answers and write a book and do talks and make it hard because then maybe, just maybe, I'll have earned that love. The love I crave from you.

But I don't think it is love I crave. I've asked too

much. I've wanted you to reach out so I can feel your power. So you can give me your power and I think you've known that? Maybe not consciously but on some level you've known that. I've asked too much. I see that now, I have to find my own power. I have to fight, not for you, not for anyone, but for me.

When I was at the protest the other week some bit of me thought I was there for you, for trans liberation, for the union. But I was there for me. To let the rage out. To scream and dance for the boy who loved to dance and question and who wished he could've maybe searched for answers without being so afraid of what he might find. Mostly straight. Not much of a discovery. But it took me 31 years.

And I hate it when you call me white and I hate it when you call me straight, it feels like rejection, but I know why you do. I know we're not the same but some bit of us is. Because you're my sister. And the thought of losing you ... I just want to belong. That's all it is I guess, and my whole thing the whole Both Not Half thing has been about how belonging isn't something you find it's something you do. And you've done it. You're doing it. Quietly and loudly for you.

And I've been afraid to take that final step. Because you've always been home when home wasn't there. And I've been trying to convince you that you need to let me in, like Malachi did in that BAFTA photo, because actually, I knew I wanted to be in that photo, but I was too scared to include myself. I don't need belonging from you. I don't need home. And I'm sorry I've been asking. I just want to be your brother. There's a space by your side for that. That's what I want. I want to be your brother. I'm ready to just be your brother.

I'm ready to be me.

ACKNOWLEDGEMENTS

I sat down with a blank page to write the proposal for this book in January 2021. I submitted my final draft to my publisher in January 2024. After three intensely challenging and rewarding years, I thought sitting down to write these acknowledgements would be relatively straightforward and fun. But when I realised I had submitted my tax return ahead of writing a single thank you, I had to ask myself why. As with most of my discoveries on this journey, the root cause was fear. I was afraid I wouldn't be able to find the words. But I have tried.

Aanchal Malhotra, for showing me that history can be poetry. My ADR family, for your community. Aisling O'Connor, Mesha Stewart and Sarah Trigg at the BBC, for giving my story the green light and being by my side at the Asian Media Awards 2022. Alex, for sharing your story. Alex

Gower-Jackson, for making me feel so safe in front of your lens. Amandeep Madra, for all that the UK Punjab Heritage Association does. Amina Elbayoumi, for always celebrating my worth. Amrit Lohia, for asking the hard questions. Amrit Maan and the team at the Punjab, for every meal and for providing me with a home in the heart of Covent Garden. Andrei Airimitoaie, for introducing me to the Stoics. Andy Nyman, for our brunch in the cold and for teaching me to find joy in juggling. Anisa Subedar, for spending over an hour on the phone, giving me feedback on my essay. Annabelle Huet, for sharing your love of constitutional issues. Arend Koeditz and Joshua Davison, for making me a part of your family. Ava Patel, for warming me with your fire. Ayman Khwaja, for sitting by my side and being the first to hear so much.

Barry O'Brien, for talking to me about Anglo-Indian life. Benji Hart, for refusing to leave the economics out of diversity.

Catriona Durrell, for suggesting anonymity. Charlotte Brown, for indulging my audiobook dreams. Christian Cronauer, for always supporting me quietly (and taking the piss loudly). Ciara Garcha, for introducing me to our history and sharing your own. Clara Foster, for chaperoning me with such care and confidence. Cristian Solimeno, for opening my eyes to invisible things.

David Henry Hwang, for *Yellow Face* and your permission to share your words. Dominique Holmes, for holding space for me to learn and accepting me as your brother.

Ellen Ryan, for understanding the pain of writing 90,000

words. My Equity comrades, for giving me hope and power. Evelyn Brooks Higginbotham, for your kind permission and generous insight.

Geeta Kana, for seeing my being. Georgina Kamsika, for your sensitivity read. Gorby Jandu, for never doubting my Sikh identity.

Hannah Aria, for sharing your experiences as a working-class artist. Harpinder (Raju) Ahluwalia, for fact checking my earliest memories.

Harry Lister Smith, for offering me a place to stay when I could no longer afford the cost of living. Hashi Mohamed, for knowing what it feels like to stop writing because of the tears. My literary agent, Hattie Grünewald, for representing me and this book with quiet conviction. Hussein Kesvani, for being a dude who rocks. My Bonnier publicist, Izzy Smith, for going big.

James Penford, for being a talent agent who inspires agency. Jane MacQuitty, for keeping me gainfully employed. Jess Francis, for healing my professional heart, and then following your own. Jo Watt, for handling my initial agreement. Jordan Lees, for reassuring me in Hattie's absence.

Dr Katherine Schofield, for giving me the confidence to let go of my final draft. Kevin Shen, for always bringing the salsa. Kim Wagner, for reminding me that this book would always be an attempt, not a certainty. Kristof de Bruyn, for double checking my quantum mechanics.

Laila Woozeer, for inspiring me to view this book as a performance, not a sculpture. Leah Sheshadri, for every email and phone call. My editor, Lucy Tirahan, for only ever needing me to explain my ideas, and never myself; for pushing me further, for cutting without loss, and counselling me to leave a few things unsaid. Mark Godfrey and Soho Theatre, for the time and space to research and develop. Michelle Bullock, for proofreading.

Natalie Healy, for inspiring a core memory. Nisha Chopra, for setting my BBC documentary in motion.

My dad, Parminder Ahluwalia, for the gift of my Punjabi childhood. Parmjit Singh, for showing me what a Sikh really looks like. Paul W Fleming, for fostering my trade unionism. Peter Mitchell, for giving me the words to express what I felt (and for correcting my errors). Philip Pullman, for *His Dark Materials* and allowing me to share Lyra's conversation with Xaphania. Phoebe Scholfield, for keeping me afloat. Pritika Mehta and Simarpreet Singh, for inviting me to create magic.

Dr Rachel Pougnet, for talking to me about constitutional safeguards in the UK. My sister, Ramanique Ahluwalia, for holding my hand and leading me home. Reha Kansara, for making me feel comfortable in my own skin. Rhian Parry, for every email and DocuSign link. Dr Ritch C. Savin-Williams, for introducing me to a new way of knowing myself.

Saad Awan, for the gift of my return to Nepal. Sanjeev Bhaskar, for adopting me as your *chota bhra*. My mum, Sarah Ahluwalia, for encouraging me to fail when the fear rises. Sathnam Sanghera, for saying everything to put me off writing a book, and then doing everything to help make it happen. Satpal Singh, for teaching me to sing, listen and accept. Sebastian Solberg, for every adventure, and for respecting that I had to do this one solo. Shane Mann, for my first taste of what comes next. Sharan Dhaliwal, for always forgetting that I'm straight. Sita Balani, for your generous insight into the deadly and the slick. Sivamohan Valluvan, for challenging me to think again. The Society of Authors and Authors' Foundation, for granting me £2000. Sukhdeep Jodha, for knowing what it means to become aware of awareness. Susan Pegg, for copyediting with such care and insight. Susannah Otter, for welcoming me to Bonnier and leaving me in such good hands.

Tamara Douthwaite, for leading the marketing campaign. My therapist, for giving me the tools to heal.

Uther Charlton-Stevens, for introducing me to those who came before and being so selfless with your expertise.

Vaneet Mehta, for your answers and giving me the confidence to question.

William Dalrymple, for *White Mughals* and always answering my calls – even when you're on your own deadline.

And to you, for joining me on this journey. Thank you.

ENDNOTES

Chapter 1: Alone in the Jungle

1   Henry Waterfield, *Memorandum on the Census of British India 1871–72* (London: George Edward Eyre and William Spottiswoode, 1875), 54, http://piketty.pse.ens.fr/files/ideologie/data/CensusIndia/CensusIndia1871/CensusBritishIndia1871.pdf.

2   Nishan Canagarajah, 'Leicester – A Super Diverse-City', Higher Education Policy Institute, 10 January 2023, https://www.hepi.ac.uk/2023/01/10/leicester-a-super-diverse-city/#:~:text=Not%20for%20the%20first%20time,ethnic%20group%20has%20a%20majority.

3   John Agard, 'Half-Caste', appears in *AQA Anthology* (Manchester: Assessment and Qualifications Alliance, 2004).

4   Ira Gershwin, "Let's Call the Whole Thing Off".

5   Rudyard Kipling, *The Jungle Books* (Harmondsworth: Penguin, 1987), 95.

Chapter 2: My Name Is Jassa Ahluwalia and I Have Imperial Nostalgia

1   Charles McGrath, 'Rudyard Kipling in America', *The New Yorker*, 1 July 2019, https://www.newyorker.com/magazine/2019/07/08/rudyard-kipling-in-america.

2   Rudyard Kipling, *The Jungle Books* (Harmondsworth: Penguin, 1987), 97.

3   Rudyard Kipling, *Kim* (Public Domain, 1936), 2, retrieved from https://books.apple.com/gb/book/kim/id395539135.

4   Ibid, 6.

5   Edward Said, 'Introduction' in Rudyard Kipling, *Kim* (Harmondsworth: Penguin, 1987), 30.

6   Rudyard Kipling, *Kim* (Public Domain, 1936), 437, retrieved from https://books.apple.com/gb/book/kim/id395539135.

7   Ibid, 438.

8   Walt Disney Productions, *The Jungle Book* (1967).

9   Bradley Deane, 'Empire of Analogies: Kipling, India and Ireland (review)', *Victorian Studies* 50 (2007): 162–63, https://www.researchgate.net/publication/236706779_Empire_of_Analogies_Kipling_India_and_Ireland_review.

10 As quoted in Charles Allen, *Kipling Sahib* (London: Little, Brown, 2014), 324–26.

11 Alison Flood, 'Kipling's Poignant Jungle Book Inscription Comes to Light', *Guardian*, 9 April 2010, https://www.theguardian.com/books/2010/apr/09/kipling-jungle-book-inscription.

12 Rudyard Kipling, 'Merrow Down', in *Just So Stories*, The Kipling Society, https://www.kiplingsociety.co.uk/poem/poems_merrow.htm.

13 William Dalrymple, *White Mughals* (London: HarperPress, 2012), xlviii-xlix.

14 'Report of an Examination instituted by the direction of his Excellency the most noble Governor General, Fort St. George 7th Nov 1801' OIOC HM464, quoted in William Dalrymple, *White Mughals* (London: HarperPress, 2012), 5.

15 Ibid, 9.

16 J.H. Van Linschoten, *The Voyage of John Huyghen Van Linschoten to the East Indies* (2 vols, London, 1885; original Dutch edition 1598), p.205, quoted in Dalrymple, *White Mughals*, 12.

17 William Dalrymple, *White Mughals* (London: Harper*Press*, 2012), 13.

18 Krish Ashok (@_masalalab), 'The Amazing Story of Pav Bhaji', Instagram reel, 19 March 2023, https://www.instagram.com/p/Cp-PaQzvRCO.

19 Rituparna Goswami, 'From Batata to Aloo- the journey of potato in India', https://www.thisday.app/story/from-batata-to-aloo-the-journey-of-potato-in-india-27736.

20 John Keay, *India* (London: HarperPress, 2010), xxvii.

21 Dalrymple, *White Mughals*, 20.

22 Charles D'Oyley, *The European in India* (London: East India Company, 1813), xix–xx, quoted in Dalrymple, *White Mughals*, 35.

23 The Maratha empire was a confederacy of central and southern Indian states.

24 Dalrymple, *White Mughals*, 36.

25 Jörg Fisch, 'A Solitary Vindicator of the Hindus: The Life and Writings of General Charles Stuart (1757/58–1828)', *The Journal of the Royal Asiatic Society of Great Britain and Ireland* 1 (1985): 43, https://www.jstor.org/stable/25211769.

26 Jörg Fisch, 'A Solitary Vindicator of the Hindus: The Life and Writings of General Charles Stuart (1757/58–1828)', *The Journal of the Royal Asiatic Society of Great Britain and Ireland* 1 (1985): 43, https://www.jstor.org/stable/25211769.

27 P/Secr./253, Bengal Secret Consultations of 17 December 1813, nos. 48–72, unpaged, '1 October 1813, Fagan to Stuart, no.71', quoted in Fisch, 'A Solitary Vindicator of the Hindus', 47.

28 Maurice N. Hennessy, *The Rajah From Tipperary* (London: St Martin's Press, 1972), 33.

29 Hennessy, *The Rajah*, 42.

30 https://www.curveonline.co.uk/whats-on/shows/wipers/

31 Simon Rivers, 'Sikh Actor Changed Name to Get Acting Roles', BBC Asian Network Reports, 16 August 2016, interview, https://www.bbc.co.uk/programmes/p044vx50.

32 Peter Mitchell, *Imperial Nostalgia* (Manchester: Manchester University Press, 2021), 23, Kindle; Svetlana Boym, 'The Future of Nostalgia', in *The Svetlana Boym Reader*, eds. Cristina Vatulescu, et al. (London: Bloomsbury, 2018), 217–18.

33 Mitchell, *Imperial Nostalgia*, 19.

34 Mitchell, *Imperial Nostalgia*, 138.

35 Mitchell, *Imperial Nostalgia*, 144.

36 Rudyard Kipling, *Kim* (Public Domain, 1936), 73, retrieved from https://books.apple.com/gb/book/kim/id395539135.

37 Mitchell, *Imperial Nostalgia*, 138.

38 Edward Said, 'Introduction' in Rudyard Kipling, *Kim* (Harmondsworth: Penguin, 1987), 9.

39 Carlo Rovelli, Translated by Simon Carnell and Erica Segre, *Reality Is Not What It Seems: The Journey to Quantum Gravity* (London: Allen Lane, 2016), 115–16.

40 Jesse Emspak, 'What is Quantum Entanglement?', Space, updated 16 May 2023, https://www.space.com/31933-quantum-entanglement-action-at-a-distance.html#:~:text=Quantum%20entanglement%20is%20a%20bizarre,one%20will%20affect%20the%20other.

41 Philip Pullman, *The Amber Spyglass* (London: Scholastic, 2001), 185.

Chapter 3. Half-Casting

1   Ben Brantley and Jesse Green, 'The Great Work Continues: The 25 Best American Plays Since "Angels in America"', *New York Times*, 1 June 2018, https://www.nytimes.com/interactive/2018/05/31/theater/best-25-plays.html.

2   Kavita Bhanot (2022) 'A "Balanced" History of Empire: Sathnam Sanghera's *Empireland* and Other Colonial Anti-Colonial Histories', *Wasafiri* 37, no. 4 (November 2022): 88–100, https://doi.org/10.1080/02690055.2022.2101784.

3   William Dalrymple, *White Mughals* (London: HarperPress, 2012), 187.

4   Harper Lee, *To Kill A Mockingbird*, (London: Mandarin, 1989), 177-78.

5   Sita Balani, *Deadly and Slick* (London: Verso, 2023), 52.

6   Winyan Soo Hoo, 'Bearing the "Yellow Face": Q&A with David Henry Hwang', *Washington Post*, 22 February 2014, https://www.washingtonpost.com/news/arts-and-entertainment/wp/2014/02/22/bearing-the-yellow-face-qa-with-david-henry-hwang.

7   Richard Maltby, Jnr. and Alain Boublil, 'Bui Doi', *Miss Saigon* (1989).

8   David Henry Hwang, *Yellow Face* (New York: Theatre Communications Group, 2011), 9.

9   Ibid, 68–69.

10 The accurate Vietnamese terms are mỹ lai (mixed American and Vietnamese), con lai (mixed child), or người lai (mixed person).

11 Russell Peters, 'Excerpt From *Call Me Russell*', Penguin Random House Canada, 21 Jul 2018, https://www.penguinrandomhouse.ca/books/202286/call-me-russell-by-russell-peters/9780385669658/excerpt.

12 William Dalrymple, *White Mughals* (London: HarperPress, 2012), 50.

13 As quoted in Barry O'Brien, *The Anglo-Indians A Portrait of a Community* (New Delhi: Aleph Book Company, 2022), 21.

14 OIOC, Sutherland Papers, Mss Eur D547, pp.133-4, undated but c.1803, as quoted in William Dalrymple, *White Mughals* (London: HarperPress, 2012), 382.

15 NAUK, WO/32/6889, handwritten note on file: 'on 5983', signed '29-12-86 Wolseley', as quoted in Uther Charlton-Stevens, *Anglo-India and the End of Empire* (London: C. Hurst & Co., 2022), 75.

16 Natalie Morris, *Mixed/Other* (London: Trapeze, 2021), 91.

17 Ciara Garcha, 'Mixed Histories: Understanding and Managing Mixed Identities in Colonial Societies', *Broad Street Humanities Review* (January 2022, issue 6), 14.

18 Leah Myers, 'Blood-Quantum Laws are Splintering My Tribe', *The Atlantic*, 21 June 2023, https://www.theatlantic.com/family/archive/2023/06/blood-quantum-laws-native-american-tribal-communities/674461.

19 Millicent D, 'Confidential submission 640, South Australia: WA Woman Removed in 1949', Bringing them Home, Indigenous Law Resources, Australasian Legal Information Institute, April 1997, http://www.austlii.edu.au/au/other/ IndigLRes/stolen/stolen13.html.

20 Healing Foundation, 'About Us', 27 May 2013, https://healingfoundation.org. au/about-us.

21 Glenn D'Cruz 'Christopher Hawes in Conversation with Glenn D'Cruz', International Journal of Anglo-Indian Studies 3, no. 1 (1998): 2–10, https:// www.international-journal-of-anglo-indian-studies.org/index.php/IJAIS/article/ view/122/115.

22 Uther Charlton-Stevens, Anglo-India and the End of Empire (London: C. Hurst & Co., 2022), 39–40.

23 Anvarsadhath Valiyaparambath, Ethnic Articulations in Contemporary Indian English Fiction: A Study of Selected Novels. Unpublished Ph.D. dissertation. Malappuram: U of Calicut, Dec 2005, 125-26, as quoted in Susheel Kumar Sharma, 'Does the Name "Anglo-Indian" Matter?: Problematic of Prodigal Literature' in Diversity in Indian Literatures in English: Recent Reflections (New Delhi: Prestige Books International, 2019), 39.

24 Dispatch from 'Court of Directors to the President of Madras …1687', cited in E. Hedin, 'The Anglo-Indian Community', American Journal of Sociology 40:2 (1934), pp. 166–7, as quoted in Uther Charlton-Stevens, Anglo-India and the End of Empire (London: C. Hurst & Co., 2022), 37.

25 Charlton-Stevens, Anglo-India and the End of Empire, 40.

26 J. Stocqueler, 'The Crime of Colour', ch. 6, Patriotic Fund Journal 1:7 (27 January 1855), p.117, quoted in Charlton-Stevens, Anglo-India and the End of Empire, 47.

27 Valerie E.R. Anderson, 'The Eurasian Problem in Nineteenth Century India', (PhD diss., SOAS, University of London, 2011), https://doi.org/10.25501/ SOAS.00013525.

28 Letter signed A.H., in The Calcutta Journal, November 6, 1821, quoted in Rosinka Chaudhuri, '"Why, Sir, Am I Not An Indian?": Identity, Liberation And Nationalism In Early Nineteenth-Century India', International Journal of Anglo-Indian Studies 15, no. 1 (2015): 4–12, https://www.international-journal-of-anglo-indian-studies.org/index.php/IJAIS/article/view/9.

29 Letter signed 'An Indian', in The Calcutta Journal, November 7, 1821, quoted in Ibid.

30 BL, F/4/1115, Extract of Fort St. George Military Correspondence (30 November 1827), folio 12839, no. 39, pp. 333–55, quoted in Charlton-Stevens, Anglo-India and the End of Empire, 79.

31 Ibid.

32 Charlton-Stevens, *Anglo-India and the End of Empire*, 82.

33 E.A. Gait, Census of India 1911, Volume 1, Part 1 – Report (Calcutta: Superintendent Government Printing, 1913), 139, http://piketty.pse.ens.fr/files/ideologie/data/CensusIndia/CensusIndia1911/1911%20-%20India%20-%20Vol%20I%20(HQ).pdf, quoted in Charlton-Stevens, *Anglo-India and the End of Empire*, 21.

34 *The Hollywood Reporter* (@THR), 'Michelle Yeoh has Made History', X, 24 January 2023, https://x.com/THR/status/1617907514405974016?s=20.

35 Variety (@Variety), 'Michelle Yeoh is the Second Asian Woman Nominated', X, 24 January 2023, https://x.com/Variety/status/1617952959928864768?s=20.

36 Sarah Broughton, *Brando's Bride* (Cardigan: Parthian, 2019), 34.

37 Andrew Lawrence, '"She Had to Hide": The Secret History of the First Asian Woman Nominated for a Best Actress Oscar', *Guardian*, 7 March 2023, https://www.theguardian.com/film/2023/mar/06/merle-oberon-oscars-best-actress.

38 Lawrence, '"She Had to Hide"'.

39 Otto Friedrich, *City of Nets: A Portrait of Hollywood in the 1940s*, pp. 354–355, as quoted in Broughton, *Brando's Bride*, 32.

40 Stephen Prince, 'Appendix B: The Production Code', *Classical Film Violence Designing and Regulating Brutality in Hollywood Cinema, 1930–1968* (Piscataway: Rutgers University Press, 2003), 294.

41 *Northern Territory Times*, cited in D. Groves, *Anna May Wong's Lucky Shoes: 1939 Australia through the Eyes of an Art Deco Diva* (Ames IA, 2011), p. 8, quoted in Charlton-Stevens, *Anglo-India and the End of Empire*, 2–3.

42 BFI, 'BFI Discovers World's First Interracial TV Kiss', updated 8 May 2019, https://www2.bfi.org.uk/news-opinion/news-bfi/announcements/bfi-discovers-world-first-interracial-tv-kiss.

43 *Othello* (1955), 'Othello (1955) | Gordon Heath | BBC Television', https://youtu.be/p09pW2k8Y6M?si=YThBKenP5k8W0_EA&t=3091

44 Charlton-Stevens, *Anglo-India and the End of Empire*, 66.

45 Charlton-Stevens, *Anglo-India and the End of Empire*, 66; my emphasis.

46 Broughton, *Brando's Bride*, 53.

47 Frank Morriss, *Here There and Hollywood* (September 1955), as quoted in Broughton, *Brando's Bride*, 69.

48 *Photoplay* (January 1958), as quoted in Broughton, *Brando's Bride*, 107.

49 *The New York Times* (13 October 1957), as quoted in Broughton, *Brando's Bride*, 29.

50 Simon Hattenstone, 'Sir Ben Kingsley's Identity is as Colourful as His
Characters', *Radio Times*, 19 June 2016, https://www.radiotimes.com/tv/drama/sir-
ben-kingsleys-identity-is-as-colourful-as-his-characters.

Chapter 4. Both Not Half

1 Rabindranath Tagore, 'The Meeting', *The Religion of Man* (New York: The
Macmillan Company, 1931), 155.

Chapter 5. Useful Fictions, Dangerous Narratives

1 https://www.britannica.com/technology/printing-press

2 Wales History, 'The 1536 Act of Union', BBC Wales, https://www.bbc.co.uk/
wales/history/sites/themes/periods/tudors_04.shtml; Joe Goodden, 'The Law and the
Welsh Language', BBC Wales, 22 October 2012, https://www.bbc.co.uk/blogs/wales/
entries/020f5be9-73a7-3491-a4dd-57fc6875eade.

3 https://web.archive.org/web/20200808120632/https://www.bl.uk/british-
accents-and-dialects/articles/accents-and-dialects-of-scotland.

4 UN, History of the Question of Palestine, 28 Dec 2023, https://www.un.org/
unispal/history.

5 Ilan Pappé, *Ten Myths About Israel* (London: Verso, 2017), 21, Kindle.

6 'Shaheen Bagh an Organic Protest to Save Constitution, says Asaduddin Owaisi',
Hindustan Times, Feb 22, 2020, https://www.hindustantimes.com/india-news/
shaheen-bagh-an-organic-protest-to-save-constitution-says-asaduddin-owaisi/story-
b7vrweUmPxTjkHDFFUf8rO.html.

7 George Orwell, *The Lion and the Unicorn: Socialism and the English
Genius* (Harmondsworth: Penguin, 2018), 29. Kindle.

8 The Whigs were a faction of Protestant aristocrats who had secured their position
by engineering The Glorious Revolution in 1688, toppling James II, a Catholic,
in favour of his Protestant daughter and her husband, Mary II and William of
Orange. Not content with ousting one Catholic monarch, they made it illegal for
any Catholic to ever be sovereign. Since 2015, members of the Royal Family were
permitted to marry Catholics, but it is still against the law for a Catholic to ascend
the throne.

9 ONS, 'England and Wales Population Estimates 1838 to 2014',
Census 2021, 6 July 2015, 004358, https://www.ons.gov.uk/
peoplepopulationandcommunity/populationandmigration/populationestimates/
adhocs/004358englandandwalespopulationestimates1838to2014.

10 ONS, 'England and Wales Population Estimates 1838 to 2014', Census 2021, 6 July 2015, 004358, https://www.ons.gov.uk/ peoplepopulationandcommunity/populationandmigration/populationestimates/ adhocs/004358englandandwalespopulationestimates1838to2014.

11 Donald Eugene Smith, *India as a Secular State*, 337–38; and Percival Spear, *India, Pakistan and the West*, 163, as quoted in Benedict Anderson, *Imagined Communities: Reflections on the Origin and Spread of Nationalism* (London: Verso, 2016), 91.

12 Thomas Babington Macaulay, *The History of England*, (Leipzig: Tauchnitz, 1849), 1-2, https://www.google.co.uk/books/edition/The_History_of_England_from_the_ Accessio/yZlRAAAAcAAJ?hl=en&gbpv=0

13 Bragg, *The Progressive Patriot*, 170.

14 Angus Hawkins, *Victorian Political Culture* (Oxford: Oxford University Press, 2015), 143.

15 Sally-Anne Huxtable, et al., eds., 'Interim Report on the Connections Between Colonialism and Properties Now in the Care of the National Trust, Including Links with Historic Slavery' (Wiltshire: National Trust, 2020), 4, https://nt.global.ssl.fastly. net/binaries/content/assets/website/national/pdf/colonialism-and-historic-slavery- report.pdf.

16 Peter Mitchell, 'The National Trust Is Under Attack Because It Cares About History, Not Fantasy', *Guardian*, 12 November 2020, https://www.theguardian.com/ commentisfree/2020/nov/12/national-trust-history-slavery.

17 Geraldine Kendall Adams, 'National Trust Members Reject Pressure Group Proposals at AGM', Museum Associations, 14 November 2023, https://www. museumsassociation.org/museums-journal/news/2023/11/national-trust-members- reject-pressure-group-proposals-at-agm/#.

18 Brendan O'Neill, 'Equity's Shameful Treatment of Laurence Fox', Spiked, 13 March 2020, https://www.spiked-online.com/2020/03/13/equitys-shameful- treatment-of-laurence-fox.

19 Chloe Seivwright, 'Rakie Ayola on Her Welsh Background, Imposter Syndrome & Black Women In TV', Black Ballad, 20 November 2020, https://blackballad. co.uk/people/rakie-ayola-actor-hermione-anthony?listIds=591b37f155fd6dc14e461 ae7.

20 Bragg, *The Progressive Patriot*, 63.

21 René Grotenhuis, 'A Program for Nation-Building in Fragile States', in *Nation- Building as Necessary Effort in Fragile States* (Amsterdam: Amsterdam University Press, 2016): 153–82, https://doi.org/10.2307/j.ctt1gr7d8r.13.

22 John Carvel, 'Tebbit's cricket loyalty test hit for six', *Guardian*, 8 January 2004, https://www.theguardian.com/uk/2004/jan/08/britishidentity.race.

23 As quoted in Colin Yeo, 'Deprivation of citizenship justified by treasonous conduct finds Court of Appeal', *Free Movement*. 27 September 2018, https://freemovement.org.uk/deprivation-of-citizenship-justified-by-treasonous-conduct-finds-court-of-appeal/

24 Lord Goldsmith, 'Citizenship: Our Common Bond', 11 March 2008, http://image.guardian.co.uk/sys-files/Politics/documents/2008/03/11/citizenship-report-full.pdf.

25 Home Office, 'Nationality and Borders Bill: Deprivation of Citizenship Factsheet', updated 13 October 2023, https://www.gov.uk/government/publications/nationality-and-borders-bill-deprivation-of-citizenship-factsheet/nationality-and-borders-bill-deprivation-of-citizenship-factsheet.

26 Sayeeda Warsi, 'Behold the New "Hostile Environment" – With the Power to Rob Millions of British Citizenship', Guardian, 15 February 2022, https://www.theguardian.com/commentisfree/2022/feb/15/new-hostile-environment-british-citizenship-government-islamic-state.

27 Electoral Reform Society, 'Replace the House of Lords', https://www.electoral-reform.org.uk/campaigns/elected-house-of-lords/

28 Luke Raikes, 'The Devolution Parliament: Devolving Power To England's Regions, Towns And Cities', February 2020, https://web.archive.org/web/20210818101951/https://www.ippr.org/files/2020-02/the-devolution-parliament-feb-20-summary.pdf.

29 Louise Cullen, 'Ireland Could Give Nature Constitutional Rights', BBC News, 16 December 2023, https://www.bbc.co.uk/news/articles/cd1d959wkq0o.

30 Refugee Action, 'Turning Words into Action', June 2019, https://www.refugee-action.org.uk/wp-content/uploads/2019/06/Turning-Words-into-Action.pdf.

31 Refugee Action, 'Turning Words into Action'.

Chapter 6. Adventures in Masculinity

1 This system is known as cis-heteropatriarchy, see: York University, 'Cis-Heteropatriarchy', 7 April 2021, https://www.yorku.ca/edu/unleading/systems-of-oppression/cis-heteropatriarchy.

2 BBC Breaking News (@BBCBreaking), 'Florida Police Confirm Multiple Injuries From Shooting', X, 12 June 2016, https://twitter.com/BBCBreaking/status/741904107968049153?s=20&t=Ov0XdyFmckx8n6XwhRbTYQ.

3 Robin DiAngelo, 'White Fragility', International Journal of Critical Pedagogy 3, no. 3 (2011): 54-70, https://libjournal.uncg.edu/ijcp/article/viewFile/249/116.

4 Evelyn Brooks Higginbotham, *Righteous Discontent: The Women's Movement in the Black Baptist Church 1880–1920* (Cambridge: Harvard University Press 1993), 187.

5   Merriam-Webster, 'Singular "They"', September 2019, https://www.merriam-webster.com/words-at-play/singular-nonbinary-they.

6   Anna Nelson, 'Genital Normalising Surgeries on Intersex Infants: A Scandal in Waiting?', University of Manchester, 10 May 2018, https://blog.policy.manchester.ac.uk/posts/2018/05/genital-normalising-surgeries-on-intersex-infants-a-scandal-in-waiting.

7   Bi.org, 'Freddie Mercury', American Institute of Bisexuality *Journal of Bisexuality*, 6 June 2020, https://bi.org/en/famous/freddie-mercury.

8   Giorgina Ramazzotti, 'In Pictures: Freddie Mercury's Beautiful Relationship with Mary Austin', Smooth Radio, updated 26 April 2023, https://www.smoothradio.com/artists/freddie-mercury/mary-austin-photos-relationship.

9   Movement Advancement Project, 'Invisible Majority', 15 September 2016, https://www.lgbtmap.org/file/invisible-majority.pdf.

10 ONS, 'Sexual Orientation, UK: 2020', Census UK, 25 May 2022, https://www.ons.gov.uk/peoplepopulationandcommunity/culturalidentity/sexuality/bulletins/sexualidentityuk/2020.

11 Brandon Ambrosino, 'I Am Gay – But I Wasn't Born This Way', BBC Future, 28 June 2016, https://www.bbc.com/future/article/20160627-i-am-gay-but-i-wasnt-born-this-way.

12 Yash Bharati, 'This Is How Much Akshay Kumar Earned To Be the Only Indian on the Forbes Highest-Paid Actors List 2020, *GQ India*, 12 August 2020, https://www.gqindia.com/entertainment/content/how-much-akshay-kumar-earned-to-be-the-only-indian-on-the-forbes-highest-paid-actors-list-2020.

13 Brynn Tannehill, 'Is Refusing to Date Trans People Transphobic?', *Advocate*, 14 December 2019, https://www.advocate.com/commentary/2019/12/14/refusing-date-trans-people-transphobic.

14 Ritch C. Savin-Williams, *Mostly straight : sexual fluidity among men* (Cambridge, Massachusetts: Harvard University Press, 2017), 178.

15 Ibid, 201.

Chapter 7. Occupy the Back Seats

1   Edzia Carvalho, Kristi Winters, 'I Went with What I Always Do …': A Qualitative Analysis of 'Cleggmania' and Vote Choice in the 2010 British General Election, *Parliamentary Affairs*, Volume 68, Issue 2, April 2015, 425, https://doi.org/10.1093/pa/gst050.

2   Kate Stevenson, Music Education under Threat, *FORUM* 53, no. 2 (2011), https://journals.lwbooks.co.uk/forum/vol-53-issue-2/article-4688.

3   Ibid.

4   Francis Green and David Kynaston, *Engines of Privilege* (London: Bloomsbury, 2019), 101, as quoted in Hashi Mohamed, *People Like Us* (London: Profile, 2020), 290, Kindle; The Sutton Trust and the Social Mobility Commission, 'Elitist Britain 2019', 24 June 2019, https://www.suttontrust.com/wp-content/uploads/2019/12/Elitist-Britain-2019.pdf; Independent Schools Council, 'Research', 4 October 2018, https://www.isc.co.uk/research.

5   TalkTV (@TalkTV), 'Actor Laurence Fox has Received an Apology from Equity', X, 13 March 2020, https://twitter.com/TalkTV/status/1238402152801992705?s=20&t=Fs8DNO5soyXaT2uGrIKBPA.Danyal; Hussain and Phoebe Eckersley, 'Actors Union Equity Brands Laurence Fox a "Disgrace" and Calls for the Industry to "Unequivocally Denounce" Him Over Question Time Megxit Comments - Then Deletes Tweets Blaming "Two Rogue Members"', Mail Online, updated 3 June 2020, https://www.dailymail.co.uk/news/article-7904115/Actors-union-Equity-brands-Laurence-Fox-disgrace-deletes-tweets.html.

6   Jade Anouka (@JadeAnouka), 'Accuracy tho', X, 8 April 2021, https://twitter.com/JadeAnouka/status/1380087445530755072?s=20.

7   Ben Lamb (@therestis_), 'Depressingly accurate!', X, 8 April 2021, https://twitter.com/therestis_/status/1380137020354404353?s=20.

8   Emma Williams (@Williamstweet), 'And Then There are the Times', X, 10 April 2021, https://twitter.com/Williamstweet/status/1380997283274166283?s=20.

9   Michael Ordoña, 'Nudity, Stunts and Cost: Why Self-Taped Auditions are a Lightning Rod in the Actors' Strike', *Los Angeles Times*, 25 July 2023, https://www.latimes.com/entertainment-arts/business/story/2023-07-25/sag-aftra-strike-self-taped-auditions.

10 Eve Livingston, *Make Bosses Pay* (London: Pluto Press, 2021), 30–31, Kindle.

11 Kenan Malik, *Not So Black and White* (London: Hurst Publishers, 2023), 13–14), Kindle.

12 Malik, *Not So Black and White*, 23.

13 Valerie E.R. Anderson, 'The Eurasian Problem in Nineteenth Century India', (PhD diss., SOAS, University of London, 2011), https://doi.org/10.25501/SOAS.00013525.

14 Jeroen Robbe, 'Leaderful Organizing Tool: Race Class Narrative Checklist', *The Commons' Social Change Library* (2023), https://commonslibrary.org/leaderful-organizing-tool-race-class-narrative-checklist/#:~:text=An%20early%20and%20influential%20thinker,of%20a%20global%20class%20structure.

15 Lareau, sociology.sas.upenn.edu/sites/sociology.sas.upenn.edu/files/Lareau_
Question&Answers.pdf (https://web.archive.org/web/20100622145733/sociology.
sas.upenn.edu/sites/sociology.sas.upenn.edu/files/Lareau_Question&Answers.pdf), as
quoted in Mohamed, *People Like Us*, 48.

16 Theresa May, 'Britain, The Great Meritocracy: Prime Minister's Speech', Prime
Minister's Office, 9 September 2016, https://www.gov.uk/government/speeches/
britain-the-great-meritocracy-prime-ministers-speech#:~:text=I%20want%20
Britain%20to%20be,their%20hard%20work%20will%20allow.

17 Heather Stewart, 'Corbyn to Drop Social Mobility as Labour Goal in Favour
of Opportunity for All', *Guardian*, 8 June 2019, https://www.theguardian.com/
politics/2019/jun/08/jeremy-corbyn-to-drop-social-mobility-as-labour-goal.

18 Joanna Williams, 'The Myth of Social Mobility', *Spiked*, 19 June 2019, https://
www.spiked-online.com/2019/06/19/the-myth-of-social-mobility.

19 Livingston, *Make Bosses Pay*, 18.

20 Trades Union Congress, 'Why we are marching on 18 June?', https://www.tuc.
org.uk/why-we-are-marching-18-june.

21 Joseph Lee, 'Rail Strike: Grant Shapps Dismisses Calls for Government
Involvement as a "Stunt"', BBC News, 21 June 2022, https://www.bbc.co.uk/
news/uk-61874811; Jedidajah Otte and Rachel Hall, 'Train Strikes: Boris Johnson
Calls Union Action "Unnecessary" Amid Second Day of Rail Disruption – As It
Happened', *Guardian*, 22 June 2022, https://www.theguardian.com/uk-news/
live/2022/jun/23/train-strikes-railways-rail-disruption-britain-latest-updates.

22 Eric Hobsbawm, *Labouring Men: Studies in the History of Labour* (New York:
Anchor Books, 1967), 164.

23 Jake Jooshandeh, 'Key Workers in the Pandemic: Security traps among
Britain's essential workers', *Trust for London*, September 2021, https://tfl.ams3.cdn.
digitaloceanspaces.com/media/documents/keyworkers-in-the-pandemic.pdf.

24 Enough is Enough, https://wesayenough.co.uk.

25 Gurpreet Narwan, 'Rising public support for unions despite widespread
strikes, Sky News poll suggests', *Sky News*, 31 January 2023, https://news.sky.com/
story/rising-public-support-for-unions-despite-widespread-strikes-sky-news-poll-
suggests-12799325.

26 'Combination Acts', *Britannica*, updated 18 December 2017, https://www.
britannica.com/event/Combination-Acts; Livingston, Make Bosses Pay, 19.

27 Gavin Hawkton, 'The Media Versus the Miners', *Tribune*, 18 June 2022, https://
tribunemag.co.uk/2022/06/the-media-versus-the-miners.

28 David Conn, 'We were fed lies about the violence at Orgreave. Now we need the truth', *Guardian*, 22 July 2015, https://www.theguardian.com/commentisfree/2015/jul/22/orgreave-truth-police-miners-strike.

29 Gavin Hawkton, 'The Media Versus the Miners', Tribune, 18 June 2022, https://tribunemag.co.uk/2022/06/the-media-versus-the-miners.

30 Ibid.

31 John Moylan, 'Union Membership Has Halved Since 1980', BBC News, 7 September 2012, https://www.bbc.co.uk/news/business-19521535.

32 'Fall in trade union membership linked to rising share of income going to top 1%', *The Institute for Public Policy Research*, 10 Jun 2018, https://www.ippr.org/news-and-media/press-releases/fall-in-trade-union-membership-linked-to-rising-share-of-income-going-to-top-1.

33 Ibid.

34 John Logue, Trade unions in the Nordic countries, nordics.info, 18 February 2019, https://nordics.info/show/artikel/trade-unions-in-the-nordic-region.

35 Trading Economics, 'United Kingdom Corporate Profits', 23 Apr 2014, https://tradingeconomics.com/united-kingdom/corporate-profits.

36 Emily Gosden, 'Shell Profits Double to Record $40bn After Energy Prices Soar', *The Times*, 2 February 2023, https://www.thetimes.co.uk/article/shell-profits-results-2022-stock-share-price-uk-2gq6rqt5j.

37 Joint Committee on Human Rights, 'Strikes Bill Fails to Meet Human Rights Obligations – JCHR', UK Parliament, 6 March 2023, https://committees.parliament.uk/committee/93/human-rights-joint-committee/news/186524/strikes-bill-fails-to-meet-human-rights-obligations-jchr.

38 Tim Sharp, 'Fighting the anti-strike law', *Trades Union Congress*, 20 January 2023, https://www.tuc.org.uk/blogs/fighting-anti-strike-law.

39 Malik, *Not So Black and White*, 341.

40 Robbie Shilliam, *Race and the Undeserving Poor* (Newcastle upon Tyne: Agenda Publishing, 2018), 6.

41 Nick Morrison, 'Liz Truss Appoints Most Diverse Cabinet In History - With One Big Exception', *Forbes*, 8 September 2022, https://www.forbes.com/sites/nickmorrison/2022/09/08/liz-truss-appoints-most-diverse-cabinet-in-historywith-one-big-exception.

42 Douglas Murray, 'Who cares about Liz Truss's 'diverse' cabinet?', *The Spectator*, 10 September 2022, https://www.spectator.co.uk/article/who-cares-about-liz-truss-s-diverse-cabinet/

43 Eve Livingston, '"Old White Men?" Labour and the Question of Representation', *New Socialist*, 28 November 2017, https://newsocialist.org.uk/old-white-men-labours-representation-question.

44 Vyara Apostolova, et al., 'General Election 2017: Results and Analysis', House of Commons Library, Briefing Paper, no. CBP 7979, updated 29 January 2019, https://researchbriefings.files.parliament.uk/documents/CBP-7979/CBP-7979.pdf.

45 Robert Wright, Mary McDougall and George Parker, 'Rishi Sunak paid more than £400,000 in tax last year', *Financial Times*, 22 March 2023, https://www.ft.com/content/ae674691-296a-43cf-8ad5-7cf4e6ceb3ae.

Chapter 8. One Not Both

1   Seneca, *Letters from a Stoic* (London: Penguin Classics, 2004) 69.

2   Seneca, *Letters from a Stoic* (London: Penguin Classics, 2004) 67.

3   Robin Campbell, 'Introduction', *Letters from a Stoic* (London: Penguin Classics, 2004) 15.

4   Singh, P. (2016). Sikh Empire. In *The Encyclopedia of Empire* (eds N. Dalziel and J.M. MacKenzie). https://doi.org/10.1002/9781118455074.wbeoe314

5   Puri, Harish K. "Scheduled Castes in Sikh Community: A Historical Perspective." *Economic and Political Weekly* 38, no. 26 (2003): 2693–2701. http://www.jstor.org/stable/4413731.

6   Major A. Barstow, *Handbook for the British Army* (1928), as quoted in Eleanor Nesbitt, *Sikhism: A Very Short Introduction* (Oxford: Oxford University Press, 2005), 72.

7   'Sikh Community Faces "Existential Crisis" in Pakistan', *Hindustan Times*, 31 May 31 2022, https://www.hindustantimes.com/world-news/sikh-community-faces-existential-crisis-in-pakistan-101654007355224.html.

8   Imma Ramos, 'What is Tantra?', British Museum, 23 January 2020, https://www.britishmuseum.org/blog/what-tantra.

9   Sikhi Wiki, 'Guru Nanak in Nepal', 7 March 2012, https://www.sikhiwiki.org/index.php/Guru_Nanak_in_Nepal.

10 Manjeev Singh Puri, 'Foreword', *Sikh Heritage of Nepal*, September 2019, 4, https://www.indembkathmandu.gov.in/docs/Sikh%20Heritage%20of%20Nepal.pdf.

11 Sri Guru Granth Sahib, 525, https://www.srigranth.org/servlet/gurbani.gurbani?Action=Page&Param=525.